Additional praise for

A Scheme of Heaven

"Educated in both the humanities and the sciences, Boxer is uniquely qualified to guide his readers into a fascinating story of mathematical complexity. The overarching theme of our human destiny is inspirational."

—**Norman Austin**, emeritus professor of classics, University of Arizona

"Astrologers as the first and most ambitious quants and data scientists? Alexander Boxer's remarkable book reveals astrology's mathematical, scientific, historical, philosophical, and literary roots. He shows that astrology is not only an indispensable part of science history but also springs from the same mixture of motives: the desire to control the world and to wonder about it."

—**Robert P. Crease**, author of *The Workshop and the World*

"Through multidisciplinary lenses, Alexander Boxer frames astrology as one of the most ambitious and daring of all human intellectual endeavors. This stellar book is a probe launched into the mysteries of the cosmos, venturing out to rekindle our timeless capacity to marvel at the universe."

—**Ferdinando Buscema**, magic experience designer and magician in residence, Institute for the Future

A
SCHEME
OF
HEAVEN

A
SCHEME
OF
HEAVEN

ASTROLOGY and **THE BIRTH** of **SCIENCE**

ALEXANDER
BOXER

P

PROFILE BOOKS

First published in Great Britain in 2020 by
Profile Books Ltd
29 Cloth Fair
London
EC1A 7JQ

www.profilebooks.com

First published in the United States of America in 2020 by
W. W. Norton & Company, Inc

1 3 5 7 9 10 8 6 4 2

Printed and bound in Great Britain by
Clays Ltd, Elcograf S.p.A.

The moral right of the author has been asserted.

ISBN 978 1 78125 963 4
eISBN 978 1 78283 409 0

FSC
www.fsc.org
MIX
Paper from
responsible sources
FSC® C018072

To my family:
To my parents, Betsy (♈) and Michael (♋), who've always believed in me,
To my sister, Abby (♉), who's always been there for me,
To my wife, Dara (♓), the love of my life,
And, newly, my darling Naomi (♐).

CONTENTS

A HOROSCOPE

Upon Opening This Book
for the Very First Time

♓   ♒   ♑   ♐   ♏   ♎

Today you find yourself presented with a mysterious opportunity. Take it, even if you're not sure it was really meant for you. The focus you apply at this moment has the potential to reveal a number of unexpected connections, each of which can give you new insights into how things stand around you. Go ahead, trust your instincts. Your intuition has always been a faithful guide whenever you've been true to yourself. Yes, mischievous Mercury has been in and out of retrograde more than once this past year, and this hasn't made justifying yourself to others any easier. But Jupiter, ruler of the sky, is there to reassure you that, right now, it's your opinion which matters most. And the Moon? Don't mind her. That scary aspect of hers will look completely different by the time she glides into a new sign in just a few days. Besides, if all of this year's transitions have amounted to anything, it's that you've emerged from them even more resilient and receptive. Your whole being is now perfectly tuned to appreciate the new perspectives that come with a challenging new endeavor. But remember: even if it was the stars which brought you here, only you can decide how much further you'll go.

♈   ♉   ♊   ♋   ♌   ♍

A
SCHEME
OF
HEAVEN

INTRODUCTION

Do the stars and planets really have something to tell us about the cycles of history, the secrets of love, the reasons your last job was no longer right for you, and why everyone born in May is so incredibly amazing? Astrology's unflinching reply is: yes, yes, yes, and definitely yes. That the configurations of the heavens above can influence our lives here on Earth below is, of course, the basic idea of astrology. Modern science has flatly rejected astrology's claims but this hasn't hobbled astrology's charms, certainly not if the continued popularity of online and magazine horoscopes is anything to go by. Let's leave to one side for a moment all the arguments about whether astrology is wrong, or right, or still wrong even when it's sometimes right. I'm here to make the case that astrology is fascinating and still tremendously relevant as a challenge to what we think we know and why we think we know it.

For starters, the questions astrology asks—questions about the patterns of the universe and our place within them—are about as deep and as captivating as they come. If there really is a way to tap into the hidden rhythms of the cosmos, wouldn't you want to know about it? But even more intriguing, at least from where I stand, is how astrology uses mathematics and data to investigate these questions. Over two thousand years ago, astrologers became the first to stumble upon the powerful storytelling possibilities inherent in numerical data, possibilities that become all the more persuasive when presented graphically in a chart or figure. Although it took a while for the rest of the world to catch on, the art of weaving a story out of numbers and figures, often to encourage a specific course of action, is used everywhere today, from financial forecasts to dieting advice to weather models.

And yet numbers still mislead, figures still deceive, and predictions still fail—sometimes spectacularly so—even those that rely on exceptionally sophisticated mathematics. So, are the techniques being used today to parse and package quantitative information any more effective than what was devised by astrologers millennia ago?

In order to make that assessment, it's first necessary to have a basic understanding of what astrology is and how it works. But that sort of understanding—one that's at least adequate to resolve some seemingly straightforward technical questions—is surprisingly hard to come by for such a long-lived and influential craft. Being frustrated in my own search for a simple yet competent overview of astrology, I decided I might just as well write one myself. This, curious reader, is the book you now hold in your hands.

My own interests in astrology stem from several directions, but mainly it's my enchantment with any sufficiently musty book from the history of science that nudged me to investigate astrology in a more detailed way. Astrology was the ancient world's most ambitious applied mathematics problem, a grand data-analysis enterprise sustained for centuries by some of history's most brilliant minds, from Ptolemy to al-Kindi to Kepler. Just consider that for much of the last two thousand years, the word "mathematician" (*mathematicus*) simply meant an astrologer; there was no distinction.

Throughout its history, astrology's aim has been nothing short of a systematic account linking the nature of the heavens to our own human nature. And from the computations of Copernicus to the sonnets of Shakespeare, even to the sculptures in Rockefeller Center, there are, quite simply, recesses of our culture that can't be accessed without astrology's key. This is especially true in fields such as math and astronomy, where so many of the principal innovators were themselves practicing astrologers. Take, for instance, the Renaissance physician and mathematician Girolamo Cardano, who, when he wasn't busy laying the foundations of algebra and probability theory, compiled one of the first collections of celebrity horoscopes. Here, for example, is his horoscope for King Henry VIII of England.

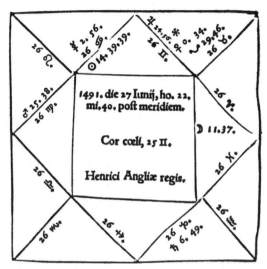

Birth horoscope of King Henry VIII. Girolamo Cardano, *Libelli Quinque* (Nuremberg: Johannes Petreius, 1547), Geniture 46.

Diagrams like this appear seemingly everywhere in books and pamphlets from the Renaissance and scientific revolution. For the longest time, I would skip over them, unable to make heads or tails of what seemed to me like graphical gibberish. But to an expert interpreter like Cardano, these inscrutable hieroglyphs evidently had the capacity to brew a bottomless pot of juicy gossip. Were you taken aback by Henry's break with the Catholic Church? Well, now, who's being naive? According to Cardano, Venus in the Ninth House in a sextile aspect to Mercury is just screaming a major change to the laws. His six wives? They really ought to have known better than to get involved with someone whose Moon was in the Seventh House in square with the Sun, while Saturn was in aspect with Venus at the same time Mars was in aspect with Jupiter, the very lord of the Seventh House! Talk about asking for marriage troubles!

I find horoscopes such as Henry's exciting on several levels. First, there's the exquisitely complex astronomical calculations needed to generate a horoscope, which is really a map of the sky as seen from a particular spot on Earth at a particular moment in time. The millennia-long project to refine these calculations led directly to Copernicus's revolution and, from there, to modern science as we know it today.

Then there was the problem of how to condense and arrange all of this information. Typically this was done visually. The graphical depiction of the positions of the Sun, Moon, and planets constituted what William Lilly—by far the most notorious astrologer in England during the 1600s—referred to colorfully as a "scheme of heaven." As an homage to this art, I've included a number of these heavenly schemes throughout this book as a way to show how the solar system was configured at key moments in astrology's history. The graphical style I've adopted, which is a bit different from Cardano's, takes the outputs of the most modern astronomical computations and displays them according to the design of a very ancient and very beautiful astronomical instrument called an astrolabe (plate 1). Presented in this format, King Henry's horoscope now looks like the diagram on the opposite page.

No doubt about it, there's a tremendous amount of information here. But astrology's particular genius is that it can encode all of the complex astronomical data needed for its operations so perfectly within a single, abstract image. To a remarkable degree, then, the exercise of understanding astrology is really the exercise of learning how to "read" one of these figures. As this book unfolds, I'll describe how to do this piece by piece so that, by the end, you'll be able to visualize the sky in these charts as intuitively as you can see your house in its floor plan, or navigate your way through a city with a street map.

To sketch out a scheme of heaven like this was, however, only the beginning of the astrologer's art. It was still necessary to interpret the data once it had been reduced to graphical form, and this is where things really got interesting. As Cardano's reading of Henry VIII's horoscope shows, these sparse diagrams somehow contain within themselves a wild multitude of possible plotlines. But which ones are expressed and which ones suppressed? To borrow a term from biology, horoscopes are like the "pluripotent cells" of

An Astrolabe-Style "Scheme of Heaven" for Tuesday, June 28, 1491
The Birth of England's King Henry VIII

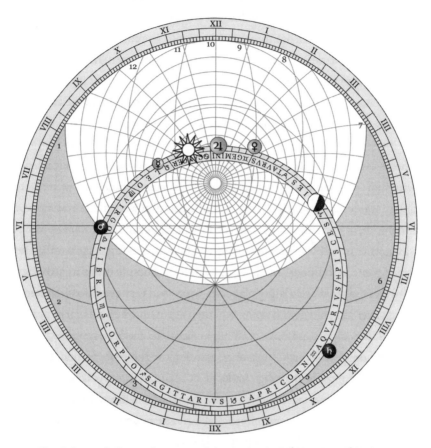

The Palace of Placentia, Greenwich, England: 51°29'01"N, 0°00'21"W
JD: 2265823.94722
10:44 UT
ΔT: 311s
Local Time: 10:40 AM
Local Apparent Sidereal Time: 5:44

		λ	β	RA J2000	Dec J2000	Az	El	House
♄	Saturn	≈ 6°42'↓	0°44'	21ʰ 05ᵐ 59ˢ	-17°25'	297°04'	-43°22'	⑤ 13°17'
♃	Jupiter	♊ 24°24'	0°17'	6ʰ 06ᵐ 34ˢ	23°12'	184°00'	61°34'	⑨ 27°49'
♂	Mars	♍ 26°16'	0°21'	12ʰ 12ᵐ 54ˢ	-1°00'	88°17'	0°58'	⑫ 29°01'
☉	Sun	♋ 14°39'	0°00'	7ʰ 34ᵐ 02ˢ	21°44'	144°22'	57°21'	⑩ 20°27'
♀	Venus	♊ 0°50'	-2°41'	4ʰ 26ᵐ 26ˢ	19°01'	222°00'	50°11'	⑨ 0°50'
☿	Mercury	♌ 6°45'	1°17'	9ʰ 06ᵐ 54ˢ	17°56'	116°26'	43°41'	⑪ 13°08'
☽	Moon	♈ 10°59'	3°30'	1ʰ 01ᵐ 13ˢ	10°21'	264°46'	13°50'	⑦ 13°53'

storytelling, capable of producing many, but still not quite every possible outcome. Considered this way, horoscopes offer up neatly wrapped little packages for examining the mischief that can arise when words are translated into numbers and numbers are translated back into words, even if the numbers themselves are handled with the utmost precision and care. The various ways the borders get blurred between numbers and words, whether innocently or otherwise, can be thought of as a second type of scheme, one that astrologers were the first, but by no means the last, to grapple with.

As someone who analyzes data for a living, my curiosity about these schemes of heaven—"schemes" in their double sense of both a graphical blueprint and an interpretive sleight-of-hand—ultimately became too much to resist. I wanted to understand them, to know how they work, to take them apart and put them back together again. And so, perhaps not fully aware of what I was getting myself into or where it all would lead, I took a deep breath, I set aside my preconceptions, and I began in all seriousness to examine astrology.

I can't say that calculating planetary aspects to high precision was something I ever pictured myself doing but, then again, maybe it all makes perfect sense. I love opportunities to mash up ancient and modern technology, and when it comes to archaic high-tech, astrology is the most formidable and therefore the most tantalizing challenge of them all. Also, with astrology, it helps to have a somewhat eclectic knowledge of both math and dead languages which, by an odd quirk of my upbringing (unless Fate insists on taking credit), I happen to possess. This combination isn't terribly rare, but it's uncommon enough that it seems to have left astrology surprisingly underexplored.

Of course, in a book of this scope, it's not possible to focus on more than just a few of astrology's many facets. Certain topics, such as the astrology of India and China, I've avoided altogether on account of the fact that I know very little about them. But the traditions of Greek, Roman, and Renaissance astronomy and the modern-day arts of statistical analysis are subjects which I know quite well, the latter through my profession, the former through a lifetime's fascination. Does this give me license to write about astrology—a topic for which the whole idea of expertise seems thoroughly up for grabs? That's a judgment you'll have to make for yourself. For my own part, I make no pretense to astrological mastery. My hope, instead, is simply to offer a different perspective on a subject for which it's all too easily said that there's nothing new to be said about it.

At a minimum, I want to give astrology a treatment that's open and fair. Unlike many others who have a scientific background, I've never felt any particular animus toward astrology. On the contrary, its taboo status as the arch-pseudoscience makes it all the more delicious to think about. Why, for example, is astrology considered unscientific while economics— which also uses complex mathematical formulas to predict the future with results that are, let's say, mixed—is regarded as a perfectly respectable field of study? Being able to articulate the distinctions, yes, but also the commonalities between astrology and other modes of asking questions about the world helps to clarify which approaches are fruitful, which aren't, and why.

Astrologers were the quants and data scientists of their day, and those of us who are enthusiastic about the promise of numerical data to unlock the secrets of ourselves and our world would do well simply to acknowledge that others have come this way before. What profession would I, or anyone who delights in numbers, have been drawn to had we lived five hundred years ago? A thousand years ago? Two thousand years ago? Astrologers were the originators, and for most of history the sole cultivators of a tradition that transmuted numbers into stories. And like any story that's been retold for generations, astrology's account of the cosmos has been refined to just its most captivating themes. Regardless of whether astrology has distilled any truth or not, what seems clear to me is that it has bottled up a certain type of magic, one that has proven time and again its ability to get us to stop and think about our connections to the wider universe. Against a backdrop of indifference, this is some magic indeed. So who's to say we can't use a little of astrology's charms for our own ends? Whether you're intrigued by astrology, repelled by it, or anywhere in between, we can interpret astrology's bold claims as an open invitation to explore some of the deepest mysteries of who we are and where we are. This book is my elaborate way of saying yes to that invitation, and now it's my turn to invite you to come explore these mysteries with me.

1

TO EVERYTHING
THERE IS A SEASON

When I behold Thy heavens, the work of Thy fingers,
the moon and the stars, which Thou hast established;
What is man, that Thou art mindful of him?
and the son of man, that Thou thinkest of him?

Psalm 8:4–5

I t's possible that in ages past, there was a common intimacy with the night, even if this has long since been lost to us in modern times. I'm not so sure. To be outside, alone, on a clear and moonless night, far from any lights, far from any trees, and looking up at the sky is not an ordinary thing. I'm skeptical that it ever was. No, I don't believe that we ever really notice the stars except in those rare moments when their possibility of being seen coincides with our openness to seeing them. But if you catch them in their splendor, glimmering across the brisk night air like icy drops of cosmic fire, then you have no choice except to stop and notice them. They engulf your vision fully. They enfold your thoughts up whole. And there you stand beneath them feeling suddenly, utterly exposed. Because if you can see the stars that clearly, might not they, then, see you too? Thus, when David sang his psalm, gazing up at the sky in wonder, it wasn't the contents of the night which moved him;

it was his astonishment that just as he was contemplating the universe, so too the universe, or rather its creator, was contemplating him right back.

This perception of a mutual regard between man and the cosmos has, from our earliest beginnings, animated humanity's efforts to understand the world and our place within it. Modern science began from studying the heavens, and in this sense we can say that, yes, the stars really have communicated to us many profound truths about the nature of things. The bigger question isn't whether the universe is speaking but, instead, how far we can ever hope to comprehend what it might be saying. Because for all the progress that's been made in deciphering the Book of Nature, what expectation can there be that humankind will ever manage more than a thin and incomplete translation? The language of the cosmos is simply not our native tongue. And if ever we wanted a reminder of the mismatch between the world as it is and the world as it is processed through the filters of our minds, all we need to do is look up at the stars.

THE STRANGENESS OF SEEING

Quick: On a clear, dark night, how many stars can be seen in the sky? A thousand? A million? A *billion*? If you're like me, you might think a million sounds high but it's probably at least in the ballpark. Actually, in the modern, high-precision *Hipparcos* star catalog there are only a paltry 5,044 stars that have a visual magnitude of 6.00 or less—that's the value generally considered to be the limit of what's visible with the naked eye. Since at any given moment roughly half of these are hidden below the horizon, seeing a couple thousand stars in the sky at any one time is as good as it gets—ever—even on a perfectly pristine night. Does this seem like a surprisingly low number to you? It did to me. So consider this our first hint, courtesy of the stars, that our natural ability to gauge large numbers is not necessarily to be trusted without question.

Now, a few thousand may sound like a small number, especially when talking about stars, but it would still be very difficult, if not impossible, to create a mental picture of the heavens that consisted of these several thousand stars regarded individually. Yet this bewildering chaos of darkness and light is immediately converted into a more intelligible map of the sky simply by grouping the stars into constellations. The specific shapes of the constellations may be arbitrary, but the tendency to cluster the stars this way can be found across the various stargazing cultures. The stars that make up the constellation Ursa Major, for example, have been seen as a bear, a dipper, a wagon, a plough, and an ox's leg, to list just a few of its varied personae.

Quite clearly, our brains have become exquisitely tuned to recognize the shapes of people, animals, and other objects meaningful to our daily lives. And when what occupies our field of view defies any discernible pattern, we tend to foist these same shapes onto otherwise amorphous scenes such as cloudscapes, rock formations, or the stars in the sky. Does the stone outcrop in figure 1.1(a) look like a human head to you? If so, then your mind has performed a remarkable act of association, one which emphasized the object's loose outlines while completely discounting other information, such as size, texture, color and situational context. Rock formations like this one, just like the constellations above, are good indicators that we rarely perceive the world in a perfectly straightforward way.

Interestingly, a very similar phenomenon occurs in computer vision applications. It's an impressive technological feat to coax a computer to recognize a class of visual objects—say, for example, dogs—within a larger collection of images. But once you succeed in doing this, it's just as hard, if not harder, to restrain the algorithm from falsely seeing dogs everywhere. Figure 1.1(b), for instance, uses an algorithm called DeepDream—originally developed by Google in 2015—to show what a computer-vision application trained to recognize dogs "sees" when looking at a photograph of clouds. The composite images generated by DeepDream are sometimes illuminating, occasionally beautiful, but mostly just delightfully bizarre. Yet what these images do reveal is that a computer that has been taught to see faces and animals like we do—namely, by emphasizing outlines above everything else—will tend to see faces and animals in the clouds just like we do, too. This suggests, not surprisingly, that our peculiarly human way of seeing the world is probably inseparable from our peculiarly human ways of misconstruing what we see.

Of course, the fact that the constellations have traditionally taken on

Figure 1.1: What Do You See?

(a) The Grey Man of the Merrick, Galloway Hills, Scotland. GARY COOK / AGEFOTOSTOCK.

(b) Doglike features in the clouds over Washington, DC, enhanced by Google's DeepDream algorithm.

the rowdy shapes of beasts and demigods doesn't mean that anyone has ever suggested that the sky is infested with lumbering space-bears or interstellar scorpions. But the constellations do illustrate nicely that there is a limit to the number of objects the human mind can handle individually before it tends to impose an additional layer of abstraction. For most people it's simply more convenient—one might even say more human—to view the night sky not as the disposition of several thousand stars but instead as the disposition of just several dozen constellations.

In general, when the number of distinct objects in a system is reduced from thousands to dozens, our minds can begin to develop a basic familiarity, identify structures, and examine how parts relate to the whole. We can even take those parts and craft that higher and most human layer of abstraction: a narrative story. As an extreme case, consider that nearly 10 percent of the night sky (plate 2) can be accounted for by retelling just one single legend, that of a hero (the constellation Perseus) who slays a monster feared for her demon eye (the star Algol) which could turn any living creature to stone. This hero then returns to rescue a beautiful princess (the constellation Andromeda)

Figure 1.2: Real and Random Star Maps

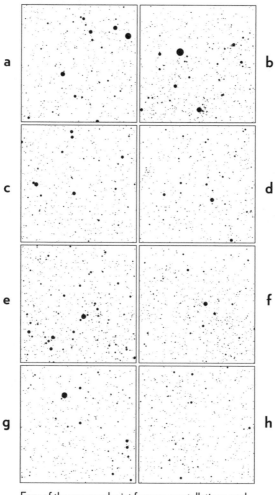

Four of these maps depict famous constellations, and four show random dots. Can you tell which are which?

chained to a rock by her parents (the constellations Cepheus and Cassiopeia) as a sacrifice to a giant sea monster (the constellation Cetus).

All the same, our propensity to group stars into constellations and constellations into stories can hardly be said to derive from the actual arrangement of the stars themselves. In fact, to a remarkable degree, the distribution of stars in the sky is completely random. Figure 1.2, for example, shows eight star maps, each depicting a roughly equal area of sky. Four snippets contain famous constellations and the other four show an alternate night where all the brightest stars of our sky have been repositioned entirely at random. Can you tell which four are real and which four are random? I'll reveal the correct answers in the next section.

KEEPING COUNT

For millennia, the stars have been our teachers in how to extract information from vast, unruly clumps of seemingly incoherent data. And if, as the stars have shown us, there are peculiarities in how our minds process quantities that are very large, or that exhibit randomness, this doesn't mean that we're unable to learn anything about systems that are large, or random, or both. Fortunately, our brains are capable of a trick or two that allows us to compensate, at least somewhat, for our occasionally skewed first impressions of things. For the most part, these tricks rely on nothing more than our innate ability to count.

As an example of what can be learned simply through careful counting, take another look at figure 1.2. The four images depicting a genuine representation of the night sky are b: Taurus and Auriga, d: Leo, e: Scorpius, and f: Cygnus. If you were brave enough to attempt to sort them, then your score, which is the number of star maps you correctly identified as being genuine, will be either 0, 1, 2, 3, or 4. For all but the most seasoned stargazers, however, it should be pretty tough to pick out all four legitimate maps. How tough? Well, your chances getting any given score just by guessing are presented in table 1.1.

Table 1.1: Star Map Sorting Scores

Number of Star Maps You Correctly Labeled as Genuine	Chances of Getting at Least This Score Just by Guessing	This Is Roughly as Likely as
0	100%	Death
1	99%	Losing at roulette
2	76%	Drawing a non-face card from a deck of cards
3	24%	Flipping a coin twice in a row and getting heads both times
4	1.4%	Flipping a coin six times in a row and getting heads each time

Oftentimes, seeing the actual numbers of how likely (or unlikely) it is for a particular event to occur can be counterintuitive, if not downright surprising. Does picking three of the four genuine star maps seem impressive? Table 1.1 indicates that it's no more remarkable than flipping a coin twice in a row and getting heads both times—in other words, not remarkable at all.

A sorting game like figure 1.2 can be extremely useful when there's a decision to be made—for instance, if we want to determine whether you're as good at recognizing constellations as you claim to be—under circumstances where other information may be hard to come by. In fact, our star map challenge turns out to be an example of what's called a statistical inference test—a carefully designed experiment that uses knowledge of the laws of probability to marshal evidence for answering a question in an informed way. More specifically, I've arranged figure 1.2 to mimic one of the most famous of all statistical inference tests, the so-called Lady Tasting Tea experiment. Its format was originally devised by Ronald A. Fisher, one of the titans of twentieth-century statistics, when a colleague of his insisted that she could tell whether her teacup had been prepared with tea first and then milk, or milk first and then tea. (Statistics lore has it that she easily sorted the eight teacups, presented in random order, into their correct groupings of four, thereby winning from Fisher a grudging acknowledgment of her exceptional tea-tasting talent.)

Today, statistical inference tests are used widely throughout science and industry, from measuring the effectiveness of new medical procedures, to identifying which website features generate the most clicks, even to ensuring the consistency of beer from one bottle to the next. So long as you have numerical data, these tests can be applied without any contextual knowledge whatsoever, since numbers are the only things that go in and numbers are the only things that come out. This feature makes them especially useful in many fast-moving fields of research—including almost any eyebrow-raising investigation into human or social trends—where there are few if any established theories on which to rely. In these scenarios, statistical tests may be the only way to gain any insight into what's going on.

Yet the tradeoff of drawing conclusions from purely numerical results, untethered to anything more solid than statistics, is that it's deceptively easy to misinterpret the significance of a rare outcome. The temptation to ascribe a deeper meaning to an unlikely event, to insist that some seemingly incredible coincidence couldn't possibly be the result of chance alone, can be extremely hard to resist, especially if it supports an interpretation we deeply want to believe is true. But what's rare is a relative notion. If a process is repeated enough times, otherwise rare events are almost guaranteed to occur, and this can be very misleading if we're not also keeping a tally of every time something rare does not occur.

Referring back to our star map example, it turns out that there are exactly seventy ways to sort the eight images into two groups of four. There is a famous mathematical formula for this: the number of ways to make a group containing k items from a larger set of N items (an operation called "N choose k") is equal to

$$\frac{N!}{k! \, (N - k)!}$$

(The exclamation points here stand for the factorial operation. For example, 4!—read as "four factorial"—is equal to $4 \times 3 \times 2 \times 1 = 24$.)

Out of the "8 choose 4" = 70 ways to sort the star maps, only one correctly assigns every image to its proper group. The probability of choosing this sorting just by guessing is, therefore, one out of seventy, or about 1.4%. This result may meet our threshold for being called statistically significant. That is, witnessing this outcome, which is expected to happen by chance only 1.4% of the time, may be deemed sufficiently improbable that we conclude, instead, that it's more likely to have arisen for some other reason. Perhaps we'll take this result as evidence for an actual knowledge of the stars.

But the risk here is that while an expert stargazer can be expected to sort the four genuine and four fake star maps correctly, correctly sorting all of the star maps doesn't guarantee any stargazing expertise whatsoever. In fact, the only thing this test does guarantee is that among all the people who try to sort these images using nothing more than dumb luck, one out of seventy can be expected to guess them all exactly right. Thus, through sheer force of numbers, the unlikely outcome of someone labeling each image correctly is not just possible, it's practically inevitable.

UPS AND DOWNS

Statistical inference tests provide a powerful tool for interrogating the behaviors of an otherwise inscrutable system. For a proper account of astrology they are absolutely indispensable, because when we're searching for something extraordinary, we don't want to be deceived by chance occurrences which the laws of probability insist are predictably ordinary. This isn't always easy to do. The eight star maps of figure 1.2 generated a universe of possibilities limited to just seventy outcomes. Yet the implications of even this small system required a fair amount of nuance to convey. So what happens when the number of possibilities becomes much, much larger? Suffice it to say, with astrology this predicament gets very sticky very quickly.

Astrology has just a few basic pieces: seven planets, twelve signs of the zodiac, and twelve Houses of Heaven. But together these can be combined in an almost infinite number of ways. The chance that any one celestial configuration will occur is fantastically unlikely, and yet the heavens are graced by one of these fantastically unlikely configurations at every instant in time, including right now. Just think how incredible it is for the planets to have entered into such a unique alignment at the exact moment you find yourself reading a book about astrology. A mere coincidence? As with our star map example, it's not possible to gauge the significance of any one outcome unless we are prepared to examine it in the context of all possible outcomes. For astrological questions in general, then, the enormous number of potential configurations means we had better buckle in for some pretty enormous calculations.

Astrology's ability to generate a dizzying array of possibilities from just a few simple rules is a quality it shares with many of the world's most popular pastimes, like chess, Sudoku, and poker. As with any good game, the basic operations of astrology are easy enough to grasp after just a few explanations, but to execute those operations in full is an enormous and occasionally impossible challenge. This layered quality means that astrology can be enjoyed as a few minutes' diversion, a lifelong obsession, or anything in between. However, astrology possesses one fundamental feature that sets it apart from any mere game: its intimate connection with the passage of time.

Through their risings and settings, their cycles and orbits, the stars and planets trace out patterns in time. These patterns unfold over intervals ranging from mere minutes to tens of thousands of years, and no two cycles, however similar, are ever exactly the same. This means that each astrological moment is at once both unique and yet always reminiscent of countless earlier moments in time. And each sequence of such moments, though never repeated, contains the echoes of countless earlier sequences (plate 3).

Previously, we pointed to the constellations as an example of how our minds impose familiar patterns onto otherwise disorganized visual scenes. The merest hint of a visible outline was all our brains needed to suggest an association, however bizarre or unlikely. When confronted with disorganized events in time, this impulse remains exactly the same. Our minds still insist on imposing a familiar pattern, although a pattern not in space but in time. And all our minds need to suggest an association, however implausible, is the merest hint that one sequence of events unfolded at roughly the same time and with roughly the same rhythm as another.

Astrology's reliance on time, its deep structure of endlessly overlapping yet never identical cycles, allows it to mirror the ups and downs of our lives in an eerily convincing way. Astrology can therefore plausibly combine two powerful human tendencies—our compulsion to find connections in everything, and our irrepressible fascination with ourselves—into a recipe for some exhilaratingly potent brain candy. Or, to put it another way, we humans are pattern-matching animals, and astrology is the universe's grandest pattern-matching game. This combination, I believe, and as this book will explore, is what has kept astrology so captivating and fertile in spite of every effort to eradicate it. Acknowledging this, and recognizing some of the patterns that characterize our own pattern-matching tendencies, is hardly without relevance in a world that puts ever more stock in the ability to pick out just the right patterns from all the information around us.

Astrology offers us an outlet for these impulses. It provides an almost totally uninhibited template for linking the vast number of possible states of the solar system with the stories that matter most in our lives: love, money, power, and the true identities of who we really are. But no matter how complicated astrology can seem, every one of its operations is, at root, nothing more than the assertion of a linkage in time. Do you sometimes get the impression that the craziest people you know all have November birthdays? How odd is it, then, that they each took their first breath when the Sun was in Scorpio? Remember those few weeks not long ago when nothing seemed to go your way? Wasn't that right around when Mercury was in retrograde? And couldn't you just swear that, almost like clockwork, there's some major geopolitical upheaval every twenty years or so? Strangely enough, that's the interval between successive conjunctions of Jupiter and Saturn.

TIME'S PETTY TYRANTS

The statistics term of art for describing how closely two signals in time rise and fall together is correlation. In essence, then, what astrology proposes is an elaborate system of correlations between the positions of the stars and planets in the sky and various phenomena here on Earth. Some of these correlations have a physical justification, like the connection between the Sun's apparent orbit and the seasons of the year, or the phases of the Moon and the tides. But beyond these examples, it becomes much less clear which heavenly bodies should be held responsible for the current political landscape, the financial markets, or the love lives of your friends. Astrology addresses this worrisome lack of celestial oversight by bestowing a broad sovereignty over earthly affairs onto entities variously called rulers, despots, lords, or most loftily of all, chronocrators.

Chronocrator (from χρόνος, *chronos* = time, and κράτωρ, *krator* = ruler) is a Greek word that translates literally as "time ruler" or "time lord." However, a more accurate translation (and one that happily avoids any confusion with the television show *Doctor Who*) might be something more like "interval lord." This is because *chronos* refers to a set period of time with a beginning, middle, and end, as opposed to the more free-flowing sense of the English word "time." In astrology, a chronocrator is the planet, star, or combination of planets and stars which governs a particular interval of time. There are chronocrators for general time periods, such as days and years, and there are also chronocrators for personal time periods such as the first year of your life, the second year of your life, and so on. When Shakespeare mused that "All the world's a stage . . . And one man in his time plays many parts," it was no accident that he insisted the number of these parts was seven. Astrologers had long averred that the seven ages of man, from infancy through senility, were governed by the seven classical planets in their sequence from the Moon to Saturn.

The astrological role of a chronocrator actually maps quite well onto the modern notion of correlation, since in each case there is the assertion of a temporal link between two distinct sequences of events. In astrology, specifically, one of these sequences will be a list of earthly events, and the second will track the waxing or waning influence of the relevant celestial chronocrator. Of course the trick has always been to figure out which chronocrator is the appropriate one for a given time and scenario. The lines of authority within the heavenly bureaucracy can be exceedingly convoluted, especially since the chronocrator of a more immediate period of time may find itself at cross-purposes to the chronocrator of the longer interval to which it belongs. But expressly because the temporal structure of the solar system is so intricate, there is never a shortage of plausible candidates for any conceivable occasion. So long as your earthly concerns have ups and downs, some celestial cycle can be found that correlates with it, even if the match is never perfect.

THE ASTROLOGICAL ORIGINS OF THE WEEK

Since the cycles of the stars and planets create patterns over an enormous range of timescales, the temporal jurisdiction of the chronocrators likewise extends from the briefest of instants all the way to eons and eras. At the short end of this range, it was customary to assign planetary rulers even to each hour of the day. In fact, it was this practice that gave us the modern week as we know it.

As anyone who is familiar with a Romance language such as French, Spanish, or Italian knows, most of the days of the week are named after planets. For instance, the days of the week in Italian are *domenica, lunedì, martedì, mercoledì, giovedì, venerdì, sabato*. Translated literally, these are "the Lord's Day," "Moon Day," "Mars Day," "Mercury Day," "Jove (= Jupiter) Day," "Venus Day," "Sabbath." Norse mythology buffs will recognize that the English week follows the same sequence, once the Roman deities that correspond to the planets are swapped for their Germanic equivalents, and allowing for the fact that in most Romance languages Saturday and Sunday are designated by their Judeo-Christian titles. By merging these lists of day-names, it's fairly simple to reconstruct the old astrological week, which had become the de facto standard during the Roman Empire, and which serves today as the template for the week in all Western languages.

Table 1.2: The Astrological Week

The Week in Italian	domenica	lunedì	martedì	mercoledì	giovedì	venerdì	sabato
Meaning	The Lord's Day	Moon Day	Mars Day	Mercury Day	Jove (= Jupiter) Day	Venus Day	Sabbath
The Week in English	Sunday	Monday	Tuesday	Wednesday	Thursday	Friday	Saturday
Meaning	Sun Day	Moon Day	Tiw's (= Mars) Day	Odin's (= Mercury) Day	Thor's (= Jupiter) Day	Freya's (= Venus) Day	Saturn Day
Astrological Week	Sun Day	Moon Day	Mars Day	Mercury Day	Jupiter Day	Venus Day	Saturn Day

In the astrological week, each of the seven days was ruled by one of the seven classical heavenly bodies. From Sunday through Saturday, the chrono-crators of each day are the Sun (Sunday), the Moon (Monday), Mars (Tuesday), Mercury (Wednesday), Jupiter (Thursday), Venus (Friday), and Saturn (Saturday). These associations are reasonably well known, but what's a bit less familiar is why the days are ordered in such an odd way. In the ancient world, the seven "planets" had a fixed sequence based on their perceived distance from the Earth. From nearest to farthest, the old geocentric order-ing was 1. Moon; 2. Mercury; 3. Venus; 4. Sun; 5. Mars; 6. Jupiter; 7. Saturn. Using these numbers, the week that starts on Monday would be represented by the following strange sequence: 1, 5, 2, 6, 3, 7, 4. What is going on? Actu-ally, there's a hidden pattern here, but one that only comes into focus when we realize that it was the hours of the day, and not the days of the week, that were assigned planetary rulers in their proper sequence. How this works is shown in table 1.3.

Beginning from the first hour of Saturday, each of the twenty-four hours of the day is assigned to one of the seven planets in their sequence from far-thest (Saturn) to nearest (the Moon). But because twenty-four (the number of hours in a day) is not evenly divisible by seven (the traditional number of planets), the sequence of planets ends abruptly, with the twenty-fourth hour

Table 1.3: Order of the Week as Determined by the Planetary Hour-Lords

DAY OF THE WEEK

	Saturday	Sunday	Monday	Tuesday	Wednesday	Thursday	Friday
1	Saturn ♄	Sun ☉	Moon ☾	Mars ♂	Mercury ☿	Jupiter ♃	Venus ♀
2	Jupiter ♃	Venus ♀	Saturn ♄	Sun ☉	Moon ☾	Mars ♂	Mercury ☿
3	Mars ♂	Mercury ☿	Jupiter ♃	Venus ♀	Saturn ♄	Sun ☉	Moon ☾
4	Sun ☉	Moon ☾	Mars ♂	Mercury ☿	Jupiter ♃	Venus ♀	Saturn ♄
5	Venus ♀	Saturn ♄	Sun ☉	Moon ☾	Mars ♂	Mercury ☿	Jupiter ♃
6	Mercury ☿	Jupiter ♃	Venus ♀	Saturn ♄	Sun ☉	Moon ☾	Mars ♂
7	Moon ☾	Mars ♂	Mercury ☿	Jupiter ♃	Venus ♀	Saturn ♄	Sun ☉
8	Saturn ♄	Sun ☉	Moon ☾	Mars ♂	Mercury ☿	Jupiter ♃	Venus ♀
9	Jupiter ♃	Venus ♀	Saturn ♄	Sun ☉	Moon ☾	Mars ♂	Mercury ☿
10	Mars ♂	Mercury ☿	Jupiter ♃	Venus ♀	Saturn ♄	Sun ☉	Moon ☾
11	Sun ☉	Moon ☾	Mars ♂	Mercury ☿	Jupiter ♃	Venus ♀	Saturn ♄
12	Venus ♀	Saturn ♄	Sun ☉	Moon ☾	Mars ♂	Mercury ☿	Jupiter ♃
13	Mercury ☿	Jupiter ♃	Venus ♀	Saturn ♄	Sun ☉	Moon ☾	Mars ♂
14	Moon ☾	Mars ♂	Mercury ☿	Jupiter ♃	Venus ♀	Saturn ♄	Sun ☉
15	Saturn ♄	Sun ☉	Moon ☾	Mars ♂	Mercury ☿	Jupiter ♃	Venus ♀
16	Jupiter ♃	Venus ♀	Saturn ♄	Sun ☉	Moon ☾	Mars ♂	Mercury ☿
17	Mars ♂	Mercury ☿	Jupiter ♃	Venus ♀	Saturn ♄	Sun ☉	Moon ☾
18	Sun ☉	Moon ☾	Mars ♂	Mercury ☿	Jupiter ♃	Venus ♀	Saturn ♄
19	Venus ♀	Saturn ♄	Sun ☉	Moon ☾	Mars ♂	Mercury ☿	Jupiter ♃
20	Mercury ☿	Jupiter ♃	Venus ♀	Saturn ♄	Sun ☉	Moon ☾	Mars ♂
21	Moon ☾	Mars ♂	Mercury ☿	Jupiter ♃	Venus ♀	Saturn ♄	Sun ☉
22	Saturn ♄	Sun ☉	Moon ☾	Mars ♂	Mercury ☿	Jupiter ♃	Venus ♀
23	Jupiter ♃	Venus ♀	Saturn ♄	Sun ☉	Moon ☾	Mars ♂	Mercury ☿
24	Mars ♂	Mercury ☿	Jupiter ♃	Venus ♀	Saturn ♄	Sun ☉	Moon ☾

HOUR OF THE DAY AND PLANETARY HOUR LORD

of Saturday ruled by Mars. The convention for what happens next was to keep the planetary sequence unbroken, and thus to assign the next planet in line (in this example, the Sun) to the first hour of the next day (in this example, Sunday). Since the chronocrator of the first hour of the day was also the chronocrator for the entire day, the result is that each day's ruler (and hence its name) jumps three planets ahead of the day before it.

Another consequence of the fact that seven and twenty-four have no common factors is that seven is therefore the fewest number of days in which this pattern of assigning every hour to a planet can be completed. From an astrological perspective, then, a universe of seven planets and twenty-four-hour days necessarily requires a seven-day week. This little mathematical constraint is actually of tremendous cultural significance, because unlike the other standard calendrical units—the day, the month, and the year—the week is not based on any natural cycle. On the contrary, the week is handy expressly because it doesn't require astronomers, mathematicians, or priests to compute when it begins and ends. And yet, since its length is arbitrary, there's no particular reason to have a seven-day week as opposed to some other number. The ancient Egyptian week, for example, was ten days long, while the Roman week was originally eight days long.

Instead, it was likely only the curious coincidence that two of the trendiest creeds within the Roman Empire—astrology and another Eastern upstart named Christianity—both preferred a seven-day week that this system was able to supplant its eight-day precursor without much fuss. So, if previously you scoffed that astrology and its chronocrators couldn't possibly exert any real influence over your life, think again. It's the planetary hour-lords who are directly responsible for structuring society's most basic unit of work and social life: the seven-day week. And the next time Monday rolls around after a weekend that seems much too short, you can be totally justified in blaming the planets.

THE AGE OF AQUARIUS

In the same way that no moment is too short for astrological governance, chronocrators are also found at the opposite end of the temporal spectrum, ruling over time periods that are very, very long. The longest of these is the nearly 26,000-year cycle of the precession of the equinoxes. Now, unless you happen to have an unusually avid interest in astronomy, this is probably a pretty unfamiliar term. But precession is absolutely critical for a proper understanding of astrology, so it's not out of place to introduce it right here, at the beginning of this book. And, besides, I promise it's not nearly as complicated as it sounds.

To begin, and with a little imagination, you can convince yourself that even during the daytime there are still stars overhead. It's only the Sun's brightness that prevents them from being seen. But if the Sun came with a dimmer, a simple turn of the dial, much like a solar eclipse, would render these stars visible again. In fact, we could use the stars closest to the Sun at any given moment as a handy way of marking the Sun's position in the sky.

Taking this idea further, imagine that whenever a star was sufficiently close to the Sun, the star's color turned bright purple and stayed purple for the rest of the year. Over the course of a single day, the Sun might change only one or two stars to purple, but over the course of an entire year, the Sun would trace out a complete circle of purple stars in the sky. The astronomical name for this imaginary circle (purple or otherwise) is the ecliptic. (It's called the ecliptic because it plays a role in eclipses, but more on that in chapter 3.) The stars along the ecliptic circle have traditionally been given a special significance because these are the stars which make contact with the Sun during its yearly orbit. Not surprisingly, the constellations made from these stars also have a special significance—they are the twelve signs of the zodiac.

The zodiac signs can be thought of like tick marks on the face of a clock, but instead of marking the hours of a day, they serve to mark the Sun's progress during the year. Each day, the Sun advances a little on its yearly orbit along the ecliptic to a new position within one of the zodiac constellations. By tradition, the starting point of the Sun's annual orbit is its position on the first day of spring, also called the spring equinox. This is the day when the hours of daylight have increased to become exactly equal to the hours of night. (Note the name: equinox = "equal night.") The corresponding equinox when the days are getting shorter is, of course, the autumnal equinox, which marks the first day of fall.

This year, on the first day of spring, the Sun will be positioned within the constellation Pisces. Next year, after making a complete orbit through the zodiac, the Sun's position on the first day of spring will again be in the constellation Pisces. In fact, to an extremely fine approximation, the Sun will return to the same spot within Pisces on the first day of spring year after year after year. However, it turns out that this spot, which is called the vernal point ("vernal" from the Latin word for spring), doesn't quite stay fixed from one year to the next. It's actually making a very slow revolution around the ecliptic—so slow, in fact, that it will take nearly 26,000 years to make one complete cycle.

This extraordinarily slow motion is called the precession of the equinoxes and it was first noted by the astronomer Hipparchus around the year 130 BC. Whenever I think about it, I can't help but feel amazed—dumbfounded, really—at how early in history this discovery was made, because in order to recognize this motion, Hipparchus, who seems ancient to us, had to rely on the accuracy of stargazers who would have seemed ancient even to him. Hipparchus's discovery is thus a humbling example of how science is a collaborative endeavor in time, with each generation building upon the efforts of those who came before. It's also a powerful reminder that knowledge from the past, however out-of-date or obsolete it may seem, ought not to be dismissed lightly, since one never knows just when, or in what context, it may yet prove insightful.

Because of the precession of the equinoxes, the Sun's location on the first day of spring (that is, the vernal point) will eventually pass through all twelve zodiac constellations, spending about 2,150 years in each. This roughly 2,150-year period defines the longest temporal unit of astrology: an astrological age. Each astrological age takes its name and, so the story goes, its overall characteristics from whichever constellation contains the vernal point at that time.

Currently, and for approximately the last two thousand years, the world has been living in the Age of Pisces.

"Precession" is an unusual word, but it means more or less the same thing as procession, that is, an advance or progression. However, when compared to the sequence of the Sun's transit through the zodiac during the year, the vernal point precesses through the zodiac constellations backward: Pisces, Aquarius, Capricorn, Sagittarius, Scorpio, Libra, Virgo, Leo, Cancer, Gemini, Taurus, Aries, and then back to Pisces. This is because the phenomenon was originally envisioned as the stars precessing slowly ahead of the Sun, and not the other way around. Consequently, the next astrological age after this one is destined to be the much heralded Age of Aquarius.

Although the precession of the equinoxes has been noted for over two thousand years (or, to put it another way, since the Age of Aries), the idea that the imminent arrival of the Age of Aquarius is an event of great cosmic significance is actually quite modern. References to it begin bubbling up toward the close of the nineteenth century, particularly in the United States, and particularly in the exuberant and often highly eccentric religious periodicals circulating widely at the time. In a story that quickly took shape along familiar lines, they tell of a "Taurian Age" and the rise of the ancient bull-worshipping civilizations, how the transit of the equinox into Aries, the ram, presaged God's covenant with Abraham, while the "Piscean Age" of the last two thousand years was characterized by the teachings of the Christian Gospels. (Indeed, the fish is a long-standing Christian symbol.) But it was the pronouncements of an upcoming "Aquarian Age," expected to be an era of spiritual rebirth, which truly captured people's imaginations and gave a unifying theme to the mystic and transcendental groups which came to be called, simply, New Age—an indirect though still unmistakable reference to the astrological idea.

Over the years, there have been many, wildly varying estimates for when the Age of Aquarius will begin or, indeed, has already begun. The best known of these is the song "Aquarius" from the musical *Hair*, which links the Age of Aquarius to the 1960s' counterculture. Nevertheless, using modern astronomical algorithms, we can actually determine the dawning of the Age of

Aquarius a bit more definitively. The tricky part isn't the precession itself, but instead deciding where the constellation Pisces ends and where the constellation Aquarius begins.

Based on the official constellation boundaries adopted by the International Astronomical Union in 1930, of which we will have more to say in chapter 3, the spring equinox should pass the border dividing the constellations Pisces and Aquarius around the year 2600. But if we insist on waiting until the equinox enters the group of stars that actually form the figure of Aquarius, then we'll need to be patient until at least the year 2900. However, from an astrological point of view, neither of these approaches is entirely satisfactory. In astrology, the zodiac is supposed to serve as an orderly system of coordinates, with each sign covering an arc in the sky of exactly 30 degrees such that all twelve signs constitute the full, 360-degree circle of the ecliptic.

Unfortunately, there is no clean way to partition the zodiac constellations into twelve equal sections since the constellations themselves vary significantly in their breadth. The longest, Virgo, extends over 48 degrees of the ecliptic, while the most cramped, Libra, covers barely 16 degrees. But while a perfect partition of the zodiac does not exist, a best compromise can still be found. This is actually a straightforward optimization task, one that can be tackled by assigning a penalty whenever a star belonging to one zodiac constellation falls within the boundaries of its neighbor. The optimal boundary lines will then be those which minimize the total penalty. In the algorithm used here, I decided to penalize each star according to the distance it falls outside its boundary and also according to its brightness.

Following this approach, the optimal division between Pisces and Aquarius is found to lie almost exactly 3.53 degrees west from today's vernal point. (Or, more precisely, it has an ecliptic longitude of -3.53° in the ICRF/ J2000.0 reference frame used by astronomers today.) The other constellation boundaries then follow in exactly 30-degree increments. Again, it's important to stress that the output of this computation is pretty arbitrary; even tiny adjustments to how the constellation boundaries are computed can change the overall result by tens, or even hundreds of years.

Nevertheless, in the spirit of a mathematical recreation, we can use this

Figure 1.3: Precession of the Equinoxes and the Age of Aquarius

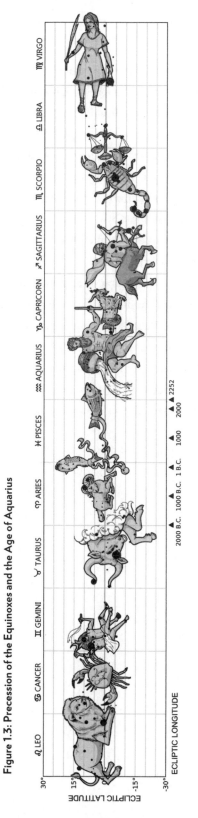

Location of the Sun on the spring equinox through the ages

value, along with the most modern equations and coefficients for precession-ary motion, to estimate when the Age of Aquarius will arrive. It's simply a matter of determining how long it will take for the equinox to precess 3.53 degrees from its present location. Taking these calculations to an extreme, unsupportable, and altogether absurd level of exactness, we can compute this moment even to the very day. And so, as a monument to questionably-spent leisure time, I offer my prediction that the Age of Aquarius will begin on August 8, 2252. This is a Sunday, by the way, in case you want to plan ahead. Whether, on that day, "peace will guide the planets, and love will steer the stars," alas, my equations were mute.

Now, if you're wondering what it means for astrology when a winter sign like Aquarius will, in a few hundred years, mark the beginning of spring, then you're ahead of the game. Because we've gotten quite a bit ahead of ourselves with all this talk of equinoxes and the ecliptic and so forth. I'll present a proper overview of the astronomical concepts needed for astrology in chapter 3. In the meantime, in chapter 2, I'll attempt to address two very primary questions: when, and where, did astrology first arise?

2

FROM OBSCURE BEGINNINGS

Amarna, Egypt, 1338 BC

Nearly 3,400 years ago, at a little past two in the afternoon, on a day that in our modern calendar would be Saturday, May 14, 1338 BC, a thick darkness descended over the land of Egypt. All up and down the Nile, from the pyramids at Giza to the temples of Karnak, the light of day was extinguished as the Moon passed directly in front of the Sun. It was a total solar eclipse.

The timing of this eclipse is especially intriguing. Egypt in 1338 BC was in the midst of a religious revolution, one sparked a decade earlier when the pharaoh Akhenaten, together with his glamorous queen Nefertiti, abandoned the Egyptian faith and its horde of animal-headed deities. From the moment of Akhenaten's spiritual awakening, there was to be only one god: Aten, the deified Sun. On Akhenaten's orders, the old gods were banished and their temples barred shut. All religion was henceforth to be centered at Amarna, a shining new city built solely to worship the Sun. Most curiously of all, though, it's this tumultuous period that Sigmund Freud saw as the historical backdrop for the story of Moses. Might it be possible, then, that this eclipse was remembered as the ninth plague, the plague of darkness, as recounted in the biblical book of Exodus?

Figure 2.1: Akhenaten and his family worshipping the Aten. EGYPTIAN NATIONAL MUSEUM, CAIRO, EGYPT / BRIDGEMAN IMAGES.

For very ancient eclipses, such as this one, it's not possible to pinpoint with certainty the parts of the globe lying directly within the Moon's shadow. Nevertheless, the best estimate of the most modern astronomical models is that Amarna and its Great Aten Temple were situated squarely within the eclipse's path of totality that afternoon. This means that after about an hour of gradual darkening, the Moon's obscuration of the Sun would become total, complete, 100 percent. In fact, out of the 2,440 total solar eclipses which have occurred between 2000 BC and the year 2020, the eclipse of 1338 BC was the twelfth most intense, at least as measured by eclipse magnitude. At the peak of the eclipse, which occupied nearly seven whole minutes of the afternoon, the air would have cooled as the Sun's warming rays were blocked from the Earth. A conjunction of Venus and Mars above the western horizon, previously concealed by the light of day, now shone as brightly as if it were dusk, an invisible sight made visible by the perfect conjunction of the Sun and Moon within the stars of the constellation Taurus.

What would the Egyptians have made of such a spectacle? Were the ancient gods reasserting their superiority over the impudent Aten? Or did the Sun's reemergence following the eclipse signify that Akhenaten's final triumph over his enemies was at hand? Or, then again, maybe it was cloudy that day and nobody noticed. Whatever the interpretation, Akhenaten, the "heretic pharaoh," had only a few more years to live. Upon his death, his memory was cursed, the old gods were restored to their temples, and Amarna was abandoned to the wind and sand.

Figure 2.2: A Scheme of Heaven for Saturday, May 14, 1338 BC
A Total Solar Eclipse During the Reign of the Pharaoh Akhenaten

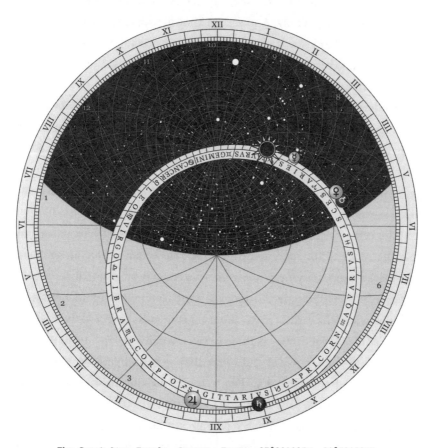

The Great Aten Temple, Amarna, Egypt: 27°39'03"N, 30°53'52"E
JD: 1232852.00232
12:03 UT
ΔT: 31890±1500s
Local Time: 2:15 PM
Local Apparent Sidereal Time: 4:44

		λ	β	RA $_{J2000}$	Dec $_{J2000}$	Az	El	House	
♄	Saturn	♐ 25°16'↓	0°09'	20ʰ 56ᵐ 13ˢ	-17°30'	284°58'	-76°57'	④	12°36'
♃	Jupiter	♐ 5°11'↓	0°12'	19ʰ 32ᵐ 55ˢ	-21°56'	50°12'	-80°27'	③	22°38'
♂	Mars	♓ 22°54'	-1°14'	2ʰ 28ᵐ 29ˢ	13°37'	260°20'	9°30'	⑦	9°38'
☉	Sun	♉ 9°50'	0°00'	5ʰ 43ᵐ 02ˢ	23°49'	255°02'	56°16'	⑧	27°10'
♀	Venus	♓ 24°29'	-2°07'	2ʰ 35ᵐ 47ˢ	13°17'	259°18'	11°00'	⑦	11°11'
☿	Mercury	♈ 23°14'	-1°27'	4ʰ 32ᵐ 05ˢ	20°50'	256°27'	39°38'	⑧	10°26'
☽	Moon	♉ 9°50'	0°00'	5ʰ 43ᵐ 02ˢ	23°50'	255°03'	56°16'	⑧	27°10'

It's fun to speculate about whether this eclipse played any role in Egyptian history or, for that matter, biblical history. Unfortunately, there aren't any records of it happening. And yet, we know it happened. The same astronomical computations that successfully guide spacecraft to distant planets leave no doubt there was an eclipse that day (even if some doubt remains regarding where, exactly, this eclipse could be seen).

Modern astronomy's ability to reconstruct the ancient sky is a little like opening a portal to the past. And positioning the stars and planets on a diagram according to their ancient configurations can feel a lot like tuning the dials of a cosmic radio. Does the simple act of contemplating the heavens as they appeared at a distant time and place make us more receptive, somehow, to the sentiments of that time and place?

The eerie thrill of mapping a sky that's been unseen for thousands of years becomes all the more uncanny whenever we have, from an age long ago, the written testimony of someone who actually viewed that very same pattern of planets and stars. Astrology is significant in this regard, because it provided one of the earliest motivations for stargazers to record their observations of the sky in detail. As these celestial records became more precise, our ability to pinpoint when and where they were written down gets more precise as well. It would be nice, then, to trace these transmissions backward in order to triangulate the origin of astrology itself. But beyond a certain point, the signals we have from the past are just too faint and garbled. Finding a narrative thread to tie them all together would be a lot like . . . well, a lot like clustering a patch of random stars into a constellation.

But if all that's known about astrology's origin is merely a constellation of scattered facts, then maybe the most honest way to describe it is simply to focus on the stars themselves, so to speak, and not on whatever artful lines can be drawn connecting them together. Here, then, is a star catalog of sorts. It consists of six physical artifacts from astrology's dawn which, to me at least, seem best positioned to both illuminate and constrain whatever historical narratives might be sketched around them.

THE ORIGINS OF ASTROLOGY IN SIX OBJECTS

α. The Pyramid of the Pharaoh Unis

Date: ca. 2350 BC

Original location: Saqqara necropolis, Egypt

Current location: Saqqara necropolis, Egypt

Significance: An early and unambiguous expression of man's regard for the stars.

When did humans first take an interest in the movements of the sky? The beginning of our species several hundred thousand years ago seems like a reasonable guess, but what actual evidence is there? Since there aren't any definitive records, we'll instead regard any physical evidence that has survived as a *terminus ante quem*, a "boundary-line before which," meaning that whatever origin date we're looking for must, logically, have happened beforehand.

Choosing the pyramids as our terminus may seem surprising, since there are a number of much older sites that are famous (or, perhaps, infamous) for their astronomical associations. Stonehenge in the U.K., for example, which dates to around 3000 BC, may have been built to align with sunrise on the summer solstice. And the even more ancient Göbekli Tepe in southern Turkey, built around 9000 BC, has also been hypothesized to have served some sort of calendrical function. But sites like these two, which consist of vaguely circular arrangements of large stone pillars, are the archaeological version of astrology's fundamental question: how do you know it's not just random?

To put it another way, the sky is a pretty target-rich environment, so any imaginary line drawn on the ground is guaranteed to point, at least approximately, to some intriguing star or celestial arc in the sky. Are you exploring an ancient structure that's oriented east–west? Well, maybe it was built that way to align with the equinoxes. And if the alignment isn't exactly east–west, then perhaps the builders had in mind the summer solstice somewhat to the north, or the winter solstice a bit to the south, or maybe even some ritually significant constellation as it would have appeared thousands of years ago.

Yet while there are plenty of things in the sky worth pointing to, the angular slop involved when sighting a line between large objects—two pillars, for example, or a row of hilltops—won't have anywhere near the precision needed to pick out a specific celestial body from its surroundings. And this makes it very hard to know if a site was built with a cosmic motivation at all.

For instance, suppose we situate ourselves at a key observation point and regard as significant just the four cardinal compass directions (north, south, east, and west), as well as sunrise and sunset at the two solstices. If we allow each of these eight directions a very reasonable 5-degree measurement window (2.5 degrees on either side), then we've already marked 8 × 5 = 40 degrees, out of a total 360 degrees, as cosmically significant. That's more than 10 percent of all possible compass directions. If we were to take a prehistoric temple and spin it around like a bottle, then it would have more than a 10 percent chance of settling in a direction that we'd be tempted to conclude was celestially motivated. And this is even before we've

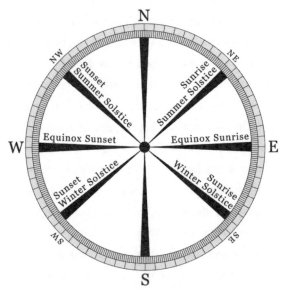

Figure 2.3: Sunrise and sunset directions for the latitude of Stonehenge. Even with very minimal assumptions, over 10 percent of the compass is quickly filled up by lines that may seem to be celestially significant.

considered the risings of the Moon and major stars. Statistically speaking, obtaining a result that can happen by dumb luck more than 10 percent of the time is simply not a significant outcome. This doesn't mean that prehistoric archaeological sites were not aligned cosmically—it's actually a perfectly plausible premise. It does mean, however, that it's difficult to argue this convincingly from their physical layout alone.

Which brings us to the pyramids. We'll skip over as no less speculative the various theories about how the pyramids' interior passageways may once have lined up with key stars, or how, taken as a group, they form a sort of primeval star chart. Actually, the pyramids' cosmic connection is much more obvious. For one thing, they're literally giant arrows pointing up at the sky. But even more definitively, we can be certain that the pyramids attest to a celestial awareness because they tell us so. A number of the earliest pyramids contain inscriptions, the so-called Pyramid Texts, consisting of spells and incantations meant to guide the deceased pharaohs on a celestial

Figure 2.4: The Pyramid of Unis, Saqqara, Egypt.
WERNER FORMAN ARCHIVE / BRIDGEMAN IMAGES.

journey to the afterlife. "[P]art your place in the sky among the stars of the sky, for you are the lone star at the shoulder," exhorts one such incantation. "Now that I have swept away the night and sent off the hour-stars, the controlling powers appear and privilege me as Baboon," exclaims another.

The oldest pyramid, built for the pharaoh Djoser by his advisor and architect Imhotep, dates to around 2650 BC. The oldest Pyramid Texts, inscribed in the tomb of the pharaoh Unis, date to around 2350 BC. These inscriptions are the very oldest Egyptian literature known. Actually, they are some of the very oldest writing known, period. And the chamber containing these inscriptions is decorated with dozens and dozens of five-pointed stars, which may be the oldest unambiguous depictions of any celestial object anywhere. While doubtless not the first expressions of mankind's regard for the heavens, these monuments provide, at least for our purposes, a rock-solid starting line from which to track astrology's subsequent rise.

β. An Ancient Egyptian Coffin Lid with a Map of the Stars

Date: ca. 2000 BC

Original location: Asyut, Egypt, Tomb 20

Current location: Egyptian Museum, Cairo

Object identifier: JE 36444; SR 3/696

Significance: An early map of the heavens, and early evidence for some familiar divisions of time.

In ancient Egypt, whoever would be reborn after death, as was the Sun each morning, would need to navigate the same celestial path the Sun took through the underworld each night. It was, presumably, to assist the dead in this journey that certain Egyptian coffin lids were decorated with maps of the stars. Though they're probably knockoffs of an older, royal exemplar, these coffin lids nevertheless have the distinction of being the oldest known maps of the heavens. The stars are arranged in a table, like a spreadsheet, so they're really

Figure 2.5: An ancient Egyptian coffin lid with a map of the stars. IMAGE COURTESY OF THE ORIENTAL INSTITUTE OF THE UNIVERSITY OF CHICAGO.

more like a train schedule than a conventional, pictorial star chart. Their purpose was to show which stars would be visible in the sky at various times. In
so doing, these coffin lids also illustrate the development of the Egyptian calendar and provide early evidence for some of its very recognizable divisions
of time: years made up of 365 days and organized into twelve months, and
days made up of twenty-four hours. This latter division is of particular interest
because, despite its familiarity, it also happens to be entirely arbitrary—there's
no reason a day couldn't be divided into twenty-five, seventeen, or one hundred intervals called "hours." Indeed, during the French Revolution, "deci-
mal clocks" were made which divided the day into just ten hours. So why the
number twenty-four? The coffin lids provide the answer.

A typical coffin lid star map identifies thirty-six patches of stars, one for
each of the thirty-six ten-day weeks of the Egyptian year. (Five special days,
not belonging to any month, were tacked on to the end of the year to bring
the total number of days to 365.) The stars assigned to a given week were
those which, during that week, could be seen rising over the eastern horizon
just before sunrise. On an average night, roughly twelve of these star patches,
called decans, could be observed arcing across the sky from sunset to sunrise.
This observation was later formalized into the notion of a twelve-hour night
and, from there, a matching twelve-hour day.

It's important to note, however, that none of the surviving coffin lids
agrees completely with the idealized Egyptian calendar. The imperfections
and alterations from one coffin lid to the next evidence the frustrations in
assigning nice round numbers to the cycles of astronomy. Even the seemingly small deviation of the Egyptian year of 365 days from the actual solar
year of (approximately) 365.24 days was still large enough for its seasonal
wanderings to have been noticeable during an individual lifespan. Regulating calendars to ensure their correspondence with the cycles of the cosmos
has been one of the chief occupations of astronomers throughout history,
and it's one that still requires active maintenance even today. In order to
account for the uneven slowing of the Earth's rotation, for example, "leap
seconds" must occasionally be added to Coordinated Universal Time, or

UTC, which is the time standard regulating the world's official clocks. As of this writing, the most recent leap second was inserted into UTC by the International Earth Rotation and Reference Systems Service (IERS) on December 31, 2016.

γ. Fragments of the MUL.APIN Astronomy Tablets

Date: 687 BC

Original location: Assur, Assyria (near modern Al-Shirqat, Iraq)

Current location: Vorderasiatisches Museum, Berlin

Object identifier: VAT 9412 + 11279

Significance: A snapshot of astronomical knowledge that includes an early version of the zodiac.

After the early artifacts of the third millennium BC, the subsequent development of the celestial sciences becomes very murky indeed. To a large degree, this is simply a fluke of archaeology. In the mid-1800s, thousands upon thousands of inscribed clay tablets were excavated from the royal library of the Assyrian Empire at Nineveh, a site that dates to around 650 BC. Meanwhile, there's no comparable trove of writings known from earlier periods. It seems reasonable that the extraordinary astronomical texts discovered in this library are the products of older traditions refined over several centuries. On the other hand, who really knows?

This is the case with the astronomical tablets called MUL.APIN, named for their opening words, which mean "The Plough Star." Some forty fragmentary copies of MUL.APIN have been recovered, one of which gives a date of inscription corresponding to 687 BC. The astronomical lore they contain, however, may be much older—perhaps by as much as a thousand years.

The MUL.APIN tablets are important because they provide an early benchmark for the state of astronomical knowledge. This knowledge included an awareness of the five planets visible to the naked eye (Mercury, Venus, Mars, Jupiter, and Saturn) and simple rules for when they could be seen. The tablets also provide several constellation lists, together with their rising dates during the year. One of these constellation lists, the so-called constellations "in the path of the Moon," is significant because it's the earliest known forerunner of the zodiac. Since the Moon's path in the sky hews very closely to the Sun's path in the sky (the path known today as the ecliptic), this is the first indication that stargazers had begun to recognize the usefulness of this celestial circle for tracking the orbits of the Sun, Moon, and planets. Although MUL.APIN lists seventeen of these constellations, their kinship with the modern zodiac is impossible to miss.

Table 2.1: Constellations in the Path of the Moon

	Constellations in the Path of the Moon from the MUL.APIN Tablets	Corresponding Modern Constellations (zodiac constellations in ALL CAPS)
1.	Stars	Pleiades (in TAURUS)
2.	Bull of Heaven	TAURUS
3.	Loyal Shepherd of (the sky god) Anu	Orion
4.	Old Man	Perseus
5.	Shepherd's Crook	Auriga
6.	Great Twins	GEMINI
7.	Crab	CANCER
8.	Lion	LEO
9.	Furrow	VIRGO
10.	Scales	LIBRA
11.	Scorpion	SCORPIUS
12.	Pablisag (a god)	SAGITTARIUS
13.	Goat-Fish	CAPRICORNUS
14.	Great One	AQUARIUS
15.	Tails of the Swallow	PISCES (western fish)
16.	Anunitu (a goddess)	PISCES (eastern fish)
17.	Hired Man	ARIES

Exactly why the number of zodiac constellations was reduced to twelve may never be known. Mathematically, twelve has the useful property that it is evenly divisible by a large set of smaller numbers, namely, 1, 2, 3, 4, and 6. It's also worth pointing out that Jupiter, frequently the brightest object in the night sky and associated by the Babylonians with their chief god Marduk, takes very nearly twelve years to complete its orbit around the ecliptic. This may have suggested the idea of dividing the ecliptic into twelve sections such that each section housed Jupiter for roughly an entire year, even if such a system could never have been maintained consistently.

δ. A Collection of Eclipse Omens

Date: ca. 650 BC

Original location: Nineveh, Assyria (near modern Mosul, Iraq)

Current location: British Museum, London

Object identifier: K.3563

Significance: An early example of celestial divination.

Assyria, as the tablets from its archives attest, was an empire entranced by all manner of prognostication and divination. In every corner of the kingdom, seers were asked for their interpretations of omens, which they dutifully reported to the capital at Nineveh. For biblical context, Nineveh is also where Jonah was commanded to prophesy—though, to no avail, he attempted instead to flee by ship. From the rubble of Nineveh, multi-tablet tomes have been excavated detailing how to predict the future from dreams, smoke patterns, deformed births, the color of ants crossing a doorway, and, of course, everything and anything observed in the sky.

The name for the main, seventy-tablet collection of Babylonian celestial omens is *Enūma Anu Enlil*, from its opening words, "When the gods Anu and Enlil." The astronomer-priests charged with observing the sky and interpreting its signs held the title of *ṭupšar Enūma Anu Enlil*, "scribe of the omen series *Enūma Anu Enlil*." The discipline as a whole, by extension, was called *ṭupšarrūtu Enūma Anu Enlil*, "the art of the scribe of *Enūma Anu Enlil*." So if you're looking for the earliest name for astrology, however imperfect the correspondence, this is probably as good as it gets.

A closely related tablet which contains an especially interesting list of celestial omens is K.3563. The tablet's origin is Babylonian, but this copy was housed, perhaps by royal request, at the Assyrian library at Nineveh. Whether it was ever consulted by the king's diviners is impossible to say. What is known is that it lay buried along with the rest of the library for nearly 2,500 years before being excavated and carted off to the British Museum in London, where it's held today. K.3563 contains a list of lunar eclipses arranged according to the months and days in which they might occur, together with the events they foretell. One example is for the lunar month of Elul (or Ulūlu), and it goes like this:

59. If on either the 13th or 14th day of Ulūlu . . . the moon is dark; the watch passes and it is dark; his features are dark like lapis lazuli; he is obscured until his midpoint; on the west (quadrant) as it is covered, the west wind blew; the sky is dark;

61. his light is covered; the son of the king will become purified (i.e., will perform *elēlu*-rituals) for (accession to) the throne but will not take the throne; an intruder will . . . princes in the west; for 8 (gloss: 16) years he will exercise kingship; . . . ; he will conquer the enemy army; there will be abundance and riches in his path; he will continually pursue his enemy, and his luck will not run out.

In other words, if you're the king and there's a lunar eclipse on the 13th or 14th of Elul while the west wind is blowing, you had better keep a very close eye out for any lucky intruders from the princes in the west.

Omen texts like tablet K.3563 reveal an impressive commitment to a close observation of the natural world, even if they display a rather bold conception of cause and effect. But how bold is too bold? Figuring out which phenomena are suitable for modeling and prediction and which aren't is a question that, in many ways, remains contentious within the sciences even today. As we'll explore in this book, astrology, which has a long history of making predictions ranging from the perfectly reasonable to the patently absurd, offers one of the richest sources of material for probing this very question.

ε. A Cuneiform Horoscope

Date: April 29, 410 BC

Original location: Babylon (near modern Baghdad, Iraq)

Current location: Ashmolean Museum, Oxford

Object identifier: AB 251

Significance: The oldest known personal horoscope.

Figure 2.6: A cuneiform horoscope. IMAGE © ASHMOLEAN MUSEUM, UNIVERSITY OF OXFORD.

The excavation of the Assyrian library at Nineveh, and specifically the discovery of the MUL. APIN tablets and celestial omen lists, offers a snapshot of celestial knowledge as it existed around the year 650 BC. The development of this knowledge over the next several centuries is actually much better understood, again thanks entirely to fairly recent archaeological discoveries. Of particular importance is the collection of tablets from Babylon known as the "astronomical diaries." These are compilations of nightly observations of the positions of the Moon and planets, together with notes on eclipses, equinoxes, and solstices. Occasionally, the diaries record the weather (such as when it's too cloudy to make an observation), the river level of the Euphrates, grain prices, and even certain newsworthy political events.

It's generally agreed that these diaries are the long-lost records which Ptolemy referred to in his *Almagest* when he wrote that the reign of the Babylonian king Nabonasser was "the era beginning from which the ancient

observations are, on the whole, preserved down to our own time." Nabonasser's reign began in 747 BC, the oldest surviving astronomical diary dates to
652 BC, and the last surviving one dates to 61 BC. Rivaled only by the extraordinary astronomical records from ancient China, the Babylonian astronomical diaries are one of, if not the longest continuous research program ever
undertaken. To properly convey the enormity of this achievement, I yield to
two of its foremost historians, Hermann Hunger and David Pingree:

> That someone in the middle of the eighth century BC conceived of such
> a scientific program and obtained support for it is truly astonishing;
> that it was designed so well is incredible; and that it was faithfully car-
> ried out for at least 700 years is miraculous.

Inevitably, perhaps, the increased observational sophistication of the
astronomical diaries was combined with the deep-rooted celestial omen tradition to produce an entirely new genre of text: the personal horoscope. The
oldest of these goes as follows:

1 Nisannu, night of the 14th(?), . . .
2 son of Šumu-uṣur, son of Šumu-iddina, descendant of Dēkē, was born.
3 At that time, the moon was below (lit.: the lower part of) the Pincer of
   the Scorpion,
4 Jupiter in Pisces, Venus
5 in Taurus, Saturn in Cancer,
6 Mars in Gemini. Mercury, which had set, was not vis[ible].
7–8 [observations of lunar visibility for the month]
[reverse of tablet]
1 (Things?) will be propitious for you.
2–4 [omitted]

This tablet is also remarkable for being one of the very first documents
to show the full evolution of the zodiac from just another constellation list
to a regular system of celestial coordinates. Using the zodiac signs this way

becomes increasingly common in the astronomical diaries starting around the year 450 BC. In fact, reporting only the zodiac signs in which Saturn, Jupiter, Mars, Venus, and the Moon were located, as this horoscope does, is sufficient to narrow down its date to just a handful of possibilities, with the night of April 28/29, 410 BC, representing the most likely match. Although the name of the child born that night is missing, given how old this tablet is, and the lucky fortune it foretold, we may just as well regard it as the birth horoscope of astrology itself.

ζ. Astronomical Diary Chronicling the Conquest of Alexander the Great

Date: 331 BC

Original location: Babylon (near modern Baghdad, Iraq)

Current location: British Museum, London

Object identifier: BM 36390 + 36761

Significance: An extraordinary conjunction of history and astronomy.

Figure 2.7: Astronomical diary chronicling the conquest of Alexander the Great. IMAGE © THE BRITISH MUSEUM.

We end this chapter as we began it: with an eclipse. This eclipse, however, was not an eclipse of the Sun, but of the Moon. And unlike the eclipse at Amarna, for which there are no historical records, the eclipse we're about to describe was remarkably well documented in eyewitness accounts. This was the famous total lunar eclipse that occurred shortly before Alexander the Great's final victory over Darius III at the Battle of Gaugamela, a battle which marked the completion of his conquest of Persia. A scheme of the heavens as they would have appeared to the stargazers in Babylon on that fateful night is plotted in color plate 4.

In their astronomical diary, those same Babylonian stargazers recorded the river level of the Euphrates, the prices of sesame, mustard, and wool, and a synopsis of planetary positions for the month: Jupiter was in Scorpio; Venus was in Leo, then at the end of the month in Virgo; Saturn was in Pisces; Mercury and Mars, which had set, were not visible. But for the 13th of Elul, as Alexander's army closed in on Darius, the diary records something more than a little ominous:

1' [. . . .]. . . . [. . . .]
2' [. . . .]. . . . [. . . .] The 13th, moonset to sunrise: 8°. . . . [. . . .]
3' [. . . . lunar] eclipse, in its totality covered. 10° night [totality². . . .]
   (broken) Jupiter set; Saturn [. . . .]
4' [. . . .] during totality the west wind blew, during clearing the east
   wind. [. . .] fourth². . . . ; during the eclipse, deaths and plague²
   [occurred²] in [. . . .]

Recall that a total eclipse of the Moon on the 13th day of Elul while the west wind blew was precisely the scenario described some three hundred years earlier in omen tablet K.3563. The events registered next in the diary are quite well known: battle was joined eleven days later, on the 24th of Elul (October 1, 331 BC), resulting in a total victory for Alexander, the intruder from the princes in the west. He conquered the enemy army and there was, indeed, abundance and riches in his path. For exactly eight years, he exercised kingship over the known world until he died, in Babylon, in the year 323 BC, at the age of thirty-two. And during his life, brief though it was, his luck never once ran out. In other words, everything happened more or less exactly as the heavens foretold. A pretty extraordinary coincidence, wouldn't you say?

3

A QUICK SPIN AROUND THE CELESTIAL SPHERE

Syracuse, Sicily, 212 BC

A s far as topics of history go, astrology pretty much has it all: mystery, intrigue, romance, and, every so often, a rollicking, old-fashioned naval assault—like the one the Roman general Marcellus waged against the Sicilian fortress of Syracuse, whose citizens had sided with Rome's arch-foe, the North African empire of Carthage. But most of all, the history of astrology is filled with astronomy. It's the starry thread that unites these stories and makes them sparkle. Being familiar, therefore, with even a little astronomy can help clear up a lot of astrology's blurriness. And this is what brings us to Syracuse: because all the astronomy we'll need in this book is hunkered behind those walls, inside the workshop of the great Archimedes.

THE WORLD IN ROME'S HANDS

At the time of Rome's wars against Carthage, the island of Sicily wasn't Italian but Greek. In fact, Cicero, the Roman orator, once described Syracuse as "the greatest and most beautiful of all the Greek cities." While Rome and Carthage duked it out for dominance of the Mediterranean, Sicily lay right in the middle—an urgent, strategic prize. Thus, even though Rome had more immediate concerns, such as Hannibal and his elephants pillaging unchecked throughout Italy, an alliance between Carthage and Syracuse could not be permitted at any price. The Senate and the people of Rome, therefore, dispatched Marcus Claudius Marcellus with a fleet of ships and orders to bring Sicily to heel.

Yet the Roman armada of quintuple-decked warships soon discovered just how outclassed they were. Archimedes, the most brilliant engineer of the ancient world, had personally designed his city's defenses. The same genius who proved the law of the lever, and who declared that he could lift the entire Earth so long as he had another to stand on, had devised a terrifying machine which (so it's said) could hoist the Roman ships straight into the air and plunge them back into the sea. Thwarted by Archimedes' contraptions, Marcellus settled in for a siege.

If this contest had been decided by engineering alone, no doubt the Sicilians would still be speaking Greek today. But Marcellus was the master of a craft even more powerful than mechanics: treachery. Through informants he learned that Syracuse's north wall would be lightly defended during the city's festival to Artemis, the virgin huntress and goddess of the Moon. And so, unnoticed amid the nighttime revels, the Romans scaled the walls and snuck into the city. The ancient sources don't give a precise date for this, but we can offer what's probably a pretty good guess. First, the walls were breached sometime around the beginning of spring in 212 BC—this much we're told. Second, Artemis, being a lunar goddess, likely preferred her celebrations when the Moon was full. Connecting these dots, it's possible that Syracuse's fate was sealed in the predawn hours of April 1, 212 BC, during the Syracusans' springtime lunar month of Artemisios, under a canopy of planets and stars resembling the scheme depicted in figure 3.1.

Even as his troops plundered the city, Marcellus still hoped to meet the man whose creations had both baffled and amazed him. He was too late. One of his soldiers had slain the old engineer—still working, it's said, on a problem of geometry. But we can imagine Marcellus's wonder when he stepped into the great man's study. Amid scattered diagrams and half-built prototypes,

Figure 3.1: A Scheme of Heaven for the Full Moon of Saturday, April 1, 212 BC
The Romans Breach the Walls of Syracuse (Conjectured)

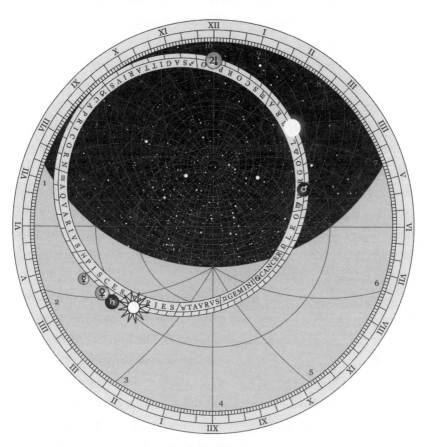

The Hexapylon Gate, Syracuse, Sicily: 37°06'07"N, 15°15'38"E
JD: 1644080.58597
2:03 UT
ΔT: 12906s
Local Time: 3:00 AM
Local Apparent Sidereal Time: 15:27

		λ	β	RA $_{J2000}$	Dec $_{J2000}$	Az	El	House	
♄	Saturn	♓ 26°38'	-2°17'	1ʰ 44ᵐ 52ˢ	8°32'	69°07'	-30°24'	②	2°07'
♃	Jupiter	♏ 23°53'↓	0°53'	17ʰ 36ᵐ 41ˢ	-22°44'	179°59'	34°47'	⑩	0°00'
♂	Mars	♍ 10°49'↓	2°46'	12ʰ 46ᵐ 48ˢ	-2°04'	265°02'	23°23'	⑦	23°28'
☉	Sun	♈ 7°18'	0°00'	2ʰ 22ᵐ 28ˢ	14°21'	56°31'	-32°10'	②	7°01'
♀	Venus	♓ 20°45'	-1°30'	1ʰ 21ᵐ 37ˢ	7°05'	74°46'	-27°07'	①	27°57'
☿	Mercury	♓ 10°54'	-2°19'	0ʰ 46ᵐ 28ˢ	2°31'	84°42'	-23°03'	①	23°09'
☽	Moon	♎ 12°40'	1°48'	14ʰ 45ᵐ 48ˢ	-14°19'	230°57'	35°26'	⑧	12°30'

two strange-looking objects attracted his gaze. They were two models of the cosmos in miniature. The first was a small, solid sphere whose surface was dotted with stars. The second was an entire clockwork universe complete with orbiting planets.

Out of all the spoils Marcellus shipped back, the clockwork planetarium was the only item he kept for himself. The starry sphere, meanwhile, he gifted to the Temple of Virtue in Rome. Surprisingly, the Roman descriptions of these two little universes provide some of the best information we have about the otherwise forgotten beginnings of Greek astronomy. And it's Cicero who offers the fullest sketch. He writes that Thales (ca. 550 BC) was the first to fabricate a spherical globe, while Eudoxus (ca. 350 BC), a student of Plato's, was the first to engrave one with a map of the stars. Aratus, the poet (ca. 250 BC), immortalized Eudoxus's sphere in a much-loved poem called *Phaenomena*. But it was Archimedes who was the first to bring one to life with mechanical motions for the Sun, Moon, and planets.

Remarkably, as recently as the twentieth century, two artifacts from around the time of Cicero turned up which may very well be copies or descendants of Archimedes' cosmic models (plate 5). The first is a silver sphere, about the size of a tennis ball, adorned with the constellations. The second is the extraordinary Antikythera Mechanism—a multifunctional, crank-operated, astronomical calculator, and the only clockwork gadget to have survived from classical antiquity. So what information did these cosmic contrivances encode? This is the question we now turn to.

STAR LAW AND STAR LORE

From Archimedes' era right up through the Renaissance, the universe was thought to look more or less like figure 3.2. Anchored at the center was the spherical Earth (the Greeks were certainly aware that the Earth was round), which never moved, not even to spin around on its axis. Farthest away were the stars, which made a clockwise, or east-to-west, revolution around the Earth once per day. Between the stars and the Earth were the seven classical planets, each nestled in their own spherical shell. Through a sort of celestial friction, the stars dragged each of these shells or "spheres" along with them in their revolution around the Earth. Thus, the movement of the outermost, starry sphere set in motion the sphere of Saturn, albeit with a bit of a lag. Saturn's motion in turn dragged Jupiter's sphere, but again at a slightly slower rate. Jupiter then dragged Mars, Mars the Sun, and so on down to the Moon.

Because each celestial shell revolved a little bit slower than the one above it, the effect was that, in addition to their daily east-to-west revolution, each planet appeared to slip backward, or west-to-east, at different speeds as measured against the background of the "fixed" stars. Saturn slips the most slowly, such that it takes nearly thirty years for it to make a complete lap around the stars. Next is Jupiter, which orbits in approximately twelve years. The interval needed for the Sun to overlap the same stars twice defines exactly one year. Lastly, and swiftest, is the Moon, which falls completely backward around the stars once every month.

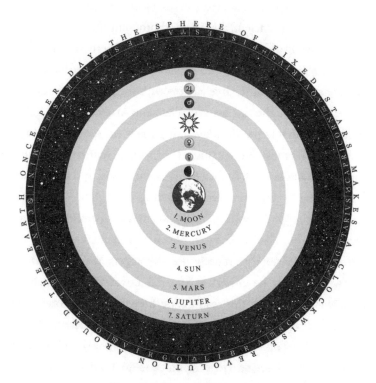

Figure 3.2: The geocentric cosmos.

The Babylonians, as far as is known, never had a use for cosmic models like this. Speculating about the physical arrangement of the heavens appears to have been a peculiarly Greek pastime, one they enjoyed so much they had two different names for it: *astrologia* (astrology) and *astronomia* (astronomy). These two words emerged early on as synonyms despite being formed from different etymological elements. *Astronomia* (ἀστρονομία) is a compound of *aster*, meaning "star" or "planet," and *nomos*, meaning "law." Meanwhile, *astrologia* (ἀστρολογία) derives from *logos*, which means "word" or "speech." Very literally, then, astronomy is "star law" while astrology is "star lore." The word *logos*, however, is notoriously versatile and often carries the added nuance of "system." Thus, a more meaningful translation of *astrologia* might be "a systematic account of the stars and planets."

Yet why have two different words to mean exactly the same thing? There's really no other ancient Greek word pair that's comparable. Today we have "economy" and "ecology," both from *oikos*, meaning "house," but while the first word is genuinely ancient, the latter is thoroughly modern. (And, indeed, these words have little connection to each other.) There may not be a good answer here. Nevertheless, we can make note of the fact that the earliest astronomy-astrology split in Greek aligns with the great chasm dividing all of ancient Greek thought: that between Plato and Aristotle. Plato, in his writings, and most notably the *Republic*, relies solely on the word *astronomia*. Meanwhile, Plato's most famous student, Aristotle, exclusively uses the word *astrologia* in his books, such as the *Physics*, *Metaphysics*, and *On the Heavens*.

It's tempting to interpret these competing word choices as a reflection of their competing philosophies. Did Plato envision *astronomia*, "star law," as approaching his ideal of a pure, abstract, and mathematical science? Conversely, did Aristotle purposely use *astrologia*, "star lore," to counter that knowledge must be empirical and inductive? Unfortunately, there's not a whole lot to support this reading. Both Plato and Aristotle categorize *astronomia–astrologia* as a branch of mathematics, and neither indicates that he is using anything other than a common and commonly understood word.

Besides, even if there is a deeper significance to this distinction, it doesn't do much to explain the subsequent histories of these words. For one thing,

Aristotle influenced the development of the natural sciences in a way that Plato, quite simply, did not. Thus, it was Aristotle's vision of the cosmos, and his terminology, which constituted the scientific consensus when Archimedes constructed his celestial models. This doesn't mean, however, that there weren't alternative ideas orbiting around. In fact, it's through Archimedes that we learn about another thinker, a certain Aristarchus of Samos, who argued that the Sun, not the Earth, stood at the center of the universe.

It's amazing to consider, but Copernicus's idea of a Sun-centered cosmos was actually proposed thousands of years before the scientific revolution. Even more amazingly, the question of whether the Earth orbits the Sun or vice-versa—the very question on which the whole scientific revolution is supposed to have hinged—may not have been viewed as particularly important, at least not to Archimedes. At that time, the abstract cosmological speculations of those whom Archimedes called "astrologers" (*astrologoi*)—that is, those who studied *astrologia*—had no real bearing on the practical problems of computing when and where the various heavenly bodies would appear in the sky. For this, there existed an entirely separate and more mathematical tradition, one whose intricate, numerical methods provided the perfect matrix for astrology (meant here in our modern sense of the word) to establish its roots and multiply.

MAPPING THE SKY

Suppose you saw something dazzling in the sky, like a planet or a beautiful star. How would you point it out? If gesturing does the trick, great. But if not, you're left with, "See such and such off to the right? OK, stop. Now look up just so high." All things considered, it's not an ineffective method. Note, though, that it would never occur to anyone to add, "and look for it at a distance of so many millions of miles away." Because when we look up at the sky, everything beyond the clouds—the Sun, the Moon, the stars, the planets—seems equally far away, as if it had all been painted on the inside surface of an enormous sphere. This sphere has a technical name: the celestial sphere. It's basically a giant, fictitious globe centered around the globe of the Earth, which provides a reference for locating distant objects in the sky.

And it's between these two globes—the celestial, above, and the terrestrial, below—that astrology makes its home.

Often it's objected that astrology must be wrong because it relies on geocentric (that is, Earth-centered) concepts like the celestial sphere, whereas it's been known since Copernicus that the Earth revolves around the Sun and not the other way around. Leaving astrology's fundamental soundness aside, there's nothing at all backward about adopting a geocentric framework. Geocentric coordinates are still used every day in the most advanced applications of satellite navigation, mapping, and even astronomy. If anything, the Copernican revolution emphasized the importance of finding the most appropriate coordinate system for a given problem. And when it comes to measuring the positions of heavenly bodies *as they are seen from the Earth*, geocentric coordinates are often the most convenient choice. Thus, despite millennia of scientific upheaval, the basic geocentric coordinates that we'll use throughout this book will be as familiar to astronomers today as they were to Archimedes thousands of years ago.

In fact, a big reason why the celestial sphere has remained so useful for so long is precisely because it doesn't require any assumptions about the actual physical arrangement of the cosmos. It's simply a handy framework for modeling motions in the sky. And we don't need to look very far, either, for an effective method to specify points on its surface. The system of latitudes and longitudes we're familiar with from geography is as effective in heaven as it is on Earth. But there's one important wrinkle: Here on Earth, the Earth's daily rotation provides a natural orientation around which to construct a latitude–longitude coordinate system. Due to the heavens' multiple motions, however, there is no single, obvious orientation to choose. Actually, there are three. These three choices yield three separate geocentric coordinate systems, each tailored to treat a separate set of celestial phenomena with maximum ease.

The system of *equatorial coordinates* is what would result if the Earth's latitudes and longitudes were extended out to the heavens. The system's fundamental midplane coincides with the Earth's equator, and its central axis coincides with the Earth's axis of rotation. Lines of longitude are called right ascensions and are measured in terms of hours, minutes, and seconds. Lines of latitude are called declinations. By design, equatorial coordinates are constructed to line up with the sky's apparent daily rotation, which makes these coordinates the simplest and most natural system with which to treat this motion.

Ecliptic coordinates are constructed around the Sun's yearly motion in the sky. And as a quick glance at figure 3.3 shows, the plane of this motion—the plane of the ecliptic—doesn't line up with the equatorial coordinate system at all. Instead, the ecliptic is inclined to the equator at an angle of about 23.4 degrees. But if it weren't for this angle, there wouldn't be any seasons. This is because the Sun's orbit along the ecliptic carries it further north of the equator at certain times of the year, and further south at others, making the Sun appear higher or lower in the sky depending on your latitude.

Astronomy would undoubtedly be simpler, albeit much more bland, if the ecliptic weren't inclined to the equator at such a funny angle. But one advantage of having two fundamental circles in the sky—the equator and the ecliptic—instead of just one, is that the two locations where these circles intersect offer two natural points of reference. These are the spring and fall equinoxes. On the two days of the year when the Sun crosses the equator at one of these points, the Earth experiences a perfectly even twelve hours of daylight and twelve hours of night. These days therefore define, astronomically, the first day of spring and the first day of fall.

By tradition, both the equatorial and ecliptic coordinate systems take the spring equinox, or vernal point, as their prime longitude. Here on Earth, by contrast, our system of longitudes has no natural staring point. The Earth's zero-longitude, or prime meridian, is the line that runs through the U.K.'s Royal Observatory at Greenwich—a cosmologically arbitrary compromise agreed upon by the nations of the world in 1884 at the International Meridian Conference in Washington, DC.

Latitude lines in the ecliptic coordinate system are called, not very creatively, ecliptic latitudes. Similarly, the longitude lines are called ecliptic longitudes and they're measured as degrees from the spring equinox in

Figure 3.3: The Three Geocentric Coordinate Systems of Observational Astronomy

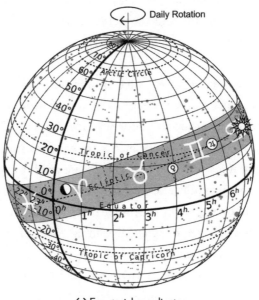

(a) Equatorial coordinates

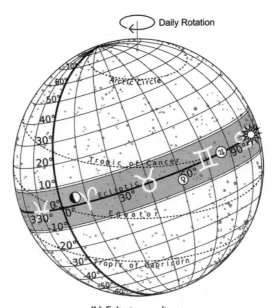

(b) Ecliptic coordinates

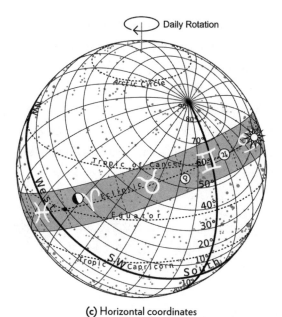

(c) Horizontal coordinates

Three identical, "god's eye" views of the celestial sphere, showing the exact same configuration of stars and planets. The images differ only in their coordinate grids. (a) The *equatorial coordinate system* is based on the Earth's plane of rotation (the equator) and divides the sphere into *right ascensions* and *declinations*. (b) The *ecliptic coordinate system* is based on the plane of the Sun's apparent orbit (the ecliptic) and divides the sphere into *ecliptic longitudes* and *ecliptic latitudes*. (c) A *horizontal coordinate system* is based on the plane of an observer's horizon and divides the sphere into *azimuths* and *elevations*. The horizontal system shown here is for an observer at the latitude of Greenwich, England.

the direction of the Sun's annual motion. But recall that the stars along the ecliptic—those which the Sun touches during its yearly orbit—are the stars which form the zodiac constellations. By virtue of its location, therefore, the zodiac offers a complementary way of denoting ecliptic longitudes. Traditionally this is done by fixing the "first point," or "cusp," of Aries at the vernal point. The other signs then follow in 30-degree increments according to the system laid out in figure 3.4. Thus, the fall equinox (ecliptic longitude 180°) coincides with the cusp of Libra, while the cusps of Cancer (ecliptic longitude 90°) and Capricorn (ecliptic longitude 270°) coincide with the solstices.

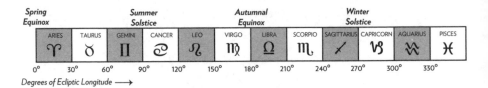

Degrees of Ecliptic Longitude ⟶

Figure 3.4: The zodiac as a rational partition of the ecliptic

One remnant of this tradition has persisted right down to modern times, in that the circles traced out by the Sun on the summer and winter solstices are still called the Tropics of Cancer and Capricorn. These celestial circles, projected back down to Earth, define that warm and sunny region we call tropical, and whose boundaries correspond exactly to the obliquity of the ecliptic, namely, the latitudes 23.4° north and 23.4° south of the equator. The word "tropic," meanwhile, comes from the Greek word τροπή (tropé) signifying a turn. It's related to the word "trophy," which was a marker showing where the enemy's army had been turned on the battlefield. By analogy, the Tropics of Cancer and Capricorn mark the northernmost and southernmost excursions of the Sun before it turns back toward the equator.

Ecliptic coordinates are designed to make it easy to track the Sun's apparent yearly orbit. But they are handy for tracking the Moon and the planets, too. Due to the way the solar system first formed, the Earth, Moon, Sun, and planets are all situated very nearly on the same plane in space: the ecliptic plane. This gives the whole solar system a disk-like structure, as no planet strays from the ecliptic by more than 9 degrees of ecliptic latitude. This behavior is often encoded on celestial globes in the breadth of the zodiac band drawn around the ecliptic.

To give a specific example: the Moon orbits the Earth on a plane that is offset from the ecliptic by about 5.1 degrees. Were it not for this small offset, there would be a solar eclipse each and every month during the new moon, when the Moon and Sun align in ecliptic longitude. Clearly this isn't the case, and the reason is that at most new moons, the Moon is ever so slightly offset from the Sun in ecliptic latitude. Since the Sun is always, by definition, exactly on the ecliptic, it follows that no eclipse can occur unless, at the precise instant of new moon, the Moon is also on the ecliptic and not a smidgen above or below. (You can see an example of this in the coordinates computed for the solar eclipse at Amarna in chapter 2.) And this connection with eclipses is how the ecliptic got its name.

Predicting eclipses is a tricky business, in part because it requires an ability to accurately model the Moon's ecliptic latitude as well as its ecliptic longitude. But in situations where that level of detail isn't needed, the disk-like structure of the solar system means that the positions of the Sun, Moon and planets can be communicated effectively simply by reporting their ecliptic longitudes. This practice is especially characteristic of astrology, which simply adds a little pizzazz to the matter by using the zodiac symbols to denote longitude increments of 30 degrees. For example, an ecliptic longitude of 127° can be written equivalently as ♌ 7°, since the zodiac sign of Leo (♌) begins at the ecliptic longitude of 120°.

During the course of a day, the ecliptic longitudes of the Sun and planets remain more or less unchanged. But over longer time periods, each of these bodies makes its slow, west-to-east orbit through the zodiac in the direction of increasing ecliptic longitude, that is, in the direction of Aries → Taurus → Gemini. Occasionally, however, each of the planets (but never the Sun or Moon) will appear to make a small loop-de-loop in the zodiac. When a planet wanders backward through the zodiac—that is, in the direction of decreasing ecliptic longitude, or Aries → Pisces → Aquarius—it is said to be in retrograde. Today, it's known that this behavior is simply the result of the Earth orbiting the Sun. But in the geocentric cosmos, modeling retrograde motion wasn't a simple matter at all. Nevertheless, it was this and other orbital anomalies which spurred the stargazers of antiquity to continually improve their models and predictions of the complex motions of the planets as seen from the Earth.

The third and final system of standard, geocentric coordinates are *horizontal coordinates*. These are based around you, the observer, wherever you happen to be. The fundamental midplane of the system is your local horizon. The system's north pole is the spot in the sky directly over your head, called your local zenith. Latitude lines, counting from horizon to zenith, are called elevations. Longitude lines are called azimuths, and they correspond to the directions you would read off a map, with local north (or, just as often, local south) serving as the zero-longitude. Horizontal coordinates are especially important from a practical standpoint, since these are the values you would read directly off an astronomical instrument. Converting to equatorial or ecliptic coordinates requires trigonometric formulas which, traditionally, might be approximated by handy algorithms, tables in a book, or the mechanical operations of a device like an astrolabe.

Table 3.1 summarizes the three geocentric coordinate systems just described. In the schemes of heaven I've included throughout this book, the positions of each of the seven classical planets are reported as latitude–longitude pairs in each of these three systems. That's a total of six coordinates per planet. (The presence of a downward-pointing arrow ↓ indicates that a planet is in retrograde.) The seventh, rightmost column in these schemes lists the astrological House of Heaven in which each planet is located. These Houses are astrology's unique system of local coordinates; we'll discuss them in greater detail in chapter 8. In the meantime, simply by observing the schemes which appear in each chapter and getting more comfortable with their coordinates, you'll feel increasingly at home inside the celestial sphere as you make your way through this book.

Table 3.1: The Geocentric Coordinate Systems of Astronomy

	EQUATORIAL	ECLIPTIC	HORIZONTAL
Orientation			
Fundamental Midplane	Equator	Ecliptic	local horizon
North Pole	in URSA MINOR	in DRACO	local zenith
South Pole	in OCTANS	in DORADO	local nadir
Longitude Coordinate			
Name	Right Ascension	Ecliptic Longitude	Azimuth
Abbreviation	RA	λ	Az
Prime Meridian	longitude containing the vernal point	longitude containing the vernal point	local north (or local south)
Span	$0^h\ 0^m\ 0^s$–$24^h\ 0^m\ 0^s$	0°–360°	0°–360°
Latitude Coordinate			
Name	Declination	Ecliptic Latitude	Elevation
Abbreviation	Dec	β	El
Span	–90°–90°	–90°–90°	–90°–90°

SUN-BASED OR STAR-BASED ASTROLOGY? ZODIAC SIGNS VS. ZODIAC CONSTELLATIONS

If you've been paying extra-close attention, then perhaps you've noticed a very subtle, but very important inconsistency in what's been discussed so far. In just three chapters, I've already mentioned two separate ways of dividing the zodiac. In chapter 1, when discussing the Age of Aquarius, I described a method for dividing the ecliptic which ensured that as many stars as possible from a particular zodiac *constellation* ended up in the partition assigned to that zodiac *sign*. And in this chapter I've referenced an entirely different system, in which the spring equinox defines the cusp of Aries. As it turns out, these two methods are completely incompatible. On account of the precession of the equinoxes, the vernal point will cycle through all twelve zodiac constellations over a period of approximately 26,000 years. And if the vernal point is taken as the cusp of Aries, then Aries, the sign, must slowly but inevitably slide away from Aries the constellation. And so too for Taurus, Gemini, Cancer, etc., such that in a few more centuries, the zodiac sign of Aries will have migrated all the way into the constellation of Aquarius.

This situation is equally problematic for astronomy. The equatorial and ecliptic coordinate systems also use the spring equinox as their nominal origin, but because of the Earth's slow wobbling, which is the physical cause of precession, these systems of coordinates are in a constant state of flux. This is a really unfortunate property for any coordinate system to have. Consequently, when specifying the astronomical coordinates of an object in the sky, it's also necessary to specify the "epoch," or instant in time, to which those coordinates are referenced. Modern astronomy uses the J2000.0 epoch, which references the location of the spring equinox at noon, in Greenwich, on January 1 of the year 2000. (More precisely, beginning in 1997, astronomers finally dispensed with using equinox reference points altogether and switched to the International Celestial Reference Frame, or ICRF. The ICRF is based on a set of extragalactic radio sources and is aligned, for continuity and convenience, to the J2000.0 epoch.) In astrology, meanwhile, it's almost always preferable to give coordinates that are "of-date," that is, coordinates which are referenced to the equinox of the specific moment in question. In our schemes of heaven, ecliptic coordinates are always given "of-date," whereas equatorial coordinates are always given with respect to the ICRF/J2000.0 reference frame.

In practice, the precession of the equinoxes is so slow that, at least in astronomy, a given epoch can be handy for fifty or a hundred years before it's worth the effort to retabulate all the star catalogs. But for astrology, precession is more than just a minor nuisance. It forces a fundamental choice as to whether you want a solar astrology, in which the solstices and equinoxes are the main thing, or a sidereal (that is, star-based) astrology, in which the constellations are the main thing—because you can't have both.

This inconsistency, which precession makes a little bit worse each year, would seem to have set the clock ticking for a pretty catastrophic crack-up of astrology's core beliefs. And yet, no such crack-up ever occurred. Instead, Claudius Ptolemy, the most authoritative astronomer *and astrologer* of the ancient world, preemptively and definitively settled the matter in favor of solar astrology. And he did this remarkably early in astrology's history—around the year 150 of the Common Era—long before the slow divergence of solar Aries from sidereal Aries would have been seen as especially glaring or problematic.

Ptolemy, whom we'll meet again later in this book, never discusses this issue in detail. He simply adopts the practice of using the spring equinox to define Aries in both the *Almagest,* his book on astronomy, and the *Tetrabiblos,* his book on astrology, without offering much by way of explanation. But such was Ptolemy's prestige within the astrological traditions of Rome, Persia, Arabia, and Europe that there has never been a serious challenge to this convention. In other words, Western astrology is, and generally always has been, emphatically solar. Occasionally, a few important stars may appear in horoscopes here or there, but they are at most bit players. This is, to be sure, a tad ironic for a discipline called "astrology," and whose most basic entities are named after constellations. Nevertheless, as early as Ptolemy's time, when the spring equinox was just beginning its precession through the constellation Pisces, a decision was made—whether controversially or not, we will never know—to dissociate the zodiac signs from their starry namesakes. And astrology has never looked back since.

A THIRTEENTH ZODIAC SIGN?

There's no denying that the zodiac signs called Aries, Taurus, Gemini, etc., share the same names as the constellations called Aries, Taurus, Gemini, etc., from which they arose. So it's not terribly surprising that news of their astrological divorce, though finalized some two thousand years ago, has never really become common knowledge. This has set the stage for a classic comedy of errors, one that has played out most publicly in the recent "discoveries"—repeated every five years or so—of the existence of a thirteenth zodiac sign. "A thirteenth zodiac sign?" you might ask. "What does that even mean?"

Think back two chapters, to our somewhat quixotic computation for when the Age of Aquarius will begin. Recall that the trickiest part wasn't projecting where the stars will be hundreds of years in the future, but rather how to draw the boundary between one constellation and the next—because, traditionally, the constellations never had precise boundaries, or, for that matter, a consistent set of names, or even an unambiguous account of which stars belonged where. Modern astronomy solves this problem, albeit in a somewhat arbitrary way.

Today, in astronomy, the constellations serve no real function. At worst, they're an embarrassing reminder of an astrological past that most astronomers would just as soon forget. Nevertheless, when observing the heavens, it's useful to have a handy way to reference large swaths of sky, and the constellations serve this purpose just as well as would any other, equally arbitrary scheme. And so, in 1922, the International Astronomical Union (IAU), which itself was only established in 1919, adopted a list recognizing eighty-eight "official" constellations. These official constellations were given official boundaries in 1930, such that the complete set covers the entire celestial sphere with no overlap.

The IAU constellation boundaries are defined in terms of equatorial coordinates, that is, right ascensions and declinations. If you were to draw theses boundaries on the celestial sphere and then unroll the sphere's surface along its equator, you'd end up with a map which looks like figure 3.5. Note that in a map like this, the ecliptic circle now appears as a sinusoid-like curve. The constellations intercepted by this curve are shown in white. Sure enough, if you count them, there are thirteen! Twelve are the familiar zodiac constellations, while the interloper here is Ophiuchus, the "serpent bearer." If we were hyperliteral types who regarded the IAU boundaries as possessing some sort of physical significance, as opposed to being an entirely arbitrary scheme of convenience, then, yes, we would be forced to conclude that there are thirteen, not twelve, zodiac signs. (Cetus, the sea monster, and Orion, the

Figure 3.5: The Celestial Sphere Divided by the 88 Modern Constellations

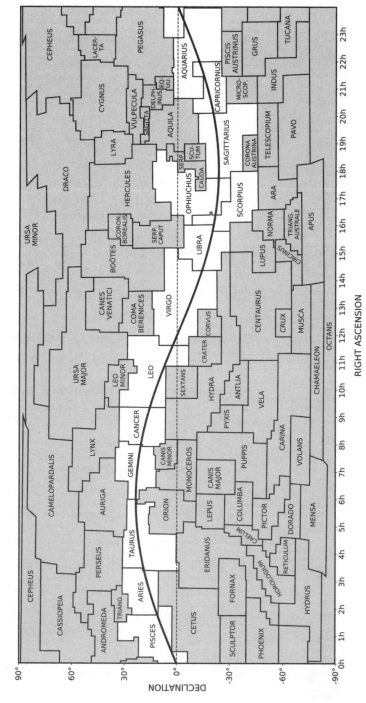

A map of the celestial sphere showing the 88 modern constellations and their boundaries as adopted by the International Astronomical Union in 1930. According to this division of the sky, the ecliptic (solid black curve) intercepts not twelve, but thirteen constellations (shown in white).

Table 3.2: Solar and Sidereal (IAU) Divisions of the Zodiac for the Year 2020

Solar Zodiac			2020 Start Date	UTC
1.	♈	Aries	Mar 20 *equinox*	3:50 a.m.
2.	♉	Taurus	Apr 19	2:46 p.m.
3.	♊	Gemini	May 20	1:50 p.m.
4.	♋	Cancer	Jun 20 *solstice*	9:44 p.m.
5.	♌	Leo	Jul 22	8:37 a.m.
6.	♍	Virgo	Aug 22	3:45 p.m.
7.	♎	Libra	Sep 22 *equinox*	1:31 p.m.
8.	♏	Scorpio	Oct 22	11:00 p.m.
9.	♐	Sagittarius	Nov 21	8:40 p.m.
10.	♑	Capricorn	Dec 21 *solstice*	10:02 a.m.
11.	♒	Aquarius	Jan 20	2:55 p.m.
12.	♓	Pisces	Feb 19	4:58 a.m.

Sidereal Zodiac			2020 Start Date	UTC
1.	♈	Aries	Apr 18	2:03 p.m.
2.	♉	Taurus	May 14	1:51 a.m.
3.	♊	Gemini	Jun 21	4:39 a.m.
4.	♋	Cancer	Jul 20	11:05 a.m.
5.	♌	Leo	Aug 10	10:47 a.m.
6.	♍	Virgo	Sep 16	2:40 p.m.
7.	♎	Libra	Oct 31	12:47 a.m.
8.	♏	Scorpius	Nov 23	4:50 a.m.
9.	⛎	Ophiuchus	Nov 29	4:30 p.m.
10.	♐	Sagittarius	Dec 18	3:01 a.m.
11.	♑	Capricornus	Jan 20	9:32 a.m.
12.	♒	Aquarius	Feb 17	3:14 a.m.
13.	♓	Pisces	Mar 12	12:42 a.m.

hunter, both miss the cut by a whisker.) We can even use these IAU bound-aries to construct a fully sidereal, thirteen-sign zodiac, as table 3.2 shows for the year 2020, simply by computing the dates when the Sun will be present in each of these constellations.

Exercises like this one have an amusing habit of throwing tabloid astrol-ogers into a sort of existential tizzy. But while astrology is often laughed at for being hopelessly irrational, it must be admitted that in this instance, the traditional astrological zodiac, constructed around the equinoxes and sol-stices, is indisputably more rational than the presumptively more "astronom-ical" zodiac, constructed around the IAU constellation boundaries, which is totally arbitrary and more than a little absurd.

4

SIGNS FROM ABOVE: MARCUS MANILIUS AND THE TRAITS OF THE ZODIAC

Rome, 44 BC

Reconstructing the ancient sky isn't merely an astrological curiosity. Historical accounts of eclipses, such as the one preceding the Battle of Gaugamela, are absolutely indispensable when calibrating modern models of the long-term fluctuations of the Earth's rotation. These models, in turn, inform our understanding of the flexing of the Earth's surface after the last ice age, the sloshing of the Earth's molten core and magnetic field, and, of course, our most basic notions of time and the length of a day.

The problem is that there are precious few incidents of any kind from ancient times, let alone detailed astronomical observations, whose exact date can be determined. The calendars and timekeeping systems of the ancient world were just too irregular and inconsistent. But this makes the few events of ancient history which can be precisely dated all the more extraordinary. And without a doubt, the most momentous exact date handed down to us from antiquity is March 15, 44 BC—the Ides of March—the day of the assassination of Julius Caesar.

The omens leading up to that day—weeping horses, birds torn apart by other birds—had become increasingly inauspicious. "Beware the Ides of March," Caesar was warned in no uncertain terms. And when the Ides arrived without incident, as Caesar observed with a laugh, he was reminded that "indeed they have come, but they have not yet gone." Moments later Caesar lay murdered, havoc was cried, the dogs of war let slip, and all of history lurched from one destiny to another.

Archaeologically, the site of Caesar's assassination, the Curia of Pompey, can be pinpointed fairly precisely. It lies very near the modern intersection of Via di Torre Argentina and Via dei Barbieri in downtown Rome. As for the timing, we're told that Caesar departed his house "at about the fifth hour," meaning the fifth out of the twelve Roman hours of daylight, corresponding roughly to 11 a.m. Assuming it took an hour or so for Caesar to arrive and take his seat in the Senate, it was probably early in the afternoon when Tullius Cimber first raised his hand in violence. But from then on the conspirators made quick work of it, stabbing Caesar twenty-three times until he fell dead, so it's written, at the feet of Pompey's statue. How the heavens appeared from that fateful spot and at that fateful moment is diagrammed in figure 4.1. Venus, the ancestral goddess of the Julian clan, though peering down from near her culmination in the sky, was nevertheless completely obscured by the Sun. Simultaneously, Jupiter, the monarch of the planets, in conjunction with the waning Moon, sank mournfully below the western horizon. Thus, with a little imagination, we can see that the tragedy of Julius Caesar was played out on the celestial no less than the terrestrial stage that day.

AN EMPIRE OF ASTROLOGY

The assassination of Julius Caesar marks one of the great turning points in world history. When the chaos subsided, the Roman Republic had ceased to exist and Octavian, Caesar's great-nephew, had emerged as Augustus, the sole ruler of a Roman Empire that stretched from Portugal to Syria. Shifting our gaze to the celestial realm, Caesar's death can be said to mark an equally significant turning point in the history of astrology, too.

Figure 4.1: A Scheme of Heaven for Wednesday, March 15, 44 BC
The Assassination of Julius Caesar

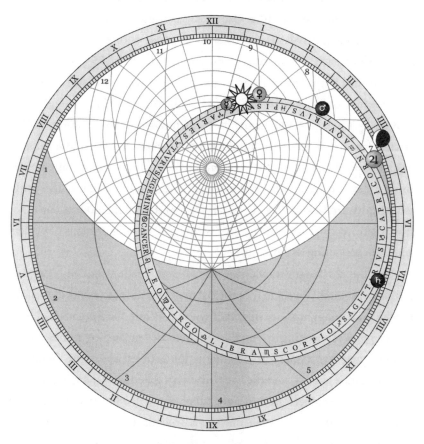

The Curia of Pompey, Rome: 41°53'43"N, 12°28'34"E
JD: 1705426.01104
12:15 UT
ΔT: 11024s
Local Time: 12:55 PM
Local Apparent Sidereal Time: 0:27

	λ	β	RA J2000	Dec J2000	Az	El	House	
♄ Saturn	♐ 19°14'	0°58'	19ʰ 16ᵐ 08ˢ	-21°33'	264°22'	-28°08'	⑥	1°44'
♃ Jupiter	♑ 25°44'	0°34'	21ʰ 46ᵐ 51ˢ	-14°09'	240°04'	0°00'	⑦	0°00'
♂ Mars	♒ 19°12'	-1°12'	23ʰ 16ᵐ 28ˢ	-6°03'	225°28'	18°35'	⑦	25°15'
☉ Sun	♓ 22°26'	0°00'	1ʰ 16ᵐ 57ˢ	8°13'	199°05'	43°21'	⑨	10°53'
♀ Venus	♓ 14°20'	-1°25'	0ʰ 49ᵐ 06ˢ	3°46'	206°01'	37°03'	⑧	29°50'
☿ Mercury	♓ 23°29'	0°47'	1ʰ 22ᵐ 03ˢ	7°53'	197°17'	43°21'	⑨	12°31'
☽ Moon	♑ 29°21'	-5°39'	22ʰ 08ᵐ 18ˢ	-17°40'	233°50'	0°01'	⑦	0°02'

For starters, in his official role as *Pontifex Maximus*, or Roman High Priest, Caesar was able to radically overhaul the Roman civil calendar. In the year preceding his murder, Caesar successfully replaced Rome's politically distorted, partly lunar, partly solar calendar with a new, purely solar one in which each "Julian year" consisted of exactly 365.25 days. This was accomplished in the familiar way, by having three 365-day years followed by a "bissextile," or leap year, of 366 days every fourth year. Minus a small clarification by Augustus, and a small refinement during the Renaissance, this calendar, with its familiar rhythms of January, February, March, and so forth, has triumphed to become the standard civil calendar used throughout the world today. Thus, from the time of Caesar's death onward, it becomes fairly straightforward to associate historical calendar dates with modern ones and, from there, to determine the precise astronomical configurations of planets and stars prevailing at those times.

But the chief significance of Caesar's assassination for the history of astrology is that this event may be the last major episode of ancient divination in which astrology *was not* directly involved. While the Romans had long made a point of checking in with the gods before even the most minor undertakings, their traditional forms of divination entailed observing the flights of birds, called augury, and the livers of sheep, called haruspicy, rather than the orbits of the planets. Accordingly, out of all the ill omens Caesar received prior to his death, not a single one was astrological. And things remained similarly non-astrological even when events took a decidedly celestial turn. At Caesar's funeral games, a comet appeared in the sky, which was said to be Caesar's soul ascending to heaven as a star. If ever an excuse was needed to mention a few zodiac signs, surely this was it. And yet, in all of its portrayals in both poetry and prose, Caesar's transformation into a star remained conspicuously astrology-free.

The existence of Caesar's star has never been corroborated astronomically. But whatever it was, even if only a rhetorical fiction, the non-astrological nature of this "comet" offers a good illustration of just how unconcerned with astrology the Roman Republic was. By contrast, the Roman Empire of just a generation later can be characterized as utterly astrologically starstruck. The emperor Augustus himself set the tone by incorporating Capricorn, his zodiac sign, into his imperial imagery. Subsequently, evidence of astrology's influence starts popping up seemingly everywhere, including in some surprisingly official settings. You can find zodiac signs stamped into coins, chiseled into public sundials and, what's particularly striking, adopted as emblems by the Roman legions, the ultimate source of the empire's power.

Figure 4.2: A silver *cistophorus* coin, ca. 25 BC, showing the head of Augustus (obverse) and his zodiac sign, Capricorn (reverse). IMAGE COURTESY OF THE AMERICAN NUMISMATIC SOCIETY.

But by far the most delicious example of Rome's newfound infatuation with astrology has to be the twelve-course astrological appetizers served at Rome's most famously decadent dinner, the feast of Trimalchio. This is the fictional banquet portrayed so colorfully in Petronius's *Satyricon*, a humorous novel written during the reign of the emperor Nero. Although several of the delicacies have never been positively identified, figure 4.3 re-creates the basic spread of what must have been a truly cosmically balanced meal.

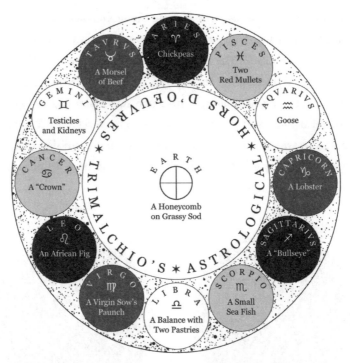

Figure 4.3: Trimalchio's platter of astrological appetizers, as described in the *Satyricon* of Petronius.

THRASYLLUS & SON, ASTROLOGERS

The Roman Republic, at least in principle, could count on an orderly transition of power. Every year, two consuls were elected to serve as joint heads of state for a one-year term. In the Roman Empire, however, the emperors had consolidated absolute power to themselves. Consequently, all of politics was reduced to: how long will the emperor live, and who will succeed him? But these were exactly the sort of questions astrology promised it could answer. This made astrology, suddenly, directly relevant to the security interests of the Roman state.

Augustus, the first of the Roman emperors, began his reign already enamored with his horoscope and his zodiac sign, Capricorn. Perhaps he initially regarded it as nothing more than a good-luck charm. Be that as it may, by the time of his death some forty years later, astrology had become a crucial component of his empire's intelligence apparatus, as indispensable, if not more so, as his vast network of spies and informants. The shadowy figure behind this operation—Rome's director, as it were, of astrological intelligence—was the mysterious Thrasyllus.

Thrasyllus first appears on the scene in 6 BC. The setting was the island of Rhodes, a few miles off the southern coast of what's now Turkey. It was there that Tiberius, Augustus's son-in-law, sought out a self-imposed exile during a period of particularly poor family relations. Desperately needing a friend, Tiberius found Thrasyllus. Whatever other qualities the astrologer may have seen in the Roman aristocrat, he quickly ascertained that Tiberius's future was destined to be very bright indeed. Sure enough, the wheels of Fate turned round, and in the year 2 of the Common Era, Tiberius was summoned back to Rome and officially named Augustus's heir. Accompanying Tiberius was Thrasyllus, who, having picked right when everyone else picked wrong, was never to be far from Tiberius's side.

With the question of his succession satisfactorily resolved, Augustus continued to rule as emperor for another decade, until his death in the year 14. During this time, Thrasyllus came to be regarded as a trusted confidant to Augustus no less than to Tiberius. Augustus, in return, demonstrated his growing appreciation of astrology's power in the most convincing way he could: he outlawed it. Or, rather, a better analogy might be that astrology became classified information: "Imperial Top Secret," so to speak, "for the emperor's eyes only." In the year 11, an empire-wide edict was put forth prohibiting all forms of divination, and explicitly all predictions pertaining to the date of someone's death. Simultaneously, Augustus made public his own horoscope, thereby signaling that astrological technology would henceforth be regarded as the exclusive purview of the Roman state. And, no less importantly, by publishing his horoscope, Augustus could demonstrate to his astrology-minded opponents that he wasn't destined to expire just yet.

It would be fascinating to know what sort of astrological advice Thrasyllus conjured up for his imperial patrons, but unfortunately, the ancient histories don't offer us any insights. We do know, however, that Thrasyllus was well honored for his skill. Incredibly, he and his son and successor, Balbillus, were able to maintain their position as imperial astrologers for a combined period of over seventy-five years. Together they served all the Julio-Claudian emperors from Augustus to Nero (with the prudent exception of Caligula). After Nero's forced suicide and the brief civil war that followed, Balbillus's predictive powers remained so highly esteemed that he was called back into service by Vespasian, the first emperor of the Flavian dynasty. On top of all this, Balbillus is known to have accompanied the emperor Claudius on his invasion of Britain, to have served as head of the library of Alexandria, and to have been appointed provincial governor of Egypt—an absolutely astounding political career for a professional astrologer. To have not only survived the assassinations, expulsions, and palace intrigue of the imperial Roman court (whose ruthlessness is well known to any fan of TV miniseries such as *Rome* or *I, Claudius*) but to have thrived, as Thrasyllus and Balbillus did, is just astonishing. It's almost easier to believe that they really could read the stars than that they somehow breezed through the first century of the Roman Empire with only their wits and a smile.

One last tidbit, just for fun: Thrasyllus evidently had at least one hobby outside of astrology, since he's reputed to have been the editor who finalized the order and groupings of Plato's dialogues. This means that Thrasyllus's preferred arrangement is the one in which Plato's dialogues are still taught today. Combine this with the idea that any number of the decisions made by Augustus or Tiberius (each, in his turn, the most powerful man in the world) could have been swayed by Thrasyllus's advice, and it may be that the influence of this obscure astrologer on our modern world is much greater than anyone suspects. Of course, we have no way of ever really knowing. Then again, that's probably just as Thrasyllus would have wanted it.

THE POETRY OF HEAVEN

It's a long way from the earliest Babylonian horoscopes to the secret counsels of the Roman emperors. How did we get here? The historical record of astrology's handoff from Babylon to the Greco-Roman world is pretty hazy, but a handful of names have been preserved. There's the Babylonian priest and astrologer

Berossus, for example. Around the year 300 BC, he is said to have relocated to the Greek island of Kos (today, just a few hours' ferry ride from Rhodes) where he made a living teaching astrology to Greek-speaking students. Then there's the Egyptian duo Nechepso and Petosiris. The first name properly belongs to an ancient Egyptian pharaoh, and the second to an ancient Egyptian high priest. Neither would have known the first thing about astrology. But their names doubtless added an aura of forbidden mystery to an astrological manuscript written in Greek which emerged sometime during the first century BC.

The salient fact about all of these characters, however, isn't that we know their names. It's that that's pretty much all we know. Berossus's books are lost, and whoever Nechepso and Petosiris were, or was, all that remains are a few measly pages preserved by later astrologers. The same can be said about Thrasyllus and Balbillus, whom we just met. Thrasyllus wrote an astrology book in Greek called *Pinax*, but only a chapter summary survives. Balbillus has left us hardly much more. And so, after going through the full astrological roll call, we come to the somewhat surprising realization that the earliest meaningful description of astrology that survives isn't Babylonian, and it isn't Greek. Instead, it's a really lovely Latin poem named *Astronomica*, authored by a certain Marcus Manilius around the year 15 of the Common Era.

Now, despite my interests in Rome, and science, and Roman science, I have to confess that I'd never read the *Astronomica* before. (It's rare to find anyone who has.) But this prompts my next confession: discovering the *Astronomica* has, for me, been one of the most delightful surprises of this entire project. I'd never appreciated the poem's significance, historically, and I definitely wasn't expecting to find it such a charming read. Certain passages, channeling the ecstasy of studying the night sky, are quite breathtaking, and the poem often reads like a beautiful love letter to science:

> *These things I wish to carry, up to the stars with breath divine;*
> *Not in the crowd, nor for the crowd, do I compose my song,*
> *But alone, as if speeding atop an empty world,*
> *And free, I'll guide my chariot. No one blocks me,*
> *Or steers a shared course on a common road.*

No, I shall sing for the sky to know, for the stars to wonder,
For the universe to rejoice in the songs of its poet;
And maybe for those (the smallest crowd in the world),
Whom the heavens have not begrudged a knowledge of themselves
  and their sacred paths.

What is the *Astronomica*? For starters, it's a fine example of what's known as a didactic, or instructional, poem. While the thought of teaching, say, quantum mechanics using a textbook written entirely in haikus sounds like an exceptionally bad idea (albeit possibly very entertaining), poetic science books had a proud tradition in antiquity. In chapter 3, for example, we mentioned the *Phaenomena* of Aratus, a Greek poem from around 250 BC which surveyed the celestial sphere in verse. Overtones of Aratus can be heard throughout the *Astronomica*. Much closer in time and spirit, however, is Lucretius's *On the Nature of Things*, from around 50 BC, to which the *Astronomica* is, in many ways, a reply.

The dueling poems of Lucretius and Manilius were written to explain the physical foundations of their dueling philosophies. Each describes a universe governed not by the whims of the gods, but by the laws of nature. Yet that's about where their similarities end. Lucretius's universe—actually, the universe of his spiritual guru, Epicurus—was infinite and eternal. Like an ancient version of John Lennon's "Imagine," there was no heaven, or hell, or life after death to vex us mortals. All natural processes were brought about by atoms moving through the void of space according to the laws of physics. Fascinatingly, these laws subjected the atoms to random, almost quantum mechanical "swerves," deemed necessary to conserve the idea of free will.

Manilius, meanwhile, was an adherent of Epicureanism's great philosophical rival, Stoicism. Rejecting a world of mindless atoms, the Stoic universe was constructed according to a divine and intelligent plan, with everything subject to the laws of Fate. *Fata regunt orbem, certa stant omnia lege*, as Manilius put it. "Fate rules the world, and by fixed law does everything stand." Because the Stoic universe was entirely predestined, it was also, therefore, entirely predictable—provided, of course, that you knew how to read its signs. In principle, these signs were everywhere, although the sky presented an especially conspicuous showcase. While a Stoic need not have swallowed astrology in all of its particulars, in practice the two were so closely linked in their insistence on fatalism that it's not much of an exaggeration to label astrology as simply Stoic astronomy.

Lucretius and Manilius are like the call and response of a cosmological duet played out with competing poems. So it's a bit surprising that Manilius is so utterly obscure, while Lucretius is, as far as Roman poets go, actually quite famous. History's snub to Manilius seems even crueler when one considers that his philosophy, Stoicism, was significantly more widespread than Lucretius's Epicureanism—which, in fact, was much despised for its atheism. And yet, one need not look far for a reason why Manilius isn't more widely read. In fact, it's a reason he himself acknowledges. Manilius's subject matter, astrology, is exceptionally technical, which is to say, mathematical. While it's often impressive to see how Manilius can explain complex topics such as ecliptic rising times, all in perfect poetic meter, it can also be downright exhausting to follow.

Yet there's a still deeper irony to the divergent fates of Lucretius and Manilius. To the modern reader, Lucretius's atomism seems centuries ahead of its time. But what's an enlightened metaphysics without the physics to back it up? It's nothing but a lucky guess. Instead, the spirit of analyzing the world mathematically—the spirit embodied in Manilius's poem—is what actually empowered science to move forward. That this advance would ultimately leave Manilius behind shouldn't cheapen, in our modern eyes, the beauty of his love for studying the stars.

ZODIAC FIRST IMPRESSIONS

The *Astronomica* is a fascinating work in its own right, but it takes on a special significance when we recognize that this poem is, essentially, astrology's grand unveiling on the historical stage. And like Minerva issuing from

Jupiter's skull fully grown and clad in armor, the *Astronomica* presents an astrology emerging from obscurity remarkably complete and fully formed. Even today, two thousand years later, there is hardly any astrological idea, no matter how sophisticated or complex, which can't trace its debut to Manilius's poem. This makes Manilius our best source for examining what's surely the most fundamental question for any investigation of astrology: where did the characteristic traits of the zodiac come from? The *Astronomica*'s treatment of this topic is quite revealing. Manilius's survey of the twelve zodiac personality types is too long and flowery to include here in full, but I've summarized the main points in the distinctly unpoetic table 4.1, which, nevertheless, will suffice for our needs.

A few things from this table leap out immediately. First, in answer to our question about where these traits came from, it's pretty clear that the qualities ascribed to people born under a given zodiac sign were, at least originally, simply the qualities associated with the sign itself. Thus Aries are timid like sheep, Tauri are hardworking like bulls, and Pisces have a love of the sea. All in all, this would seem to provide a most unlikely foundation for a theory of human psychology. And yet, within the context of a universe that's divinely ordained, this idea wouldn't have sounded so silly, or at least not irredeemably so, because nothing was the way it was by accident. If the constellation Cancer looked like a crab, then this had to be for the purpose of signifying something crabby. The alternative interpretation, that the stars' arrangement in the sky was random and meaningless, was too absurd to entertain.

But the most remarkable thing about this list is how daringly specific Manilius gets. And he's certainly not shy about including explicitly negative traits either. (Sorry, Scorpios.) This is a refreshing contrast to modern zodiac descriptions, which tend to be hopelessly wishy-washy. Even so, it's evident that the personality types sketched out by Manilius are the direct ancestors of what you would find in any modern-day horoscope. Tauri, for instance, seem to have been just as slow and stubborn in Roman times as they are today, and Libras just as legalistic.

Table 4.1: Zodiac Personalities from Manilius's *Astronomica*

Zodiac Sign	Personality Traits
♈ Aries	associated with all aspects of the garment trade • subject to financial ups and downs • optimistic • self-doubting, timid, and ready to sell themselves for praise
♉ Taurus	associated with farming • hardworking • content with silent praise • slow but strong in both mind and body
♊ Gemini	associated with music and singing • opposed to war • adept at astronomy • living easy lives full of love and pleasure
♋ Cancer	associated with finance and international trade • grasping and miserly • shrewd and combative
♌ Leo	associated with hunting and butchery • prone to anger and sullenness • honest, fair, and pure of heart
♍ Virgo	associated with the arts of writing • inquisitive and studious • adept with words and speech • held back by shyness • unlikely to have children
♎ Libra	associated with law, lawyers, and judges • associated with weights, measures, and numbers
♏ Scorpio	lovers of war, slaughter, fighting, carnage, and gladiatorial combat
♐ Sagittarius	associated with any profession that requires a mastery over animals, such as a chariot driver or shepherd • physically and mentally strong and swift • untiring in spirit
♑ Capricorn	associated with professions involving fire, such as a metalsmith or baker • restless and indecisive • prone to amorous indiscretion when young
♒ Aquarius	associated with professions involving water, such as landscaping and hydraulic engineering • gentle and sweet • neither desirous of wealth nor likely to obtain it
♓ Pisces	associated with maritime professions, such as a sailor, fisherman, or naval officer • likely to have many children • friendly, fast-moving, and in a constant state of change

WHAT'S YOUR SIGN?

The wonderful thing about making specific claims is that they can actually be tested to see if they're true. So, do Manilius's assertions stand up to scrutiny? Before we examine this, we need to say a few words about what it means to "have" a zodiac sign.

Today, everyone would agree that your zodiac sign refers to the time of year in which you were born—specifically, it's the zodiac sign in which the Sun is located on your birthday. Thus Aries have birthdays between late March and late April, Tauri between late April and late May, and so on. But all of the other planets were in a zodiac sign on your birthday too, and the notion that the zodiac sign of the Sun is always the most important is actually quite recent. In fact, this practice only became prevalent in the twentieth century, when it was found that "Sun sign" astrology provided a suitably simple yet still compelling format for newspaper horoscopes.

Ancient astrology, however, was a bespoke art, with each horoscope finely tailored to fit its individual owner. To give an especially prominent example, the emperor Augustus, a proud Capricorn as we have seen, was born on September 23, 63 BC. (Note that while the month of August was indeed named in honor of Augustus, contrary to common opinion, this was not because of his birthday.) By today's conventions, therefore, Augustus really ought to have been a Virgo. So why, then, was he a Capricorn? The truth is, no one knows. In general, ancient astrologers tended to emphasize the zodiac sign rising above the eastern horizon at the hour of birth rather than the Sun sign. But since Augustus was born a little before sunrise, his rising sign would have also been Virgo. Some commentators have suggested that because Augustus was born at night, his horoscope was actually ruled by the Moon. Yet another possibility is that Capricorn referred not to the time of his birth but to his conception.

These considerations offer a glimpse of how much more complex and personalized ancient astrology could be when compared to the popular astrology of today. Far from providing just a "Sun and done" horoscope, the goal of the ancient astrologer was to predict the entire sequence of someone's life. In Manilius's time, the most cutting-edge procedure for doing this—a procedure in which Thrasyllus and Balbillus were regarded as the unrivaled masters—entailed identifying two key points on a birth horoscope: the "starter" and the "destroyer." As time elapsed from the moment of birth, the destroyer revolved along with the heavens toward the starter's original position, all the while shooting evil rays at it. When the destroyer finally reached the starter, it was game over: death. The number of hours and minutes it took for the destroyer to reach the starter was then converted to the number of years and months the individual was expected to live.

It's pretty obvious why such a highly involved procedure, which has to be carefully customized to each individual, would never be suited for a mass-distribution medium like a newspaper or magazine. On the other hand, I'm pretty convinced it would make for a thoroughly fascinating (if not potentially terrifying) board game.

As for Augustus, it's possible that he was a Capricorn because the most important point of his horoscope, his starter, was assigned to a planet in that sign. In the end, though, these are all futile speculations. Since Augustus was born before the introduction of the Julian calendar, it's simply impossible to know which date September 23, 63 BC, actually refers to. The old Roman calendar was so confused that in order for the new calendar to begin on January 1, 45 BC, Julius Caesar had to make the preceding year, 46 BC, an eye-popping 445 days long. If anything, September of 63 BC was probably closer to our July, putting the Sun even further away from Capricorn. But even this can't be said with much certainty.

Whatever the case of how Augustus became a Capricorn, it's pretty clear that, "Hey, what's your sign?" was a much more complicated question in antiquity than it is today. So, who was Manilius describing with the zodiac traits listed above? Again, there's no way to know for sure. Manilius would have been familiar with all the latest astrological techniques, since he almost certainly belonged to the same imperial astrology clique that included Augustus, Tiberius, and the master himself, Thrasyllus. But I think there are enough internal clues within the *Astronomica* to conclude that, at least in the verses summarized above, Manilius has in mind the simple, Sun sign system that we're familiar with today. If so, this is lucky news for us, since it means we only need to know someone's birthday, and not their precise hour and place of birth, in order to examine Manilius's claims more closely.

SIGNS AND SIGNIFICANCE

Of all the astrological assertions made by Manilius, the easiest one to check is that people gravitate to certain professions because of their zodiac sign. Take Libra, for instance, which both in ancient times and today is associated with lawyers and judges. Among the most distinguished jurists, then, can we expect to find a disproportionately high number of Libras? How about the justices of the United States Supreme Court? From John Jay, nominated by George Washington in 1789, to Brett Kavanaugh, nominated by Donald Trump in 2018, there have been a total of 114 individuals appointed to the U.S. Supreme Court. Of these, 113—all except for the curiously obscure James Moore Wayne—have birthdays that are reliably known. The chart in figure 4.4 tallies the zodiac signs of these 113 justices. This count, called a histogram, takes into consideration that the start dates of the zodiac signs change a little every year, and that several of the justices were born prior to 1752, when England and its American colonies switched from the Julian to the Gregorian calendar.

What can we read from such a chart? Well, if there is a correlation between Libras and judges, our sample certainly doesn't show it. And there's no use blaming the precession of the equinoxes either, since, at most, this would have just shifted the results over by one sign. Oddly enough, though, there does seem to be a suspiciously large number of Pisces. Does this mean anything? It's hard to tell just by looking at figure 4.4. So how, then, are we to judge our histogram of judges?

This is actually a textbook case where a statistical inference test, of the sort we introduced in chapter 1, can provide some much needed clarity. In fact, we can use one of the very first statistical tests ever devised: Karl

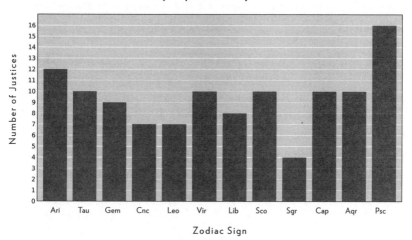

Figure 4.4: Histogram of the Zodiac Signs of U.S. Supreme Court Justices
(Sample Size = 113)

Pearson's chi-squared test, which may be familiar to those who have taken a college-level laboratory course. Pearson's test, which he refined throughout the 1890s, was initially applied to assess the fairness of coin flips, dice rolls, and, famously, the roulette tables of Monte Carlo (which, he discovered, weren't fair at all). In the amazing way in which mathematics often reveals that two seemingly dissimilar problems are actually the same, it turns out that our zodiac conundrum is mathematically identical to Pearson's question about the fairness of dice.

To make this connection more explicit, imagine that you have a twelve-sided die, of the sort that you can purchase at any game or puzzle store, and that you've rolled it 113 times, once for each of the 113 judges in our sample. If the die is fair, we would expect the rolls to be evenly distributed over the twelve possible outcomes, yet we also know that each roll is random, so we don't expect the counts to be exactly the same. But how skewed can the counts get before we should start to worry that the die is loaded? This is entirely equivalent to the question of how lopsided our histogram of zodiac signs can be before we should start to suspect that some signs are disproportionately more likely to appear than others.

Pearson's chi-squared test provides a simple check. First, we compute what's called Pearson's chi-squared statistic, denoted by χ^2 and pronounced "kai-squared":

$$\chi^2 = \text{the sum over every category of } \frac{(\text{the measured count} - \text{the expected count})^2}{\text{the expected count}}$$

In our example, the expected count for each category is simply 113 judges divided evenly by the 12 possible zodiac signs, or, 9.42 judges per sign. (This is a rather unphysical number of judges, to be sure, though one that is of no concern to the statistician.) The actual, measured counts for each zodiac sign can be read directly off the histogram. Following the formula, we have:

$$\chi^2 = \underbrace{\frac{(12 - 9.42)^2}{9.42}}_{\text{Aries}} + \underbrace{\frac{(10 - 9.42)^2}{9.42}}_{\text{Taurus}} + \ldots + \underbrace{\frac{(16 - 9.42)^2}{9.42}}_{\text{Pisces}} = 10.08$$

Evidently, the closer the measured counts are to the expected 9.42 judges per sign, the smaller our chi-squared statistic will be, and the more lopsided our sample is, the larger our chi-squared statistic will be. So where does our result, 10.08, fit in? The second step of Pearson's chi-squared test is to compare this number against the distribution of all possible outcomes. In practice, this entails simply consulting a table of critical values. For an experiment set up like ours, where there are twelve possible outcomes, it turns out that the chi-squared statistic would need to be at least as high as 20 before we might suspect that something is a bit off. And the key word here is "might," since values bigger than 20 are still expected to occur 5 percent of the time, even in data sets whose underlying distribution is perfectly uniform. If our chi-squared statistic were that high, we'd definitely want to examine some additional data to figure out what's going on. But a value like ours, which is well below the threshold for significance, is pretty much the statistics way of saying, "Move along, there's nothing to see here." In other words, regardless of how our histogram may appear, the results are perfectly consistent with there being no correlation whatsoever between being a justice of the U.S. Supreme Court and having any particular zodiac sign.

This is a reassuring result. It would be bizarre and downright unfair if a job systematically favored some people over others simply because of when they were born during the year. And yet, as I discovered to my great surprise, this is exactly what happens in a number of professions, particularly in sports, and particularly those that rely on competitive youth leagues with strict age cutoffs. The most extreme case is hockey.

Junior hockey leagues typically group players together according to the calendar year of their birth. This means that a player born on January 1 will be almost a full year older than his teammate born on December 31, even though both belong to the same age cohort. For players who are nine or ten years old, that difference represents an enormous developmental advantage, both physically and mentally. And since only the best players from any given year are likely to continue on to the next level, the cumulative effect is a system that progressively weeds out Sagittarii, Scorpios, and Libras in favor of Capricorns, Aquarii, and Pisces, even before these players ever reach the

Figure 4.5: Histogram of the Zodiac Signs of Professional Hockey Players (NHL)
(Sample Size = 7,417)

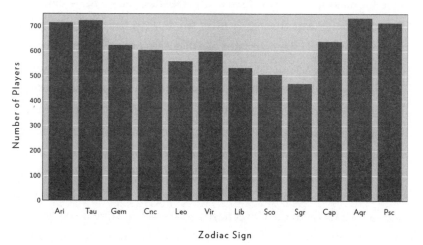

pros. And the end results are striking. Figure 4.5 shows a histogram of 7,417 current and former NHL players. The chi-squared statistic is 143.8, way above our threshold of 20, and without question a very significant departure from uniformity.

This bias is known as the relative age effect, and it can also be seen in Major League Baseball, whose players skew toward August birthdays, and the National Football League, whose players skew toward January birthdays. Interestingly, in basketball, where organized youth leagues are less important, no relative age effect is observed. Similarly, the effect often disappears if you consider only the truly elite of any sport. For instance, among the more than 1,200 individuals who have played for England's national football (soccer) team since 1872, Libra is the most common zodiac sign, but with a chi-squared statistic of only 16.7, this disparity can't be considered anything out of the ordinary.

Does the relative age effect show up anywhere outside of sports? The school year in most places has a fall cutoff, and some studies claim a bias can be found in academic achievement, job success, and a whole host of other metrics which ripple down through our lives. If so, then the effect is a small one. There are, to be sure, sophisticated statistical techniques that can be used to tease out small effects from data, but the results tend to be less persuasive. Personally, whenever I want to make a point with data, I try to keep in mind the maxim that "If you need to use statistics, you probably should have designed a better experiment." In other words, for a truly compelling result, the data should tell their own story, one that leaps from the page without any complicated analysis.

This is a good way to introduce what I think is one of the most surprising and astonishing astrological results of all: it's not just a few professions, but our entire species which exhibits an uneven distribution of zodiac signs. Figure 4.6 shows this in a histogram of more than 85 million U.S. births recorded from 1994 to 2014. The data display an almost perfect, one might even say beautiful, sinusoid pattern that rises and falls from Leo to Capricorn. Remarkably, you don't get nearly so smooth a curve if you group the data by month. The calendar months are too choppy in their lengths and, perhaps, not arrayed as naturally throughout the year as the zodiac signs,

Figure 4.6: Histogram of U.S. Births, 1994-2014
(Sample Size = 85+ million)

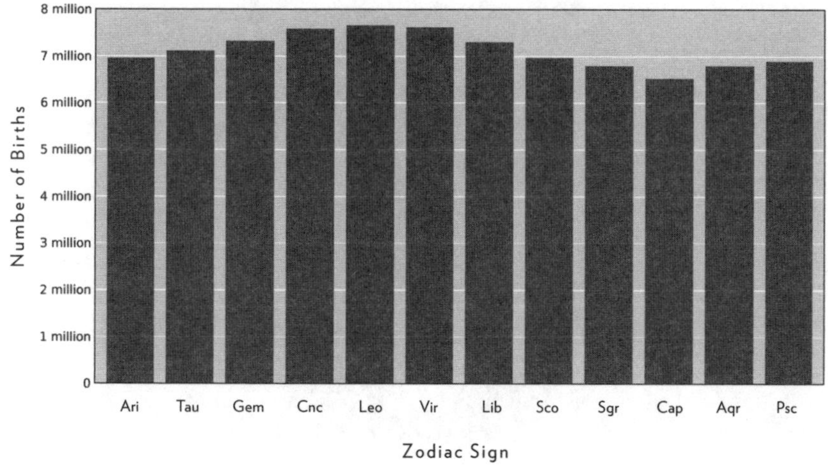

Zodiac Sign

which are pinned to the solstices and equinoxes. It's only when the data are arranged astrologically that their story comes across so clearly. And what this story reminds us is that in spite of our modern, technological lives, we are still creatures of the seasons tuned to the rhythms of the Sun—creatures with a slight but unmistakable preference for having babies in the summer and, evidently, for making them in the fall.

In the end, then, it seems that Manilius was onto something when he suggested that certain professions are linked with the zodiac. He appears to have been all wrong about the particulars, though, including when it comes to sports. For instance, a sample of 977 Olympic sailing medalists shows no correlation (χ^2 = 6.8) with Pisces or any other zodiac sign. But even here, Manilius still manages to have the last words. Because if we were to conclude from this that Manilius's assertions about Pisces have no bearing on sailors and the art of navigation, we would not be totally correct—for it's Manilius's description of the professions of Pisces that was chosen to adorn the seal of the United States Naval Observatory. *Adde gubernandi studium: pervenit in astra, et pontum caelo coniunxit,* "Then, too, the pilot's care: the stars are scaled, and sky with ocean joined." In other words, the institution that publishes each year's *Nautical* and *Astronomical Almanacs,*

Figure 4.7: The seal of the United States Naval
Observatory is emblazoned with a verse from
Manilius on the professions appropriate to Pisces.
UNITED STATES NAVAL OBSERVATORY.

and which maintains the master clock for the entire GPS satellite navigation system, has, this entire time, been operating under the subtle influence of an obscure, ancient Roman astrologer. Just think about that the
next time your phone or other GPS-enabled device successfully guides you
from point A to point B. There's no magic involved, but there is, perhaps,
a dash of astrology.

5

CLAUDIUS PTOLEMY'S ASTROLOGICAL TRAVEL GUIDE

Ultima Thule, 79

Watching from across the Bay of Naples, the Roman writer Pliny the Younger—our only eyewitness source for the events of that day—described the strange cloud rising up from one of the distant mountains as resembling "a pine tree . . . lifted up high on an extremely tall trunk and spreading out into several branches." By Pliny's reckoning, it was about the seventh hour of the day, or roughly 1 p.m. The date was August 24 in the year 79. The mountain, as Pliny would soon learn, was Vesuvius, a long-dormant volcano just then waking up from its slumber.

As Pliny goes on to narrate, it wasn't until the following morning, August 25, that an unstoppable wave of ash and debris—today called a pyroclastic surge—rumbled over and through the nearby towns. Pompeii, most famously, and Herculaneum were wholly entombed, reduced to a haunting exhibit of ancient Roman life complete with buildings, paintings, and even the contours of men, women, children, and pets, exquisitely preserved at the instant of their deaths.

Pompeii and Herculaneum received the brunt of Vesuvius's violence, but fainter ripples would have been felt much further afield. As with recent volcanic eruptions, sulfuric acid and other aerosols from Vesuvius likely contaminated the stratosphere for months, reducing the amount of sunlight reaching the Earth and causing a modest cooling of temperatures across the globe. Chemical traces of the Vesuvius eruption of 79 have even been detected in ice cores from as far off as Greenland. It's probable, then, that in distant lands that had never heard of Rome, let alone of Vesuvius, farming, trade, and the thousand facets of daily life that depend upon these activities were upended in subtle and perhaps not so subtle ways.

The strewing of Vesuvius's ash offers an apt geological analog for Rome's increasingly global reach. Even as the empire's political boundaries approached their maximum limits, Rome's role as a nexus within a surprisingly interconnected international order continued to grow. The Roman and Han Chinese empires, for instance, were certainly aware of each other, and the silk that came to symbolize Roman luxury ultimately originated in Chinese workshops, even if its export passed first through many middlemen. And in the ruins of Pompeii itself, an extraordinary ivory statuette of the Hindu goddess Lakshmi was found—evidence that the trading ships of the ancient world carried not just commercial but cultural and spiritual cargo as well. Bundled amid such freight, astrology too was doubtless transported to the far corners of the world and back many times over.

Did Roman knowledge rival Vesuvius in reaching as far as Greenland? This seems unlikely. For the Greco-Roman writers of antiquity, the northernmost spot of the known world was a place called Thule, or, as Virgil put it more melodiously, *ultima Thule* ("furthest Thule"). There's a tradition associating Thule with Greenland—the United States even maintains a military installation there called Thule Air Base—but Thule's actual location has long been a mystery. The ancient geographers were extremely vague about Thule, not only with regard to its location but even as to whether it was an island or a continent. Much like Plato's Atlantis, Thule has come to signify a lost world situated just beyond the borders of our knowledge. But though Thule lacks precise coordinates, the heavens as seen from its high northern latitude can still be reconstructed. At the moment of Vesuvius's eruption, Thule's sky would have been configured very much like figure 5.1.

Figure 5.1: A Scheme of Heaven for Tuesday, August 24, 79
The Eruption of Mount Vesuvius

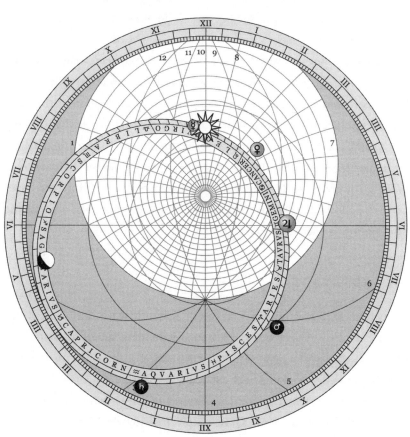

The Island of Thule, somewhere in the North Atlantic: 63°N, 0°E
JD: 1750148.00000
12:00 UT
ΔT: 9760s
Local Time: 12:00 PM
Local Apparent Sidereal Time: 10:02

		λ	β	RA J2000	Dec J2000	Az	El	House	
♄	Saturn	≈ 5°27'↓	-1°27'	22ʰ 18ᵐ 54ˢ	-12°10'	30°02'	-44°53'	③	3°18'
♃	Jupiter	♊ 3°54'	0°40'	6ʰ 02ᵐ 44ˢ	23°01'	278°19'	18°50'	⑦	19°02'
♂	Mars	♈ 4°59'↓	-4°33'	2ʰ 04ᵐ 23ˢ	7°55'	320°13'	-23°39'	⑤	25°36'
☉	Sun	♌ 28°37'	0°00'	11ʰ 42ᵐ 54ˢ	1°52'	179°36'	39°04'	⑩	0°29'
♀	Venus	♋ 24°48'	-6°19'	9ʰ 27ᵐ 30ˢ	8°28'	223°16'	36°19'	⑧	16°59'
☿	Mercury	♍ 5°44'	1°07'	12ʰ 10ᵐ 48ˢ	0°02'	170°43'	37°16'	⑩	11°57'
☽	Moon	♐ 13°33'	4°05'	18ʰ 43ᵐ 24ˢ	-19°12'	87°56'	-22°01'	①	22°01'

While the fog surrounding Thule's location is an extreme case, uncertainty about the basic contours of the globe was simply a fact of life for ancient mapmakers. These cartographic limitations doubtless seemed incongruous to an empire like Rome's, which had pretensions of being the epicenter of earthly power. But this wasn't an issue which Roman arms or Roman laws could subdue. The problem of mapping the world is, fundamentally, a problem of astronomy—because the only way to know your position on the globe with certainty is to measure it with reference to the rotating sky. Yet the only way to have accurate measurements of the sky is to first be certain of where you are on the Earth. This is a cosmographical pickle, if ever there was one. Who, then, given the technological impediments of antiquity, could ever hope to find the Earth's proper place—or, indeed, their own—within the disorienting vastness of the cosmos?

THE GREATEST

It has been said that the importance of a scientific work can be measured by the number of previous publications it renders superfluous to read. Otto Neugebauer, the historian of science who is responsible for much of today's knowledge about ancient mathematical astronomy, cited that adage to explain why essentially nothing survives of Greek astronomy prior to the time of Claudius Ptolemy. Quite simply, Ptolemy's brilliance obliterated everything that came before.

Concerning Ptolemy's life, there's not much to be said. It can be surmised that he was born around the turn of the second century—maybe a decade or two after Vesuvius—and that he lived, worked, and wrote in Alexandria, the capital of Roman Egypt. But with regard to his scientific writings, it's impossible to say too much. Ptolemy's most significant work, the *Almagest*, established a unified mathematical framework for computing the positions of the Sun, Moon, stars, and planets at any time in the past, present, or future. So comprehensive and so compelling was the Earth-centered cosmos it described that the *Almagest* would remain the final word in astronomy for nearly 1,500 years, until it was finally superseded by the Sun-centered system of Copernicus and Kepler. No scientific work, with the exception of Euclid's *Elements of Geometry*, has ever remained so authoritative for so long, and it seems safe to say that none ever will again.

The *Almagest*'s original title was *Mathematikē Syntaxis*, or "A Mathematical Treatise." But the nickname it acquired over centuries of study, the *Almagest*, is an affectionate testament to its place of honor in not one, not two, but four separate civilizations. First there's the "the"s, "il"s, "el"s, "der"s, and "le"s with which the various modern languages preface its medieval name, *Almagestum*. *Almagestum*, in turn, is a Latinization of the Arabic المجسطي (*al-Majisti*), itself an Arabization of the Greek ἡ Μεγίστη (*hē Megistē*). In Greek, *hē Megistē* means, simply, "the greatest." The *Almagest* was the greatest of all the ancient treatises on astronomy, just as Ptolemy was the greatest of all the ancient astronomers. Somewhat less well known is that Ptolemy was also the ancient world's greatest geographer and its greatest, or at least most well-respected, astrologer.

AS ABOVE, SO BELOW

It's mind-boggling to consider that one individual could stand at the summit of so many different mountains of knowledge. And yet Ptolemy would have considered his astronomy, geography, and astrology as simply separate ascents to the same destination: an unobstructed view of the cosmos in the fullness of its majesty. In this context, it becomes less surprising to learn that Ptolemy's *Almagest*, on which his fame chiefly lies, was the earliest of his major writings. But then again, neither his geography nor his astrology could have been written without it.

Ptolemy was frustrated knowing that astronomical records from cities other than his own, Alexandria, were of no use to him if their precise geographic relationship to Alexandria remained uncertain. Conversely, Ptolemy couldn't generate useful astronomical tables for other cities if their geographic coordinates were no better than rough approximations.

Accordingly, once Ptolemy completed the *Almagest*—perhaps around the year 150 or so of the Common Era—he turned his attention to his next great project, the *Geography*.

Ptolemy knew that the only way to reliably measure geographic distances was with astronomy. If two observers in two different cities record the time of the same celestial event, such as a lunar eclipse, then the difference in times can be converted to a distance on the globe. Unfortunately, the only eclipse Ptolemy notes as ever having been measured this way was the eclipse preceding Alexander the Great's victory at Gaugamela, for which Ptolemy had records from Arbela (now Erbil, Iraq) and Carthage (near modern-day Tunis, Tunisia).

The comprehensive solution to Ptolemy's cartographic conundrum would have been a global mapping survey, one that dispatched teams equipped with astronomical instruments to the far ends of the Earth, much like the eighteenth-century expeditions of Captain Cook, on his ship *Endeavour*, or Lapérouse, on his ship *Astrolabe*. But an enterprise on that scale was beyond the ambitions of even someone as far-sighted as Ptolemy. Instead, he had to settle for organizing the scattered scraps of geographic knowledge handed down to him by his predecessors. Yet it's these scraps, or at least Ptolemy's attempts to make sense of them, which give us our best peek into the far-flung trading networks of the ancient world. They even record the names of Greek and Roman explorers who ventured as far south as sub-Saharan Africa and, astoundingly, as far east as Vietnam.

Ptolemy's objective for the *Geography* was to catalog, for the first time ever, the latitudes and longitudes of the major cities and landmarks of the inhabited world. This was the region known in Greek as the *ecumene*, from which the modern word "ecumenical" derives. To this end, Ptolemy computed coordinates for locations as far west as the Canary Islands, or "Islands of the Blest," and as far east as the "metropolis of the Chinese," a city which may have referred to Luoyang, the capital of the Eastern Han dynasty. The northernmost extent of his geography was the "latitude of Thule," a line he drew at 63° north of the equator.

SQUASHING THE SPHERE

Within the *Geography*, Ptolemy managed to compile an impressive list of nearly 8,000 latitude and longitude pairs. But the purpose of the *Geography* wasn't to make a list. It was to make maps. In this, Ptolemy, even more than the explorers he described, ventured into truly uncharted terrain. By being the first to address head-on the mathematical challenges of mapping the Earth's sphere onto a plane, Ptolemy is rightfully the first true cartographer.

At issue is how to comprehend in the mind's eye the totality of the Earth's geography, both large and small, because even an accurate spherical globe shows only half the Earth in any one view. Meanwhile, on a more granular scale, it would be completely impractical to make a globe big enough to show details helpful to a traveler, like city streets or river crossings. Flat maps, in principle, can solve both of these problems. And yet, as with most things, you can't get something for nothing. It's simply not possible to transfer points from a sphere to a plane without losing important information in the process.

The simplest flat map converts the Earth's latitudes and longitudes into evenly spaced, straight lines on a rectangular grid. While this has the benefit of displaying the entire globe all at once, it doesn't do a good job showing what the continents really look like or their correct relationships to each other.

The Mercator projection (figure 5.2a), familiar from school classrooms the world over, partly solves this problem by ensuring that north–south distances are kept equal to east–west distances at every point. In particular, if you wanted to sail from, say, the Port of Shanghai to the Panama Canal, a Mercator map would tell you the right compass bearing to follow. This is a really nice property for a map to have, but the tradeoff is that regions near the poles, such as Greenland, now appear enormous.

To fix this problem, the Peters projection (figure 5.2b) shows the areas of the Earth's landmasses in their correct proportions to one another. Since the Peters map diminishes the visual importance of the more northerly coun-

Figure 5.2: Flat Maps of a Round Earth

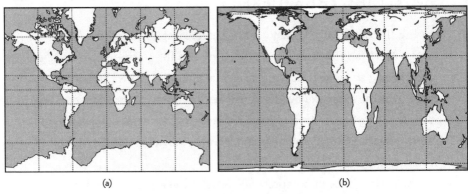

(a)   (b)

Every flat map is a compromise. The Mercator projection (a) shows angles
correctly, while the Peters projection (b) shows areas correctly. It's not possible
for a flat map to correctly represent both angles and areas at the same time.

tries, it has become popular as a sort of anti-Mercator map. But the tradeoff
here is that it doesn't represent angles correctly at all. If you were to sail from
Shanghai to Panama along the compass bearing taken from a Peters map,
you'd end up making landfall near Lima, Peru, some 1,500 miles south of
your intended destination.

Unfortunately, it's not possible, mathematically, to make a flat map that
simultaneously preserves angles, like a Mercator projection, and areas, like
a Peters projection (although it's certainly possible to make a map that preserves neither). All flat maps have to make a compromise. Ptolemy, for his
part, experimented with several mapping styles, each of which strikes a different balance of mathematical and visual characteristics. A few of these
styles remain widely used even today. In the *Geography*, for instance, he presents the first ever description of a conic projection, of which figure 5.6 is an
example. Yet terrestrial charts like these of coastlines and capitals were, to
Ptolemy, merely a warm-up. There was another sphere, beyond the Earth,
whose contours he still wished to trace.

AN IMAGE OF THE WORLD

In a separate, short treatise called the *Planisphere*, of which only an Arabic translation survives, Ptolemy gives a mathematical description of an elegant and versatile mapping technique called stereographic projection. This technique remains, even today, hugely important in disciplines ranging from mathematics and astronomy to optics, crystallography, and electrical engineering. Stereographic projection is also the basis of the astrolabe, an ancient and beautiful astronomical instrument and the graphical inspiration for all of the schemes of heaven in this book.

For a basic idea of a stereographic projection, imagine looking down on a globe from above its North Pole, and then squashing it onto its equator. The visual effect ends up looking like a scoop of ice cream that's melted onto a warm plate from the bottom out. Because there's no limit to how far outward these maps spread, it's customary to extend them only as far south as the Tropic of Capricorn.

Like the Mercator projection, stereographic projection belongs to the family of maps that preserve angles. But the special magic of a stereographic projection is that it takes any circle you can draw on a spherical globe, no matter the circle's size or location, and converts it into a corresponding circle on a flat map. In other words, stereographic projection keeps circles as circles; it doesn't transform them into more complicated curves. Since the various geocentric coordinate systems of astronomy consist entirely of circles drawn on the celestial sphere, a stereographic map provides an elegant way of displaying all of these together at the same time. Right ascensions and declinations, ecliptic longitudes and ecliptic latitudes, azimuths and elevations, even the Houses of Heaven—on a stereographic map, they're all drawn as simple, circular arcs.

Figure 5.3 shows stereographic projections of both the celestial sphere and the more familiar sphere of the Earth. To make a stereographic mapping of the entire Ptolemaic cosmos, all you would need to do is place the star map directly on top of the Earth map. The daily revolution of the

Figure 5.3: Stereographic Maps of the Celestial and Terrestrial Spheres

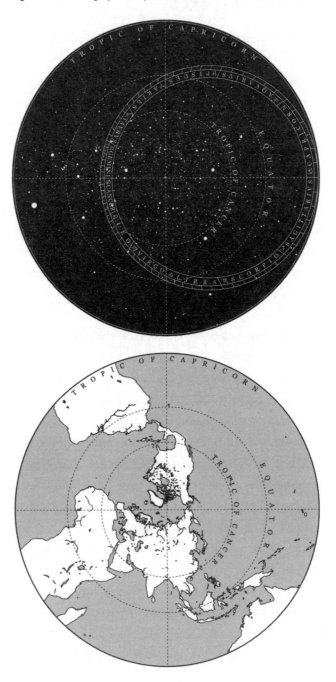

heavens can then be simulated by keeping the Earth map stationary while the star map rotates clockwise once per day.

This construction of two stacked stereographic maps provides the basic blueprint for an astrolabe. On an astrolabe, however, the terrestrial map is only implicit. What's shown instead is the horizontal coordinate grid (that is, the azimuth and elevation lines) for the spot where you happen to be. No matter where you are on Earth, you have a view of exactly one half of the celestial sphere. The plane of your horizon divides the celestial sphere into two equal hemispheres, and you can see the hemisphere above your head. What this hemisphere looks like when plotted on a stereographic map centered around the North Pole can be a little tricky to visualize. Figure 5.4 shows horizontal grids suited for observers at four different latitudes. The appearance of the grid at 90° north is probably the easiest one to intuit; the others can then be understood by comparison. In practice, astrolabes would come with several of these plates, which could be swapped in or out depending on where you were. Plates for latitudes south of the equator could be constructed in a similar way, but the Tropics of Cancer and Capricorn would need to be switched.

Now if, on top of these terrestrial plates, we keep just the ecliptic circle as an abstraction of the celestial map, we'll end up with an image of the cosmos that's starting to look a lot like the schemes of heaven which appear in this book. The most conspicuous difference is that this image would look quite barren without the Sun, Moon, and planets. Unlike Archimedes' clockwork model of the universe, astrolabes weren't designed to simulate the complicated orbits of these heavenly bodies. However, if you had a set of handy planetary tables, like the ones the *Almagest* taught you how to make, you could look up each planet's ecliptic coordinates for a given day and mark them on the ecliptic circle, just as we've done in our schemes. Then, by rotating the celestial map clockwise to simulate the sky's daily rotation, the astrolabe will tell you at what time each heavenly object will appear in different parts of the sky. In particular, the rising time of any star or planet can be determined by noting when, in its rotation, it crosses the horizon line for your latitude. This

Figure 5.4: Astrolabe Base Maps for Different Latitudes

Latitude: 90° N
The North Pole

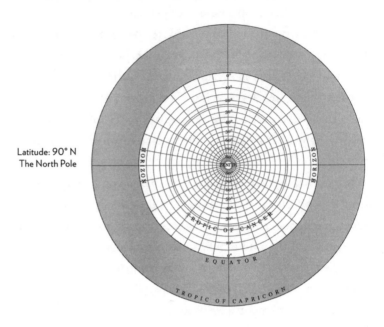

Latitude: 60° N
Cities: Whitehorse, Oslo,
Saint Petersburg

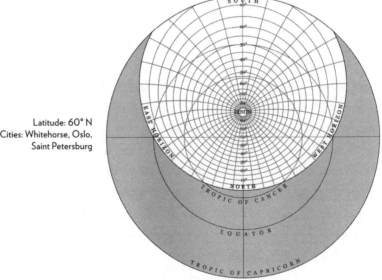

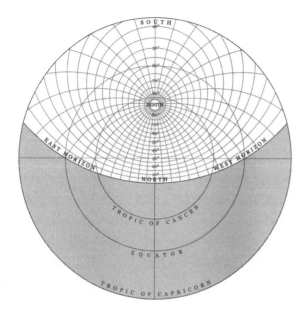

Latitude: 30° N
Cities: New Orleans,
Cairo, Shanghai

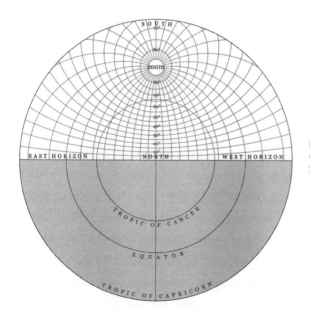

Latitude: 0°
Cities: Quito, Kampala,
Singapore

remarkable capability is of supreme importance to astrology, and we'll have more to say about it in the next chapter.

A MEANS TO AN END?

Without astronomy there can be no astrology. That much is pretty clear. In order to assess the influence of the planets, you first need to have at least some capability of determining where those planets are, were, and will be. The technological operations of astronomy are the building blocks that enable the abstract ideas of astrology to take shape. And just as a musician understands a piece of music in certain ways a pure listener does not, the ideas of astrology will be understood differently by someone who is familiar with the technological practices that give expression to those ideas. Insofar as Ptolemy's *Almagest* represents the most significant record of these practices, Otto Neugebauer, the historian of science we met earlier, draws a line in the sand:

> Any serious student of ancient or medieval astronomy must familiar-
> ize himself with these details, not only in order properly to appreci-
> ate one of the greatest masterpieces of scientific analysis ever written,
> but also to be able to understand what was common knowledge for
> every competent astronomer from the second to the seventeenth
> century.

Fighting words, to be sure. And yet a book like this is hardly the place to get into the intricacies of planetary orbit calculations, ancient or modern. For one thing, astrology is a consumer, not a producer, of astronomical data. In principle, the only astronomy an ancient astrologer needed to know was how to look up a planet's coordinates in tables compiled by an ancient astronomer (even if, in practice, these were often the same person). Similarly, today, we can take for granted that highly accurate astronomical data is never more than a mouse-click away. Specifically, all of the planetary data that I've used in this book comes from the HORIZONS online ephemeris system of NASA's Jet Propulsion Laboratory. This service provides public access to the same, high-precision data used for interplanetary spacecraft navigation and for generating the astronomical almanacs published each year by the United States Naval Observatory and the United Kingdom Hydrographic Office.

But what about the other side of this relationship? Would astronomy as we know it exist without astrology? The respectable applications of timekeeping, calendar regulation, and navigation have always been the chief motivations for observing the Sun, Moon, and stars. But the planets? Historically, there was never a single application that required knowledge of the positions of the planets other than astrology. And it was the challenge of accurately predicting the orbits of the planets that ultimately gave rise to the scientific revolution and, from there, our modern technological world. Of course, it's possible that for centuries astronomers felt compelled to address the minor inconsistencies in the orbit calculations of, say, Mars for purely theoretical reasons. I wouldn't bet too much on it, though, especially when so many of these same astronomers were so deeply committed to addressing the practical problems of astrology. In this, they were only following in the footsteps of the greatest of their predecessors, Ptolemy.

PTOLEMY'S ASTROLOGY

That Ptolemy, the most famous scientist of the ancient world, also wrote a book on astrology is a seemingly minor detail that, upon reflection, probably single-handedly ensured astrology's survival. It's as if Einstein had followed up his theory of relativity with a book on the physics of crystal healing (which, to be clear, he most assuredly did not). A millennium and a half later, when Copernicus arrived at the University of Bologna, Ptolemy's astrology book, the *Tetrabiblos*, was still required reading in the astronomy curriculum, which, in turn, was mandatory for anyone pursuing a medical degree. (This connection between astrology and medicine is one of long-standing importance; for many centuries, physicians were expected to make their diagnoses and time their prescriptions according to the planets.)

Like his geography, Ptolemy framed astrology as a natural extension of his astronomy. Or, as Ptolemy put it, his *Tetrabiblos* was about making predictions "by means of astronomy" (δι' ἀστρονομίας). According to Ptolemy, these predictions came in two varieties. The first, treated earlier in the *Almagest*, concerned the future positions of the stars and planets. The second—the subject of the *Tetrabiblos*—concerned the effects of these heavenly bodies on their surroundings.

Ptolemy's use of the word *astronomia*, "astronomy," in the opening of the *Tetrabiblos* is significant, because it contributed to the thorough blurring of "astronomy" and "astrology" that persisted right through the end of the scientific revolution. Bucking the convention established by Aristotle, Ptolemy never makes use of the word *astrologia*. Even more surprising is that in the *Almagest*, the single most important astronomy book prior to Copernicus, Ptolemy never uses the word *astronomia* either. Instead, Ptolemy insisted that the *Almagest* was explicitly a work of "mathematics." And he explicitly identifies his predecessors, including the great Hipparchus, as "mathematicians." (And let's not forget that Ptolemy's original title for the *Almagest* was the *Mathematical Syntaxis*.) Meanwhile, in literary, nontechnical writings from the Roman Empire, such as Petronius's *Satyricon*, a "mathematician" (*mathematicus*) was always and unambiguously an astrologer.

All of this is extremely confusing. But that's exactly the point. The modern distinction between astronomy and astrology is very difficult to project backward into the past. This isn't because the distinction wasn't acknowledged conceptually—it was—but more because there was rarely any distinction between an astronomer and an astrologer professionally. Indeed, Ptolemy himself was the model for this.

For Ptolemy, the more meaningful distinction was within his second type of astronomical predictions—what we would call astrology—which he divided into two subcategories: "general" predictions about the weather, the environment, and the destinies of cities and countries; and "genethlialogical" predictions (from the Greek word for "birthday") about the destinies of individuals. This notion of "two astrologies" or "both astrologies," meaning general and individual, was revived during the Renaissance and referenced frequently by thinkers like Tycho Brahe and Johannes Kepler.

In Greek, *Tetrabiblos* means "The Four Books." This signifies only that the work was divided into four extended sections. The *Tetrabiblos* is extremely detailed and, on this account, extremely fascinating. But since Ptolemy insists on keeping the *Tetrabiblos* on a high philosophical plane, it's definitely not the book you would choose as a handy, practical guide. Given its almost complete lack of examples, trying to learn about astrology from the *Tetrabiblos* is a bit like trying to learn how to cook from a cookbook with no recipes. Instead, the *Tetrabiblos* seems to have functioned as a sort of astrological referee, providing an "official" opinion on topics that were otherwise subject to a range of conflicting interpretations. We've already seen, for example, how Ptolemy's adoption of the solar over the sidereal zodiac settled the question of what to do about the precession of the equinoxes. In chapter 8, we'll see that arguments over how to draw the Houses of Heaven likewise hinged on Ptolemy's vague instructions.

Similarly, it's in his role as astrological arbiter that we too now turn to Ptolemy. Tables 5.1 and 5.2 present Ptolemy's definitive lists of some of astrology's most basic groupings: the genders and influences of each planet, and the genders and planetary rulers of each zodiac sign.

Table 5.1: Planetary Genders and Influences

	Planet		Gender	Influence
1	Moon	☽	Feminine	Good
2	Mercury	☿	Both	It depends
3	Venus	♀	Feminine	Good
4	Sun	☉	Masculine	It depends
5	Mars	♂	Masculine	Bad
6	Jupiter	♃	Masculine	Good
7	Saturn	♄	Masculine	Bad

Table 5.2: Zodiac Genders and Rulers

	Sign		Gender	Ruler
1	Aries	♈	Masculine	Mars
2	Taurus	♉	Feminine	Venus
3	Gemini	♊	Masculine	Mercury
4	Cancer	♋	Feminine	Moon
5	Leo	♌	Masculine	Sun
6	Virgo	♍	Feminine	Mercury
7	Libra	♎	Masculine	Venus
8	Scorpio	♏	Feminine	Mars
9	Sagittarius	♐	Masculine	Jupiter
10	Capricorn	♑	Feminine	Saturn
11	Aquarius	♒	Masculine	Saturn
12	Pisces	♓	Feminine	Jupiter

ASTRAL GEOGRAPHY

Earlier in this book, I suggested that all of the operations of astrology are nothing more than the assertion of a linkage in time. The effect of introducing all these extra attributes is, in essence, to open up new dimensions for expressing the ups and downs of these time-based relationships. The most important of these new dimensions are those which bring to astrology a sense of space.

The twelve zodiac signs, Aries through Pisces, are arranged around the ecliptic circle in a fixed sequence. Because of this, each sign—and, by extension, any planet that happens to be wandering through it—has a geometric relationship with every other. These relationships are called aspects, and traditionally five were recognized as being astrologically significant: conjunction, opposition, sextile, square, and trine.

Table 5.3: Astrological Aspects

Aspect	Spatial Relationship	Example	Geometric Shape	Influence
Conjunction	In the same zodiac sign	♈ ♈	Point	Harmonious
Sextile	2 zodiac signs apart	♈ ♊	Hexagon	Harmonious
Square	3 zodiac signs apart	♈ ♋	Square	Unharmonious
Trine	4 zodiac signs apart	♈ ♌	Triangle	Harmonious
Opposition	6 zodiac signs apart	♈ ♎	Line	Unharmonious

The power of an aspect found expression in the geometric shape it formed around the zodiac. For instance, all of the signs in sextile aspect with each other belong to one of two hexagons; the signs in square aspect belong to one of three squares; and the signs in trine aspect belong to one of four equilateral triangles. These triangles, also called trigons or triplicities, were, in addition, commonly associated with the four classical elements: earth, air, water, and fire (figure 5.5). Fittingly, as our scheme of heaven for this chapter shows, at the moment of Vesuvius's eruption, the three corners of the fiery trigon were all occupied: the Sun in Leo, the Moon in Sagittarius, and Mars in Aries.

Meanwhile, there's no shape you can make by connecting every fifth sign, which is why this relationship was not recognized as a meaningful aspect. Furthermore, in what would seem to be an astrologically pessimistic view of gender relations, aspects connecting signs of the same gender—conjunction, trine, and sextile—were considered harmonious, whereas aspects of mixed gender—opposition and square—were regarded as unharmonious.

The belief that spatial relationships in the sky resonated in a correspondingly spatial way over the Earth is one of the most ancient ideas in astrology. The Babylonians, for instance, held that the rival kingdoms to the north, south, east, and west of them were signified by the corresponding quadrants of the Moon during a lunar eclipse. Similarly, Manilius allotted a handful of verses in the *Astronomica* to listing which zodiac signs ruled

Figure 5.5: The Four Zodiac Trigons or Triplicities

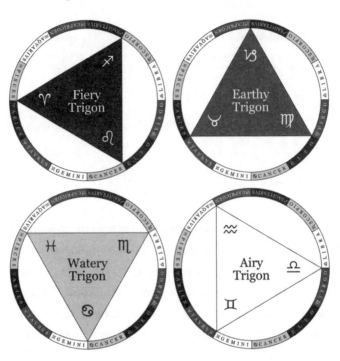

over which nations. But far and away the most elaborate system for linking celestial and terrestrial real estate was the one described, and very possibly invented, by Ptolemy.

Out of the four books of the *Tetrabiblos*, Ptolemy devotes nearly the entirety of the second, which is about "general" astrology, to his system of astral geography. It's a remarkable section insofar as it's the only place in all of his writings where Ptolemy unites his astronomy, astrology, and geography together. Ptolemy's basic idea is to assign each of the four quadrants of the inhabited world, that is, the *ecumene*, to one of the four zodiac triplicities.

The *ecumene*, according to Ptolemy, could be quartered by the line of latitude passing through the Pillars of Hercules and the Gulf of Issus (approximately 36° N), and the line of longitude passing through the Red Sea, the Black Sea, and the Sea of Azov (approximately 36° E, in modern terms). This placed the center of the *ecumene* pretty much right on top of the ancient city of Antioch, the capital of Roman Syria, not far from modern-day Aleppo. Ptolemy referred to the resulting quadrants as Europe (NW), Skythia (NE), Southern Asia (SE), and Libya (SW). Additionally, each quadrant was subject to two of the four cardinal winds, and two of the four beneficent and malefi-cent planets. I've mapped this system, along with a number of locations which play a role in our story, in figure 5.6, using Ptolemy's very own conical map projection, the same one he introduced to the world in his *Geography*.

Ptolemy's astral geography is without a doubt the most colorful part of the entire *Tetrabiblos*. After outlining his basic quadrant scheme, Ptolemy races through a remarkable list of seventy-three different regions, asserting that the quirks and idiosyncrasies of each one's inhabitants are merely the natural product of where they reside on his astrological world map. It's a little bit like reading a glossy travel guide to the ancient world, full of exotic descriptions of far-off lands. Mostly, though, it's like listening to a curmud-geonly old man spew a litany of ethnic stereotypes—except that, in this case, most of the ethnicities ceased to exist some fifteen hundred years ago. Troglodytes? They're "superstitious, given to religious ceremony, and fond of

Figure 5.6: Claudius Ptolemy's Astrological Map of the World

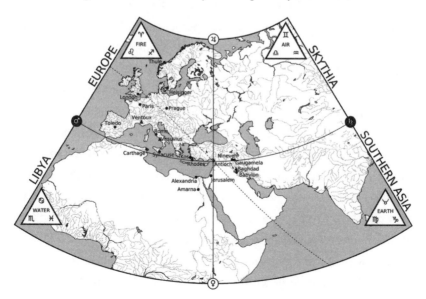

lamentation." Pamphylians? "They are exceedingly depraved, servile, laborious, rascally, are to be found in mercenary expeditions, looting and taking captives, enslaving their own peoples, and engaging in destructive wars." One can only imagine what he had to say about these groups in private!

Chauvinistic though it surely was, Ptolemy's astral geography was hardly a pointless digression. Its purpose, like that of its forerunners, was to address one of the most persistent objections to astrology: how can astrology be valid if a civilized Alexandrian like Ptolemy could, in principle, be born under the exact same stars as a savage barbarian from Germany? Assigning different regions of the Earth to different regions of the sky was a way for astrology to account for ethnic differences. Unfortunately, the inhabitants of the ancient world were hardly less fixated on race and ethnicity than are their modern descendants today, even if the *Tetrabiblos* underscores how arbitrary these divisions could be. According to Ptolemy, for instance, there were seven distinct ethnic groups around the Aegean Sea alone, whereas Britain, France, and Spain were each regarded as completely homogeneous monoliths.

What separates Ptolemy's survey from simple jingoism, however, is his attempt to ascribe the ethnic differences he perceived to a set of rational principles. On this account, the *Tetrabiblos* is one of the earliest examples of what's sometimes called anthropological ethnology. And unlike the blood-based racial theories which became especially pernicious in America and Europe in the nineteenth and twentieth centuries, Ptolemy's ethnology is entirely geographical. This makes the *Tetrabiblos* rightfully the great-grandfather of what's surely the most famous modern work of geographic anthropology, Jared Diamond's best-selling *Guns, Germs, and Steel*.

But let's not be coy here. What really makes Ptolemy's whirlwind world tour so entertaining is all the sex—or, rather, how candidly Ptolemy discusses the sexual habits of the peoples he describes. Adding to the *Tetrabiblos*'s long list of pioneering achievements, therefore, we can also credit it with being one of the first to examine "astrosexuality," which is the idea that your sexual predilections and romantic compatibilities are determined by your astrological makeup. Among the gossipy astrosexual tidbits in the *Tetrabiblos*, the one that comes closest to a general theory is the claim that attitudes toward homosexuality are distributed along a geographic gradient running northwest to southeast. The most tolerant views, according to Ptolemy, are to be found the farther you venture into northwestern Europe and the regions ruled by the fiery triplicity. Or, as Ptolemy puts it (in the standard, rather polite translation):

> Because of the occidental aspect of Jupiter and Mars . . . they are without passion for women and look down upon the pleasures of love, but are better satisfied with and more desirous of association with men. And they do not regard the act as a disgrace to the paramour, nor indeed do they actually become effeminate and soft thereby, because their disposition is not perverted, but they retain in their souls manliness, helpfulness, good faith, love of kinsmen, and benevolence.

Conversely, by the time you've reached the Middle Eastern countries of the earthy triplicity, attitudes have become downright hostile, to the point where "[they] hold in detestation such relations with males."

IN THE EYE OF THE BEHOLDER

Ptolemy's assertion that acceptance of homosexuality decreases along a line running from London to Riyadh agrees pretty well with what I imagine is the current conventional wisdom on the matter. Could he be onto something? To add a quantitative veneer to this question, we can use that favorite tool of data analysts everywhere: a linear regression.

Linear regression is one of several techniques used to gauge how strongly two lists of numbers are correlated. One of these lists, for instance, could be scores indicating how positively or negatively homosexuality is viewed in each country. As an especially detailed example, there's the Spartacus Gay Travel Index, published every year as part of the *Spartacus International Gay Guide*. In the Spartacus Gay Travel Index for 2017, each country is given points in fourteen different categories, ranging from the application of the death penalty for homosexuality to the legal status of gay marriage. Adding these points together results in a more or less continuous score from +9 (Sweden and the U.K.) to −14 (Somalia). (The U.S., incidentally, only ekes out a 4.) Of course, this list ultimately represents nothing more than the subjective assessment of the editors of the *Spartacus International Gay Guide*, but since their methodology is applied in a consistent way using publicly available data and—most importantly—it includes every country, it gives us an excellent list to use. Besides, what data set could be more appropriate for a Roman-themed regression than one named after Spartacus, the leader of Rome's most fearsome slave rebellion, who made his encampment on Mount Vesuvius?

As for the second list of numbers, these should indicate how far each country is situated in either the northwestern regions ruled by the fiery triplicity or the southeastern regions ruled by the earthy triplicity. If all we needed was an east–west measure, things would be easy. In that case we could just take the longitude of each country's capital city. Our situation is really no different. We can simply tilt the globe so that its new equator becomes the great circle passing through the center of Ptolemy's astrological world map at a 45-degree angle. (This is the dotted path drawn in figure 5.6.) Then the "longitudes" computed with respect to this new equator will serve as a measure of the "fieriness" or "earthiness" of any location.

So, are these two lists of numbers correlated? A linear regression (figure 5.7) suggests that they are. Specifically, the regression's best-fit line tells us that for every 10 degrees of "fire–earth longitude" we travel, we can expect the Spartacus Gay Travel Index score to drop by about two and a half points.

Regressions like this are a fixture of technical and scientific reports, but what do they really mean? In the previous chapter, we rejected several astrological claims when statistical tests showed that no correlation existed. So, if we're being fair, shouldn't this analysis, which indicates that a correlation does exist, compel us to accept Ptolemy's astrosexual theory? Not so fast. As the saying goes, correlation does not equal causation. With enough data sets to choose from, it's not difficult to find two that are correlated, and it can become a bit of a sport to pick out the most absurd or humorous cases. (For example, the correlation between the number of civil engineering doctorates awarded per year and mozzarella cheese consumption in the United States.)

Figure 5.7: Ptolemy's Theory of Astrosexuality Applied to Data from Modern Countries

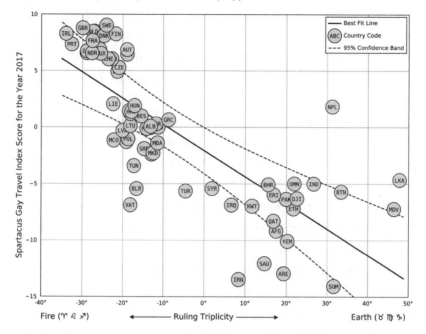

A simple linear regression (R^2 = 0.61) supports Ptolemy's claim that attitudes toward homosexuality exhibit a northwest-to-southeast gradient. Is this correlation meaningful? Who decides?

But if so many correlations are spurious, then why bother reporting them at all? This is an important question, especially since misrepresenting correlations is undoubtedly the most common way people use statistics to deceive both themselves and those around them (plate 6). One answer is that a strong correlation does indeed provide evidence in support of a theory, even if it must remain just one piece among many. How the pieces are to be weighed is ultimately a question of human judgment, one for which no single algorithm, test, or procedure will ever fully substitute.

As a case in point, the data we've plotted in figure 5.7 are hardly the only information we can bring to bear on the question of geographical attitudes toward homosexuality. It's no secret, for instance, that northwestern Europe historically, and even quite recently, was not especially welcoming toward homosexuals. Indeed, when the great Victorian explorer Richard Burton developed his own theory of geographically-influenced sexuality, the Middle East was explicitly included, and England excluded, from his map of what he termed the "Sotadic Zone"—a region where homosexuality was supposedly natural, accepted, and common. Were figure 5.7 to be redrawn with data from 150 years ago, therefore, it's altogether likely that the best-fit regression line would have entirely the opposite slope.

Yet a correlation that shifts from one moment to the next undermines any argument that there's a fixed principle at work. Instead, perhaps the only constant uniting Ptolemy's and Burton's theories is that each imagined the sexual mores of faraway lands to be radically different from what he knew back home, and each projected his disgust or desire accordingly. That's hardly the story you would get, however, if the only information you had was the cold and context-free data of figure 5.7.

Trying to figure out which story, if any, is hiding in your data is challenging expressly because there are usually multiple stories which can be crafted, and deciding which one to emphasize rarely has anything to do with the data itself. In the *Tetrabiblos*, Ptolemy intimates an awareness of this problem when he pauses to reflect upon the sheer number of astrological possibilities:

> It is of course a hopeless and impossible task to mention the proper outcome of every combination and to enumerate absolutely all the aspects of whatever kind, since we can conceive of such a variety of them. Consequently questions of this kind would reasonably be left to the enterprise and ingenuity of the mathematician . . .

But what astrology teaches us, and what Ptolemy perhaps failed to appreciate, is that with enough data, and with enough enterprise and ingenuity, the "mathematician" can generally make whatever connections he or she wants. And therein lies the danger. Because, as with exploring the world, so too with data: all too often, you find only what you were looking for.

6

HOW UNIQUE IS A HOROSCOPE? VETTIUS VALENS AND THE GOSPEL OF FATE

Alexandria, Egypt, 139

Sometime during the early centuries of the Roman Empire, a handful of disciples were inspired to write down the mystic teachings of their otherwise obscure sect. Their beliefs originated in the Near East, but these authors chose to write in Greek and Latin so as to spread their message to as wide an audience as possible. Although this faith's followers were persecuted and its practice outlawed, adherence to its teachings spread rapidly across the Roman Empire, outlasting the empire itself and ultimately becoming one of the most widespread beliefs in the world today.

Is this Christianity? Or maybe astrology? In fact, this sketch applies perfectly well to both, and the similar backstories of the two provide an important insight into what sort of creature astrology is. Astrology, despite claims of a purebred pedigree from Egyptian pharaohs or Babylonian high priests, is actually a Roman-era mutt.

A perfect portrait of this was on display in Alexandria, Egypt, during the predawn hours of Sunday, July 20, in the year 139. Only the tersest memorial remains, but with a bit of imagination we can picture a small group of temple priests, together with a few astronomers and maybe even a local official or two, keeping vigil throughout the night. Then, as the pink hues of daybreak illuminated the morning sky, each of these observers verified that Sirius, the "dog star" and brightest of all the stars, could be seen making its first appearance in the sky that year, rising above the eastern horizon just moments ahead of the Sun. Since that morning was also the first day of the Egyptian year—the first day of the month of Thoth—this meant that the Egyptian calendar had finally returned to what was believed to be its original astronomical configuration. It had only taken 1,460 years. In other words, the last time Sirius had risen this way on the first day of Thoth, it was 1322 BC, just sixteen years after the solar eclipse which signaled the demise of the pharaoh Akhenaten and his scandalous Sun cult.

The ancient Egyptian calendar, as mentioned previously, was exactly 365 days long. This is a fair but not terribly precise approximation of the true astronomical solar year, which is closer to 365.24 days. The calendar of the Roman Empire—the one introduced by Julius Caesar in 45 BC—used leap years to arrive at a better estimate of 365.25 days. When compared to the Julian calendar, therefore, the Egyptian calendar "wandered" in time, skipping ahead by one day every four years. At that rate, it takes $365 \times 4 = 1,460$ years for the Julian and Egyptian calendars to come back into alignment. Yet while the Egyptian calendar was notoriously bad at staying in sync with the seasons, its complete lack of leap years and other calendrical kludges made it an ideal timekeeper for long-term astronomical calculations. For this reason, it was the ancient Egyptian calendar, and not any of its more accurate but more complicated successors, which was used by both Ptolemy and Copernicus in their groundbreaking astronomy books. Remarkably, these two astronomers are themselves separated in time by a nearly complete 1,460-year cycle of the Egyptian calendar.

Yet how could the Egyptians of Ptolemy's time, let alone of Akhenaten's, manage to observe something as inherently imprecise as the dawn rising of Sirius to the precision of a single day? Most likely, they couldn't. The reappearance of the dog star, Sirius, had long been taken as a handy

Figure 6.1: A Scheme of Heaven for Sunday, July 20, 139
The Renewal of the Egyptian Calendar's 1,460-Year "Sothic Cycle"

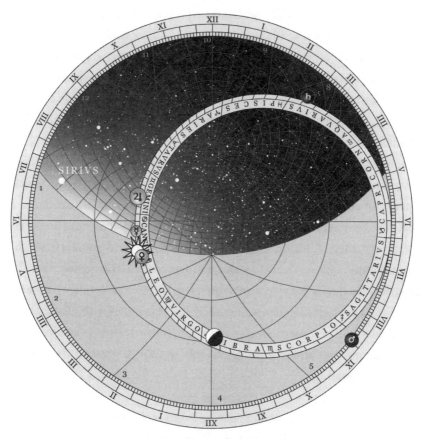

The Temple of Serapis, Alexandria, Egypt: 31°10'57"N, 29°53'47"E
JD: 1772027.60873
2:36 UT
ΔT: 9163s
Local Time: 4:34 AM
Local Apparent Sidereal Time: 0:20

	λ	β	RA J2000	Dec J2000	Az	El	House
♄ Saturn	≈ 23°44'↓	−1°56'	23ʰ 25ᵐ 00ˢ	−5°55'	223°53'	30°30'	⑧ 10°21'
♃ Jupiter	♊ 18°22'	0°12'	7ʰ 01ᵐ 57ˢ	22°42'	77°52'	26°14'	⑫ 3°14'
♂ Mars	♏ 28°58'	−4°08'	17ʰ 36ᵐ 50ˢ	−27°43'	265°54'	−45°01'	⑤ 14°54'
☉ Sun	♋ 24°45'	0°00'	9ʰ 32ᵐ 21ˢ	14°45'	60°30'	−6°00'	① 6°53'
♀ Venus	♋ 27°18'	1°13'	9ʰ 44ᵐ 00ˢ	15°04'	58°15'	−7°44'	① 9°04'
☿ Mercury	♋ 11°32'	0°48'	8ʰ 40ᵐ 27ˢ	19°22'	65°39'	6°10'	⑫ 23°13'
☽ Moon	♎ 5°10'	4°39'	14ʰ 02ᵐ 07ˢ	−7°35'	357°16'	−56°35'	④ 1°47'

way to mark the "dog days" of late summer and, vitally, the annual flooding of the Nile. But the once widely-held theory that the Egyptians based their calendar around this star is a little far-fetched. It's more plausible to imagine that the whole idea of a 1,460-year "Sothic cycle" (*Sothis* being a Greek name for Sirius) was simply invented by these latter-day astronomers of Alexandria who saw, in the happy coincidence of its completion during their lifetimes, a good excuse to have a celebration. Quite possibly Ptolemy himself, likely the chief expert in such matters, had a hidden hand in the festivities.

Whatever its historical origins, a Sothic-cycle celebration would have been an easy sell to the Romans, who, no doubt, appreciated being associated with notions of eternity. In short order, the Alexandrian mint issued a batch of commemorative coins sporting each of the zodiac signs and their planetary rulers. (This must have been a bit like our modern quarters commemorating each of the U.S. states and territories.) The quibble that the zodiac was actually Babylonian and therefore had no connection whatsoever with the Egyptian calendar would likely have been met with blank stares, particularly among Alexandria's overlords in Rome, for whom an ignorance of astronomy was almost a badge of honor. As Virgil wrote in the *Aeneid*, Rome's national epic:

> *Others will hammer out the breathing bronze more softly,*
> *(So I believe), and extract from marble living faces,*
> *They will argue their causes better, and trace the sky's meanderings,*
> *With a ray, and say which stars are rising;*
> *You, Roman, fail not to rule the nations by command;*
> *These will be your arts: to impose virtue where there's peace,*
> *To spare the conquered and crush the proud.*

And if part of the Roman art of ruling was to forge out of the cultures of its conquered peoples a unified civilization, then no city offered a more impressive display of this than Alexandria, the thoroughly multicultural capital of Roman Egypt.

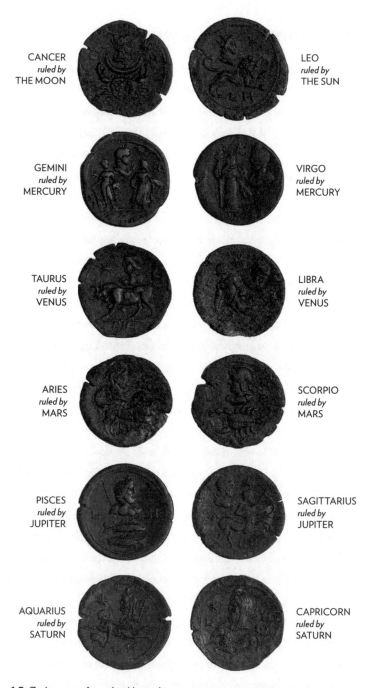

CANCER
ruled by
THE MOON

LEO
ruled by
THE SUN

GEMINI
ruled by
MERCURY

VIRGO
ruled by
MERCURY

TAURUS
ruled by
VENUS

LIBRA
ruled by
VENUS

ARIES
ruled by
MARS

SCORPIO
ruled by
MARS

PISCES
ruled by
JUPITER

SAGITTARIUS
ruled by
JUPITER

AQUARIUS
ruled by
SATURN

CAPRICORN
ruled by
SATURN

Figure 6.2: Zodiac coins from the Alexandrian mint. IMAGES COURTESY OF THE AMERICAN NUMISMATIC SOCIETY.

THE LIGHTHOUSE OF THE WORLD

Astrologers in Roman times boasted of an unbroken tradition stretching back 432,000, or 730,000, or maybe even 1,440,000 years. And yet, as we saw in chapter 2, the oldest known object that can plausibly be called a horoscope dates only to 410 BC. All things considered, this is shockingly recent. Even ignoring astrology's primeval pretensions, 410 BC is thousands of years after the pyramids, Stonehenge, and all of the other mystical sites supposed to showcase the astronomical savvy of their architects. What that crude cuneiform tablet of 410 BC really tells us is that astrology was still in its infancy when Babylon, along with all of its astral traditions, fell to Alexander the Great as a spoil of his conquest of Persia—a conquest foreshadowed, it was believed, by the lunar eclipse of 331 BC.

The marching of Alexander's armies kicked off a tremendous, east–west cross-pollination that spread to every corner of the *ecumene*, that is, the inhabited world as it was known to the Greeks. From Egypt to the borders of India, a broad swath of peoples who were not themselves Greek subsequently adopted the Greek, or Hellenic, language as an international language for politics, trade, and ideas. For this reason, the age as a whole has come to be called Hellenistic.

While literature lovers have tended to look down on the Hellenistic period—the term itself suggests a cheap knockoff of the Hellenic golden age of Plato and Sophocles—exactly the opposite is true for those of us excited about science. Practically every scientific advance of antiquity happened during this time. Euclid wrote his *Elements of Geometry*, Archimedes developed his principles of mechanics, Eratosthenes measured the circumference of the Earth, and Hipparchus discovered the precession of the equinoxes, all within two hundred years after Alexander's death.

Many of the achievements of Hellenistic science were the direct result of the integration of knowledge from the non-Greek-speaking civilizations of the ancient world into a common, Greek-language framework. Hipparchus, for instance, made extensive use of Babylonian astronomical data when constructing his model of the Moon's orbit. But what about the reverse? In particular, to what extent did astrology, so often regarded as a local Babylonian specialty, rely upon Greek or other foreign ingredients? Given the relative simplicity of the few horoscopes that survive from before Alexander's time, the answer is probably, "a lot."

The eclectic fusing of ideas and traditions that characterizes the Hellenistic age is often referred to as syncretism. And as a fitting legacy to the young conqueror who dreamed of joining east and west, the city to which he gave his name, though never lived to see, grew to become syncretism's pulsing heart. Renowned for its library and emblematic for its lighthouse, Alexandria was, by Roman times, the undisputed scientific capital of the ancient world. Whereas a budding Roman gentleman might, like Cicero, round off his education by studying philosophy in Athens, Alexandria stood out for its unrivaled accomplishments in mathematics, science, and engineering. The previously mentioned Euclid, Archimedes, and Eratosthenes lived either some or all of their lives there. To this list, we can add Hero, the creator of a steam engine and various animatronic robots, Diophantus, one of the early pioneers of algebra, and, of course, the great astronomer himself, Ptolemy.

Alexandria was no less celebrated for the cultivation of knowledge in its explicitly more mystical forms. Under the tolerant gaze of Serapis, the syncretistic, half-Egyptian, half-Greek hybrid god, a Greek translation of the Hebrew Bible, called the Septuagint, was commissioned for the library there. Hypatia, the most famous female mathematician prior to modern times, was leader of the Neoplatonists there. And Saint Anthony fought off the devil's temptations in the deserts lying just west of there. So it's hardly surprising that, far more than in any other city, astrology was able to flourish there, too.

Indeed, it's in the Septuagint, which was composed in Alexandria in the third or second century BC, that we find one of the oldest, and certainly one of the most influential, instances of the word "astrologer" to carry its modern meaning. In the prophet Isaiah's warning to "the virgin daughter of Babylon," her advisors, whom the Hebrew text calls *hovrei shamayim*—literally, "observers of the heavens"—become *astrologoi* (ἀστρολόγοι), "astrologers," when translated into Greek. Whether Matthew the Evangelist was aware of this usage is unclear, but in his Gospel, also written in Greek, he chose an altogether different word to describe the emissaries from the East who, at the appearance of a star, came to worship the newborn king of the Jews. The term that's found throughout Matthew, chapter 2, is "magi" (μάγοι), the traditional name for the diviners of Persia and also the root of the modern word "magic."

Among the ancient astrologers whose names we know, an impressive plurality called Alexandria their home. At the top of this list are Thrasyllus and Balbillus, the personal astrologers to the emperors in Rome. Balbillus, as mentioned earlier, even became head of the library of Alexandria and later governor of all Egypt. And, of course, there's Ptolemy too. Thus from the corridors of power to the apex of science, some of Alexandria's most illustrious citizens were themselves practitioners of the astral art. If pressed, it's likely that each would have pointed to astrology's extreme antiquity as one of the reasons for its success. And yet, to compare the simple horoscopes of Babylon with an Alexandrian product like Ptolemy's *Tetrabiblos* is to recognize immediately how much astrology had changed. Far from a pristine Babylonian import, astrology is much better understood as a hybrid product of Hellenistic syncretism: part Babylonian, part Greek, with perhaps a dash of Egyptian thrown into the mix. Or, to put it another way, if Babylon is where astrology was born, then Alexandria is where it came of age. In particular, Alexandria is where two of the most important astrology books to survive from antiquity were likely written. The first of these, the *Tetrabiblos*, is a book we've already met. The second, though far less known, is in almost every respect a far more interesting read. This is a book called the *Anthologies*, the work of an astrologer named Vettius Valens.

A BOUQUET OF ASTRAL FLOWERS

"Anthology" is a Greek word that means "a collection of flowers." The astrological *Anthologies* of Vettius Valens are, appropriately, not so much a systematic treatise as a potpourri of astrological advice and algorithms gathered up over several decades. Valens was probably about twenty years younger than Ptolemy, both were authors of astrology books, and both lived in Egypt during the second century after Christ. (Valens never specifies where in Egypt he lived, although Alexandria would seem the most likely choice.) Strangely enough, there's no indication that either was aware of the other's existence. And their books on astrology couldn't be more different. The *Tetrabiblos* comes across as an overview of astrology for the philosophically curious but otherwise math-phobic reader. The *Anthologies*, meanwhile, reads like a practical guide for the working astrologer. And where I can see the *Tetrabiblos* sitting impressive (and unread) on an elegant bookshelf, I imagine the *Anthologies* smudged and torn from constant use, with impromptu notes, sketches, and frazzled calculations scribbled on every page.

Astrology, however much it misdirects with its talk of stars and planets, is an art whose true subject matter has always been the stories of actual people. It's this element above all that makes the *Anthologies* such a fascinating read. Its pages are bustling with the astrological accounts of real, albeit unnamed and unknown people's lives. This is a refreshing contrast to the sterile generalities of the *Tetrabiblos*. All the more so, since there's no better way to learn a technical subject than to follow a series of worked examples. Thus, while the *Tetrabiblos* might teach you the doctrines of astrology, the *Anthologies* taught you how to *do* astrology. This is invaluable for our understanding since astrology is, and always has been, a technical craft, and not merely a set of beliefs disassociated from the practice of that craft.

Regarded in this light, astrology's principal product is, of course, the horoscope. The *Anthologies* preserve a remarkable 123 unique horoscopes, each one like an astrological epitaph for a once living, breathing, Greek-speaking inhabitant of second-century Roman Egypt (plate 7). This makes the *Anthologies* a uniquely precious document not only for illustrating the technical practices of Roman-era astrology in unprecedented detail, but also for providing one of the most intimate slices of daily life from that time. From their horoscopes we learn such voyeuristic details about these individuals' lives as their financial ups and downs:

In the first periods (or times), he had great political prestige and affairs and positions of trust . . . But later he was brought down in life and became a vagabond.

Their health issues:

> This person had mange on the head and leprosy and lichens on the body . . .

And how they died:

> This person died in the bath, choked (to death) in water.

Some of the horoscopes are charmingly colorful:

> He was a dancer and in his 25th year, he was put in confinement in the course of a public riot but he was defended before the governor and released through the help of friends and the entreaty of the crowd and became more esteemed.

Some of them are touching:

> This person began as deputy governor, but falling into the governor's disfavor in his 34th year was condemned to the quarry . . . However, his wife accompanying him affectionately comforted him and shared her possessions with him.

And some of them are just weird:

> This person was short-armed.

Admirably, for a book that focuses so much on the lives of others, Valens isn't shy about sharing a few details of his own. His life story, as befits his professional calling, seems to have fully embodied the syncretistic spirit of his times. The manuscripts call him Vettius Valens of Antioch, indicating the capital of Roman Syria (and, according to Ptolemy, the centerpoint of the four quadrants of the *ecumene*) as the city of his birth. Founded by one of Alexander's victorious generals, Antioch in Roman times was a major trading hub teeming with temples to Greek and Semitic deities and, lately, home to one of the largest communities of Christians in the empire. Antioch's patron was the goddess Fortune, or *Tyche* in Greek, the original Lady Luck. Her tutelage evidently left a lasting impression on Valens, as he would later write of the absolute supremacy of Fortune and Fate in all things.

Yet for all its worldliness, Antioch apparently proved too provincial for Valens. After wandering through many lands (he doesn't say which), his thirst for knowledge brought him ultimately to Egypt. There, it seems, no different from today, that the quest for spiritual enlightenment could be a frustrating and, above all, expensive undertaking. Valens writes of the many frauds and charlatans he encountered who were happy to take his money but were incapable of guiding him any closer to the truth. Seeking a retreat from the world, he even spent a period living as part of a monkish, and possibly Christian, commune.

In addition to what Valens says about himself explicitly, there is a specific horoscope in the *Anthologies* that is used as an example no fewer than twenty-one separate times. A recent tradition has been to identify this as Valens's own. If so, then we can add to Valens's biographical sketch that he was conceived on May 13 in the year 119, and that he was born on February 8 in the year 120. His mother predeceased his father. At the age of thirty-four he "worked abroad, was a friend of great men, and was in mortal danger because of a woman." At the age of thirty-five he survived a storm at sea but was nearly captured by pirates. In short, Vettius Valens appears to have lived the romantic, swashbuckling life one would expect of any author of a book about astrology.

But as Valens would come to appreciate, no matter how far you wander, you cannot escape your destiny. Astrology had called him, and he was duty-bound to follow. His reading of his own horoscope helped him to recognize that he would never become rich, famous, or powerful. "I know myself," he writes. "I know the foundation which my Fate has assigned me, and I know that it is impossible for anyone, contrary to Fate, to become different from what he is." According to Valens, suffering can be overcome, and balance achieved, but only by learning to accept one's lot in life. "I have abandoned all vain hopes and thoughts," he tells us, victoriously, "and I have kept the laws of Fate."

This rather bleak outlook on life—Valens goes on to compare it to being an intelligent slave of a cruel master—is actually pretty characteristic of astrology throughout its history, with the notable exception of our modern, much more cheerful variety. In the ancient debate as to the existence of free will, or of nature versus nurture, astrology has long just laughed, insisting upon an extreme form of cold, mathematical determinism. Oddly enough, it was this dispiriting attitude that probably helped astrology permeate the Roman world as thoroughly as it did. Although the Roman Empire never had an official religion—never, that is, before adopting Christianity in 380— Stoicism had a pretty good run. So much so that even the very word "stoic" tends to conjure up the image of a stern, betogaed Roman, although Stoicism itself was, like astrology, yet another Hellenistic import.

As we saw with Manilius's poem *Astronomica*, Stoicism and astrology were a natural combination. Fundamental to Stoic philosophy, and in complete harmony with astrology, was the total denial of free will and the corresponding belief in an all-powerful Fate. To the Stoic, a completely deterministic worldview implied that everything in the universe was linked together, that each past action was bound to each future one through "cosmic sympathy." Does this sound new-agey? Perhaps it does, at first, until you realize how completely antithetical it is to the idea of self-improvement, growth, or transcendence. "Everything is controlled by Fate and there's nothing you can do about it!" is just not a message that's going to motivate you to head to the yoga studio at six in the morning. It's a message that may, however, make it easier to accept that you were never going to do yoga at six in the morning anyway.

ASTROLOGY AS AN EXPERIMENTAL SCIENCE

Perusing the nativities in the *Anthologies*, it's difficult not to wonder how far our lives really are controlled by Fate, and, if so, whether that Fate is encoded in the timing of our birth. I've long had a particularly personal interest in this question because, as luck or Fate would have it, one of my dearest friends happens to have been born on the same day, in the same year, in the same city, in the same hospital, and in even in the very same hour as me. In fact, according to our birth certificates, we were born only eight minutes apart!

Yet, despite being born within feet of each other, it wasn't until high school that I was finally reunited with my long-lost astrological twin—in our high school's Latin club, no less. As time has gone by, I find myself forced to admit that our lives really do share some striking similarities. Starting with our mutual appreciation of all things dead and Roman, each of us then went on to study physics (my friend, lasers; myself, plasmas); each of us subsequently worked a series of technical jobs in similar industries; and, more recently, each of us has become especially involved in math and science outreach. Most improbably of all, however, we were both lately given the opportunity to write a book. My astral twin, you see, is none other than the talented and glamorous Olivia Koski who, along with her co-author Jana Grcevich and illustrator Steve Thomas, recently published the thoroughly charming *Vacation Guide to the Solar System: Science for the Savvy Space Traveler.* In

Figure 6.3: *Forsan et haec olim meminisse iuvabit.* "Perhaps, one day, it will be pleasant to remember even these things." University High School Latin Club, Tucson, Arizona, 1997. Olivia Koski (bottom row, right) was born at 9:28 a.m. on Friday, May 18, 1979, at St. Joseph's Hospital in Tucson, Arizona. Yours truly (top row, center) was born on the same day, at the same hospital, at 9:20 a.m. PHOTO: JANE BAMBAUER.

fact, it was Olivia's book that led, through a sequence of unlikely connections, to the inception of the book you now have in your hands. So if our fates weren't linked before, they certainly are now.

Of course, if someone asked, I could just as easily make a separate list of all the ways my life and Olivia's have been very different. So, have the stars been guiding our paths or haven't they? Unfortunately, I don't hold out much hope that this little ongoing astrology experiment otherwise known as my life will lead to any definitive answers. Statistically speaking, a sample size of two—Olivia's life and my own—isn't enough to reveal anything more than a few curious coincidences. And in the grand scheme of things, how different can we expect any two people's lives to be if they were born and raised in a similar time and place? This point, however, is one of the reasons I find the *Anthologies* so exciting. Since they contain the most detailed collection of ancient horoscopes, the *Anthologies* gives us the ability to compare, side by side, the lives of ancient and modern individuals born under the same configuration of stars. Might not the hidden influence of a shared destiny reveal itself if we could observe its effects repeated in both an Egyptian living in Roman times and, say, an American living today?

From a theoretical standpoint, the fact that astrology is impossible according to the laws of physics would seem to be all there is to say on the matter. There are only two scientifically recognized forces by which a distant object, like a planet, can influence us here on Earth: gravity and electromagnetism. And the effects of both of these forces can be calculated and shown to be absurdly small. Indeed, at the moment of birth, the gravitational pull of the obstetrician on a baby will be stronger than that from any planet, and his or her heat and reflected light will be far greater than any planetary radiation.

The problem with this argument, however, is that there are a great many things which have been discovered—quantum mechanics, continental drift, the platypus—that were also theoretically impossible right up until they weren't. As someone who is of a more experimentalist mind-set, I would want to know, in addition, to what extent astrology is, or is not, supported by observation and experimental evidence.

Yet here we run into problems as well. It's often difficult to test astrology's claims because it's often difficult to pin down what, precisely, astrology's claims actually are, especially as they apply to any specific, testable scenario. If a forecast fails to unfold as predicted, there's never a lack of countervailing nuances to blame. This slippery quality of astrology is exactly what the philosopher of science Karl Popper had in mind when he formulated his famous criterion that the difference between science and pseudoscience is that science must be "falsifiable."

Specifically, Popper contrasted Einstein's theory of relativity against Marx's theory of history, the psychoanalytic theories of Sigmund Freud and Alfred Adler, and astrology. Einstein's theory had led to a testable prediction that the bending of light by gravity ought to be noticeable as a slight shift in the apparent positions of stars when measured near the Sun. This prediction, which very easily could have proven false, was instead dramatically confirmed in observations made by Arthur Eddington during the total solar eclipse of May 1919. Meanwhile, according to Popper, there was no scenario—no observable fact or evidence—that would force a Marxist, a Freudian, an Adlerian, or an astrologer to admit their theory was wrong. This made these ideas, Popper contended, more like narrative myths than scientific theories.

Popper's idea of falsifiability has sparked decades of debate as to whether this is a meaningful way to separate science and pseudoscience. Is it really that easy to draw a line between the two? Is it even possible to identify a set of characteristics shared by all the sciences, from physics to anthropology, that is not shared by other endeavors, like history or cooking? And if it's not possible, does it still make sense to talk about "science" as a unified concept?

To muddy the waters, astrology, at least historically, has made plenty of falsifiable claims. Indeed, we've already encountered several in this book. Does this mean that astrology used to be a science? Wherever the line between science and pseudoscience lies—if, indeed, one can be drawn at all—it's worth noting that, throughout history, many astrologers were committed to the idea that astrology's validity should derive not from the divinity of its sources, nor from the antiquity of its traditions, but instead from experimental proof. One of those astrologers was Vettius Valens:

. . . I have experienced much, have expended much toil, and have personally examined and tested what I have compiled. Experience is better and more reliable than mere hearing, because one who hears has only an unreliable and doubtful grasp. One who has had experience, has tried many things, and has remembered them, validates what he has experienced.

Yet if you're Vettius Valens and you want to examine the complete arc of someone's life astrologically, how do you even begin to count, let alone analyze, all of the potential correlations? The problem is hopelessly ill-defined. Nevertheless, if that's the route you insisted on taking, it's pretty clear that the first thing you'd want is data—lots of it. I think Valens understood this intuitively, which is why he set about compiling his collection of horoscope case studies. Quite frankly, nothing could be more scientific.

Valens's 123 horoscopes weren't anywhere near the number he would have needed for the huge task he set himself. But that doesn't mean they can't be put to good use, especially today. The luxury of letting all that data marinate for two thousand years is that, in a curious way, it has reduced Valens's problem to a more manageable size. Consider, for example, the hapless individual who appears in the *Anthologies* under the heading "Violent Deaths." His horoscope recounts only the configuration of the planets at the moment of his birth, and that his demise took the form of being thrown to the lions. Would another person born with the same horoscope be doomed to be similarly devoured? Empirically, the most direct way to answer this question would be to examine the lives of multiple individuals who share the same horoscope and count how many of them were eaten by lions. And this is something we can do, at least in principle, since Valens has already done the hardest part: he's let us know exactly what such a horoscope should look like.

THE MEANINGS OF A HOROSCOPE

The word "horoscope"—no surprises here—is Greek. It comes from *hora* (ὥρα), which denotes a season, occasion, or a specific moment in time. This is as distinct from *chronos* (χρόνος), which referred to an interval of time with a clear beginning, middle, and end. The word *horoskopos* (ὡρόσκοπος), therefore, literally means "moment-watcher." To be a horoscope, that is, to be a moment-watcher, is to have the ability to distinguish each moment from the moment that came before and the moment that follows directly behind.

Yet what defines a moment? Astrologically speaking, this moment is different from another moment because the cosmic influences you're receiving right now are different from the cosmic influences you would receive at a different time or, indeed, at a different place. To specify an astrological moment, therefore, is to specify the celestial configuration which gives rise to that moment's influences. And this is precisely what our schemes of heaven do: they illustrate exactly how the heavens appear at a particular instant in time as viewed from a particular location on Earth.

But do we really need all of the information in our schemes just to mark a moment? In fact, quite a bit of it is redundant. For instance, if you know your epoch (that is, the celestial location of the cusp of Aries), then there are formulas to convert back and forth between ecliptic and equatorial coordinates. You don't need both sets. And if you know your latitude and longitude, then you can easily convert between ecliptic, equatorial, and horizontal coordinates.

So the question arises: what's the minimum amount of information we need to characterize an astrological moment? Vettius Valens gives us the answer. According to the *Anthologies*, just eight pieces of astronomical data are required to cast a horoscope. The first seven of these are the ecliptic longitudes of the seven classical planets. The eighth and final item is the part of the ecliptic which, at that same moment, is rising above the eastern horizon. In modern astrology, this is the quantity known as the ascendant. But I'm willing to bet that you're more familiar with its ancient Greek name: the horoscope (*horoskopos*).

There are a handful of examples in the *Anthologies* where the eight quantities just listed are specified to the nearest degree, or even fraction of a degree. However, in the vast majority of cases (87 out of 123), Valens is content to give only the whole zodiac sign. This suggests a template for what can be considered the minimal, but still complete, information needed to specify an astrological moment. By way of example, using this template, this chapter's scheme of heaven for the Sothic New Year at Alexandria can be reduced to the following sentence: "Saturn in Aquarius; Jupiter in Gemini; Mars in Scorpio; Sun in Cancer; Venus in Cancer; Mercury in Cancer; Moon in Libra; horoscope in Cancer." And if we agree to always list these eight quantities in the same order, then we can express this astrological moment more economically as just a sequence of eight zodiac signs: ♒♊♏♋♋♋♎—♋.

The last sign of this sequence, ♋, is the horoscope proper. It isn't tied to a celestial body, like the previous seven signs, which is why I've separated it out with a dash. It also plays a different role in characterizing an astrological moment. Although the positions of the Sun, Moon, and planets are always moving around the ecliptic, in practice these motions are sufficiently slow (it takes Saturn nearly thirty years to complete an orbit, for example) that you can easily regard them as fixed for the span of a day. The horoscope, meanwhile, tracks the much more rapid daily revolution of the sky. Over the course of a day, the horoscope will be found in each of the twelve zodiac signs in order, but precisely when and for how long will depend on your location. In our eight-sign sequence, therefore, the first seven signs can be thought of as defining the "cosmic" part of an astrological moment. These are data that are valid for the whole globe for the whole day. By contrast, the eighth sign, the horoscope, defines the "local" part of an astrological moment, since its validity encompasses only part of the globe for a part of the day.

Quite clearly, the word "horoscope" has a wonderful multivalency in astrology. In one of its usages, the astrologer himself could be the horoscope, or moment-watcher, since he was the one who tracked the changing celestial moments. More commonly, timekeeping instruments were referred to as "horoscopic," since they could be thought of as tracking the moments as they passed. It's in this sense that the word "horoscope" came to be equated with the rising sign. If you imagine the horoscope as an invisible clock hand extending eastward from your location as far as you can see, then this hand will point to the zodiac signs as they ascend above the eastern horizon. By specifying the sign in which the horoscope (in this sense of the word) is located, you therefore customize your astrology to a given time and place in a way that merely listing the positions of the Sun, Moon, and planets cannot.

Over the centuries, and in the way that parts can stand for the whole, the meaning of a horoscope has expanded to signify not just the rising zodiac sign but the entire configuration of the heavens, a graphical diagram of that configuration, and finally the predictions and life advice which derive from that diagram. But these shifts in definition serve also to reveal the astrological core of a horoscope that has never changed: the sense that there is a unique cosmic energy permeating each unique moment of time and space.

THE ASTROLOGY MACHINE

As the words themselves affirm, the horoscope, meaning the rising sign, was the indispensable part of a horoscope, meaning the astrological assessment of a moment. Unfortunately for the math-phobic, however, computing the horoscope (that is, the rising sign) was also the most mathematically challenging operation in all of astrology. In fact, nearly all of Book 2 of Ptolemy's *Almagest* is occupied with precisely this problem, offering yet another example of how developments in astronomy were, to an extent that's too easily dismissed, frequently motivated by the technological demands of astrology. Accordingly, unless you were content to cast *a* horoscope without *the* horoscope, there was zero chance that you, as an ancient astrologer, could skirt the math-heavy parts of your job description. On the bright side, though, the horridness of horoscope calculations highlights what a brilliant invention the astrolabe was, because what might previously have required several pages of calculations to determine was, by means of this instrument, dispatched with a simple mechanical rotation.

To show how this works, consider a day in the life of an astrolabe (figure 6.4). In fact, let's choose the day with which we began this chapter: the Sothic

Figure 6.4: A Day in the Life of an Astrolabe

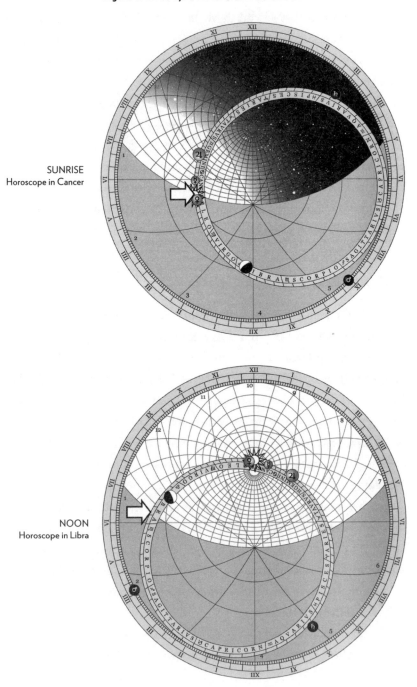

SUNRISE
Horoscope in Cancer

NOON
Horoscope in Libra

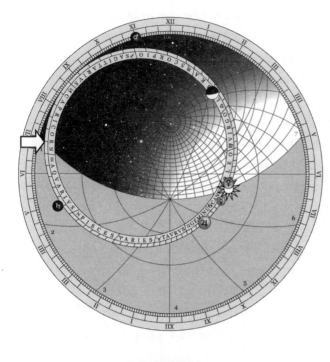

SUNSET
Horoscope in Capricorn

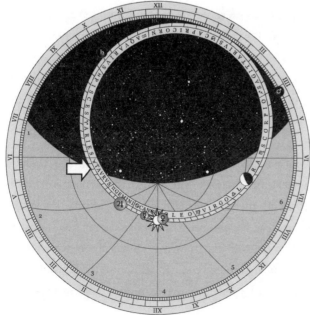

MIDNIGHT
Horoscope in Taurus

New Year of July 20, 139, as experienced at the latitude and longitude of Alexandria, Egypt. After setting the background grid of azimuth and elevation lines to Alexandria's latitude, we can fix the date by placing the Sun at 24° Cancer, since this is the ecliptic coordinate which corresponds to July 20. The day's unfolding is now modeled simply by rotating the celestial sphere (here represented by the ecliptic circle) clockwise around the instrument's center. Sunrise, for example, will occur when the Sun crosses over the eastern horizon. On the astrolabe, this is the arc extending out to the left-hand side of the instrument and located just above the small numeral 1. The horoscope, at all times, is defined as the point of the ecliptic which intercepts the eastern horizon. Thus, at the moment of sunrise, the horoscope, just like the Sun, is located in the zodiac sign of Cancer.

The rest of the day follows the same pattern. Noon, for instance, is modeled by rotating the ecliptic until the Sun arrives at the center of the sky. Looking to where the ecliptic and eastern horizon intersect, we can read directly off the instrument that the horoscope is now in Libra. And similarly for sunset (horoscope in Capricorn), midnight (horoscope in Taurus), or any other moment of the day.

Note that throughout this exercise, the configuration of the planets on the ecliptic never changed. It's not necessary to recalculate the positions of the planets minute by minute or hour by hour. To see how the sky appears at different times of the same day, you need only to compute the planets' ecliptic coordinates once, and then specify the rotation angle which the ecliptic (or, more generally, the celestial sphere) makes with respect to your location.

Those familiar with modern astronomy may recognize this rotation angle as the local sidereal time. This is the angle which the vernal point makes with your local north–south meridian. Exactly the same information is conveyed by the horoscope. The horoscope is the local sidereal time's ancient analog. Recognizing this helps to clarify why knowing the horoscope was so important: it communicated in one concise data-point the orientation of the entire celestial sphere with respect to where you stood. The genius of the astrolabe is such that both quantities, the ancient horoscope and the modern local sidereal time, can be determined simply by looking at the instrument without any additional computation.

It's not known when the astrolabe first appeared on the scene. But where? Well, Alexandria, of course! The publication of Ptolemy's *Planisphere* proved that all of the theoretical machinery was in place to build one, and Ptolemy offers a few vague hints that perhaps he may have done so. Theon, another Alexandrian astronomer, and father of the mathematician Hypatia, is known to have written a treatise on the astrolabe around the year 400, but this work is now lost. Therefore the award for the earliest surviving astrolabe manual goes to John Philoponus, a Christian theologian writing around the year 550 and living in—you guessed it—Alexandria. So whether we date the astrolabe to Ptolemy's time or somewhat later, this amazing instrument is a genuine Alexandrian original and yet another example of that city's indispensable contributions to the astral arts and sciences.

HOW UNIQUE IS A HOROSCOPE, REALLY?

As a proud (and stubborn?) Taurus, if I happen upon the horoscope section of a magazine, I'm not going to waste my time reading about Aries or Leos. I want to know what's in store for me and my fellow zodiac bulls. But these days, when even my choice of coffee is supposed to reflect my individual uniqueness, why should my horoscope leave me feeling no more special than merely one out of twelve? It's quite flattering, therefore, to consider that an ancient astrologer like Vettius Valens would agree that there's much more to me than just my Sun sign. Actually, he'd insist there were precisely seven more things to me.

Following Valens's basic template, the scheme of heaven for my birth (figure 6.5) can be reduced to a simple sequence of eight zodiac signs: ♍♌♉♉♉♉♒—♋. This is clearly more detailed than just saying I'm a Taurus. But is it unique? Maybe I really am stubborn, since analyzing this question quickly became a fixation of mine. As a preliminary to the calculations ahead, it seemed sensible to recast these sequences into an alphanumeric format that's easier for humans—and, more importantly, computers—to read (table 6.1).

Table 6.1: Zodiac ⟷ Alphanumeric Dictionary

Zodiac Sign	♈	♉	♊	♋	♌	♍	♎	♏	♐	♑	♒	♓
Alphanumeric Digit	0	1	2	3	4	5	6	7	8	9	A	B

A and B are used here instead of 10 and 11 so that each digit is exactly one symbol in length. (Anyone who has ever had an intimate conversation with a computer will immediately recognize this as simply hexadecimal notation.) Expressed in this way, my birth horoscope now becomes the following eight-digit code:

541111A-3

Having had ample opportunity to split, sort, and scrutinize these sequences, I found that the nickname "zodiac code" or "Z-code," for short, just seemed to stick. Thus, the question "How unique is a horoscope?" can be reformulated more promisingly as "How many possible Z-codes are there?"

At first glance, if each of the eight digits of a Z-code can take on any of twelve possible values (one for each of the twelve zodiac signs), then the total number of possible combinations would be $12 \times 12 \times 12 \times 12 \times 12 \times 12 \times 12 \times 12$ or 12^8. This is almost correct, except that there are certain planetary configurations which are physically impossible. Specifically, as seen from the Earth, Mercury can never be more than one sign away from the Sun, and Venus never more than two signs. For example, if the Sun is in Taurus, then the only three possible locations for Mercury are Aries, Taurus, or Gemini. And Venus in this same example can only be in Pisces, Aries, Taurus, Gemini, or Cancer, so five possibilities. Knowing this behavior, the total number of Z-codes is actually $12 \times 12 \times 12 \times 12 \times 5 \times 3 \times 12 \times 12 = 44{,}789{,}760$.

Is forty-four million, seven hundred and eighty-nine thousand, seven

Figure 6.5: A Scheme of Heaven for Friday, May 18, 1979
Birth Date of the Author

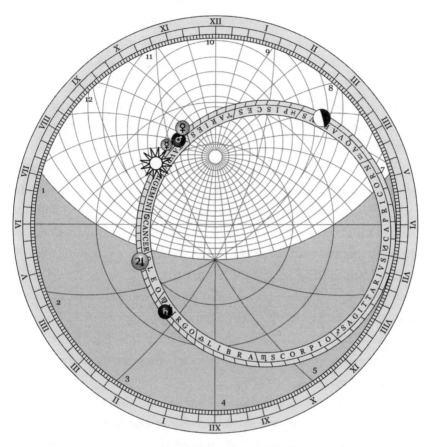

St. Joseph's Hospital, Tucson, Arizona: 32°13'35"N, 110°51'18"W
JD: 2444012.18056
16:20 UT
ΔT: 50s
Local Time: 9:20 AM
Local Apparent Sidereal Time: 00:40

		λ	β	RA J2000	Dec J2000	Az	El	House
♄ Saturn	♍	7°08'	1°56'	10ʰ 39ᵐ 28ˢ	10°35'	39°08'	-38°13'	② 21°17'
♃ Jupiter	♌	3°09'	0°40'	8ʰ 23ᵐ 40ˢ	20°02'	59°01'	-9°17'	① 10°48'
♂ Mars	♉	1°52'	0°40'	2ʰ 00ᵐ 53ˢ	11°36'	133°49'	62°15'	⑩ 20°46'
☉ Sun	♉	27°07'	0°00'	3ʰ 40ᵐ 35ˢ	19°35'	96°16'	47°56'	⑪ 11°52'
♀ Venus	♉	0°47'	-1°39'	1ʰ 58ᵐ 10ˢ	10°17'	136°37'	61°37'	⑩ 20°20'
☿ Mercury	♉	14°12'	-1°22'	2ʰ 49ᵐ 48ˢ	14°52'	113°05'	55°52'	⑪ 1°56'
☽ Moon	♒	22°10'	1°27'	21ʰ 37ᵐ 20ˢ	-12°38'	231°53'	27°12'	⑧ 3°09'

hundred and sixty a big number or a small number? Well, it's a small number when you consider that there are nearly 7.6 billion people alive today. Thus, even if the complete set of Z-codes was divvied up evenly, each one would still be shared by about 200 people. Actually, you can expect your Z-code to be much more crowded than that. Close to 400,000 people are born every day, and since the fastest-changing digit of a Z-code—the rising sign (also known as the horoscope or ascendant)—cycles through all twelve possibilities once per day, a better estimate is that each Z-code is shared by upwards of 30,000 people.

Evidently, a Z-code isn't specific enough to serve as anyone's unique address within the cosmic continuum. Maybe eight digits aren't enough? In fact, modern professional horoscopes commonly include the coordinates for lots of additional astronomical objects, some with a rich tradition, such as the ascending and descending lunar nodes, and some much more modern, such as Uranus, Neptune, and the larger asteroids. Unfortunately, none of these helps in the slightest to make your horoscope more unique. From our vantage point here on Earth, there's simply nothing moving in the sky faster than the rotating sky itself. And since this motion is encoded by the rising sign, that quantity becomes the pace-setter for how precisely you can specify a cosmic moment.

Consequently, if you absolutely insist on asserting your astrological uniqueness, your only option is to report your cosmic data with higher precision than a whole zodiac sign. This, conceptually, has long been the astrological answer to the problem of twins who lead very different lives. The Roman senator and astrologer Nigidius Figulus colorfully compared the universe to wet clay spinning on a potter's wheel. No matter how quickly you make two marks, they will always appear some distance apart when the wheel stops. Indeed, in the eight minutes between my birth and Olivia Koski's, the fastest moving astrological coordinate—the ascendant—advanced from ♋ 22°31′ to ♋ 24°12′, that is, about 1.7 degrees. Meanwhile, the fastest moving celestial body, the Moon, advanced from ♒ 22°10′ to ♒ 22°14′, or 0.07 degrees.

Thus, in principle, you could create a unique celestial serial number for yourself, even if this would be a bit unwieldy in practice. But would it be worth the trouble? For your unique astrological identity to mean anything more than, say, your unique passport number, it would need to be the case that you share meaningful similarities with people whose horoscopes are meaningfully similar to yours. And at a bare minimum, how could this not include your Z-code cousins? For my part, I'm perfectly willing to accept that Olivia and I are similar—perhaps even unusually so. But I can't see why this should extend to the roughly 30,000 other people whose horoscopes are, for all practical purposes, indistinguishable from ours merely because we all happen to have been born at roughly the same moment. Then again, maybe I need to meet more of you.

Alternatively, what if a horoscope, even if it doesn't quite seal our destiny, still offers a snapshot of the unique celestial energy which infuses a particular moment in time and space? And what if, in the way that the heavens weave patterns in time, the individuals with whom we share the strongest cosmic bond weren't born on the same day as us, but rather at some time in the past, at a moment when the celestial vibrations were the same as at our birth? Like the Alexandrian astronomers who computed the renewal of their Sothic cycle, our task now becomes one of determining how often the heavens repeat. And this is a question which can be answered exactly, at least to the precision of a Z-code. To this end, specifically, I've compiled a list of every single Z-code which has occurred, in sequence, from 10,000 BC to the present.

When counting up the number of distinct planetary configurations that have graced the heavens throughout history, the first step is to compute the total number of seven-digit, or "cosmic," Z-codes, since these represent an astronomical state of the entire solar system. As it turns out, from 10,000 BC up to the year 2020, there have been 2,515,019 distinct seven-digit Z-codes. Multiplying this number by twelve gives the total number of full (eight-digit) Z-codes, since, during each cosmic state, each of the twelve zodiac signs will be rising over some portion of the Earth. The complete count of full Z-codes is therefore 30,180,228. This is to say, in essence, that from 10,000 BC to today there have been a total of thirty million, one hundred and eighty thousand, two hundred and twenty-eight distinct astrological moments.

The most eye-opening part of this whole analysis is how extraordinarily rare it reveals each of these moments to be. Out of the millions of Z-codes counted up over the last twelve thousand years, 42.5 percent have never been repeated. Another 15.6 percent have been repeated only once. Five Z-codes share the title for the most frequent appearances during this period, which is ten times.

Altogether, our list contains a total of 19,844,460 unique Z-codes (meaning duplicates are not counted). But this isn't even half of the nearly forty-five million astronomically allowable Z-codes we computed earlier. As a hard rule, no cosmic (seven-digit) Z-code can persist for longer than 2.6 days, since that's the longest the Moon ever spends in any one zodiac sign. The actual average duration, as determined by direct computation, turns out to be more like 1.75 days. Thus, even if the seven-digit Z-codes cycled through each allowable state one by one with no repetitions, spending 1.75 days in each, it would still take nearly 18,000 years to exhaust all the cosmic possibilities.

What all of this means is that if you want to find the most recent time in history when a given celestial configuration occurred, you have to reach deep—oftentimes very deep—into the past. For example, the configuration of the Sun, Moon, and planets on Olivia's and my birthday (Z-Code: 541111A-3) last occurred on May 20, 2669 BC! That's right around the time when Imhotep is believed to have constructed the very first pyramid in Egypt. Given how rarely these Z-codes repeat, it's perhaps a bit more appealing to consider that if I were to share the same fate as anyone, maybe it was someone born on that balmy May day back in 2669 BC. At the very least, I'd like to think they could be a member of my extended cosmic family—my closest zodiac ancestor, so to speak.

Having calculated when and for how long every Z-code has occurred since 10,000 BC, it's straightforward to find the closest "zodiac ancestors" for other dates too. Plate 8 shows this for every day of the year 1979. It's fas-

Plate 1: Our schemes of heaven are based on the astrolabe, the indispensable instrument of astronomers and astrologers alike from Ptolemy's time through the Renaissance. This beautiful example was designed by the famous mapmaker Gerard Mercator around the year 1570. MUSEO GALILEO, FLORENCE, IMSS 1098. PHOTO BY FRANCA PRINCIPE.

Plate 2: The arrangement of the night sky becomes easier to remember, and more lively, when the stars are grouped into constellations and the constellations are grouped into stories. Peter Apian, *Astronomicon Caesareum* (Ingolstadt: Peter Apian, 1540). THE HUNTINGTON LIBRARY, SAN MARINO, CA, F. B3R, RB 32891.

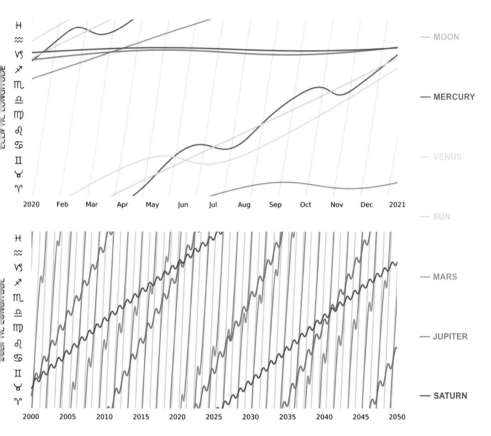

Plate 3: Top: The positions of the seven classical planets (Saturn, Jupiter, Mars, the Sun, Venus, Mercury and the Moon) during the year 2020. Bottom: the positions of the Sun, Mars, Jupiter, and Saturn over a period of fifty years, from 2000 to 2050. The location of each planet in the sky is given in terms of its ecliptic longitude. Each 30° segment of ecliptic longitude corresponds to a sign of the zodiac such that all twelve signs, Aries through Pisces, complete a full 360° circle in the sky. Against the background of stars, the positions of the planets exhibit a deep structure of endlessly overlapping, yet never identical cycles.

Plate 4: A Scheme of Heaven for Monday, September 20, 331 BC
Alexander the Great's Conquest of Persia Presaged by a Total Lunar Eclipse

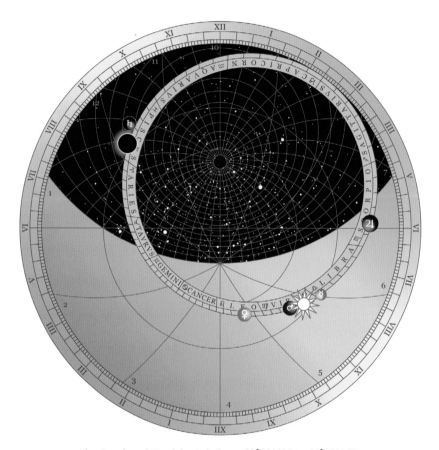

```
The Temple of Marduk, Babylon: 32°32'01"N, 44°25'16"E
                 JD: 1600788.23889
                      17:44 UT
                   ΔT: 14382s
               Local Time: 8:46 PM
        Local Apparent Sidereal Time: 20:20
```

	λ	β	RA J2000	Dec J2000	Az	El	House
♄ Saturn	♓ 14°29'↓	-2°44'	1ʰ 06ᵐ 17ˢ	4°10'	128°23'	32°36'	⑪ 20°46'
♃ Jupiter	♏ 8°56'	0°38'	16ʰ 39ᵐ 18ˢ	-21°47'	257°10'	-6°02'	⑥ 23°48'
♂ Mars	♍ 20°49'	0°46'	13ʰ 26ᵐ 51ˢ	-8°24'	300°34'	-32°10'	⑤ 23°50'
☉ Sun	♍ 22°44'	0°00'	13ʰ 32ᵐ 53ˢ	-9°50'	298°07'	-32°06'	⑤ 24°33'
♀ Venus	♌ 18°08'	0°58'	11ʰ 26ᵐ 47ˢ	4°41'	340°11'	-38°37'	④ 22°58'
☿ Mercury	♎ 2°28'	0°07'	14ʰ 09ᵐ 52ˢ	-13°25'	288°03'	-27°46'	⑥ 1°00'
☽ Moon	♓ 22°44'	0°22'	1ʰ 33ᵐ 25ˢ	9°28'	118°19'	31°45'	⑪ 24°53'

Dating from perhaps as early as the first century BC, and roughly the size of a tennis ball, this silver sphere depicting the constellations may be the oldest known celestial globe. GALERIE J. KUGEL, PARIS.

The Antikythera Mechanism, fragment A, front. This extraordinary astronomical calculator from the first or second century BC was capable of displaying the positions of the Sun, Moon, and possibly the planets. NATIONAL ARCHAEOLOGICAL MUSEUM, ATHENS, GREECE / BRIDGEMAN IMAGES.

Plate 5: The two cosmic models seized from Archimedes' workshop very likely resembled these two Roman-era artifacts.

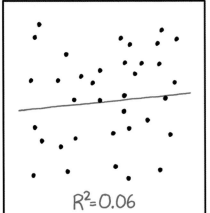

R²=0.06   REXTHOR, THE DOG-BEARER

I DON'T TRUST LINEAR REGRESSIONS WHEN IT'S HARDER TO GUESS THE DIRECTION OF THE CORRELATION FROM THE SCATTER PLOT THAN TO FIND NEW CONSTELLATIONS ON IT.

Plate 6: Linear Regression by xkcd. XKCD.COM.

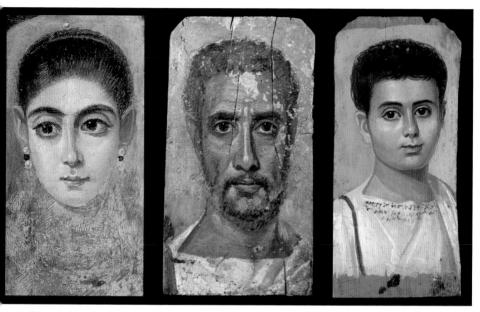

Plate 7: Hundreds of hauntingly intimate death-portraits survive from across Roman Egypt, dating from exactly the same period when the astrologer Vettius Valens was compiling his collection of horoscopes. Perhaps some of these individuals were his clients. BRIDGEMAN IMAGES / METROPOLITAN MUSEUM OF ART.

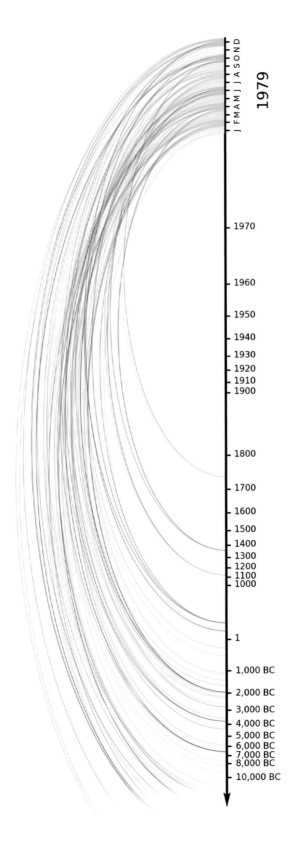

Plate 8: Nearest zodiac ancestors for every day of 1979.

Plate 9: The horoscope of Baghdad in a fourteenth-century manuscript copy of *The Chronology of Ancient Nations* by Abu Rayhan al-Biruni (eleventh century). UNIVERSITY OF EDINBURGH, OR. MS. 161, F.127V.

Plate 10: This astrolabe, which was made in Cairo by Abd al-Karim al-Misri in the year 1235–36 (AH 633), sports an exceptionally elaborate rete with plant and animal designs used to indicate the positions of bright stars. BRITISH MUSEUM, NO. 1855,0709.1.

MIDHEAVEN

| 11 Friends | 10 Power, Honors | 9 Spirituality, Voyages |

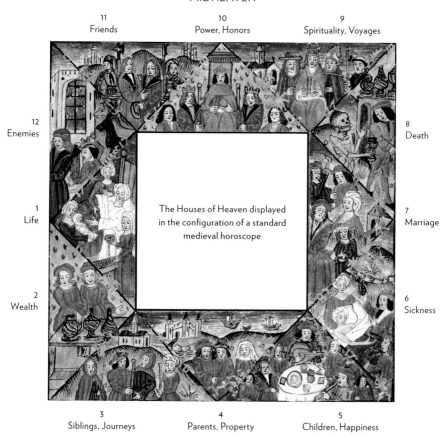

12 Enemies

8 Death

ASCENDANT

1 Life

The Houses of Heaven displayed in the configuration of a standard medieval horoscope

7 Marriage

OCCIDENT

2 Wealth

6 Sickness

| 3 Siblings, Journeys | 4 Parents, Property | 5 Children, Happiness |

LOWER MIDHEAVEN

Plate 11: Detail from William Parron, *Liber de optimo fato Henrici Eboraci ducis et optimorum ipsius parentum*, 1502–03, prepared for King Henry VII and his son, the future Henry VIII (then Duke of York). BRITISH LIBRARY, MS ROYAL 12 B VI.

Plate 12: Prague's famous astronomical clock, originally constructed around the year 1400, displays an astrolabe-style face. What modern astrologers call the Placidus method for dividing the Houses of Heaven is here used to draw the cusps of the unequal hours. PHOTO CREDIT: JOE PETERS-BURGER / NATIONAL GEOGRAPHIC CREATIVE / BRIDGEMAN IMAGES.

Plate 13: Vivid view of Tycho's supernova remnant. Spitzer Space Telescope / Chandra / Calar Alto. NASA/JPL-CALTECH/CXC/CALAR ALTO O. KRAUSE (MAX PLANCK INSTITUTE FOR ASTRONOMY) SIG08-016.

Plate 14: Johannes Vermeer, *The Astronomer*, 1668, oil on canvas, Musée du Louvre, Paris. The instruments of astronomy/astrology—the celestial globe and the astrolabe (shown resting on the table)—remained unchanged from Ptolemy's time well into the seventeenth century. Soon the telescope would become astronomy's iconic instrument and a symbol of its independence from astrology. BRIDGEMAN IMAGES.

Plate 15: Wassily Kandinsky, *Sterne (Stars)*, 1938, color lithograph. AFFORDABLEART101 FINE PRINTS.

Plate 16: Northern lights near Manicouagan Crater, Quebec, Canada, as seen from the International Space Station, February 3, 2012. The auroral lights and the crater illustrate the subtle and not-so-subtle ways the Earth is affected by particles from outer space. NASA.

cinating to see how wildly the linkages spread out in time. The shortest arcs connect several dates in the fall of 1979 back to the year 1742. The longest arcs correspond to dates whose Z-code is not repeated in our list, so all we can say is that their nearest zodiac ancestor was born sometime earlier than 10,000 BC. Using this information, we can also find the nearest zodiac ancestors for some especially famous 1979ers (table 6.2). We already knew these people were one-of-a-kind originals, but it's fun to see hard data on exactly how long it's been since the world has seen anyone like them, astrologically speaking at least.

Table 6.2: Zodiac Ancestors for some Famous 1979'ers

Name	Claim To Fame	Birthday (1979)	Z-Code	Birthday Of Their Nearest Zodiac Ancestor
DREW BREES	Quarterback, New Orleans Saints	January 15	5499894	December 27, 212
LEO VARADKAR	Prime Minister of Ireland	January 18	5499895	March 1, 7614 BC
ADAM LEVINE	Singer, Maroon 5	March 18	53BBA07	April 30, 6583 BC
NORAH JONES	Singer, songwriter	March 30	53B0BB1	March 27, 1362
HEATH LEDGER	Actor, *The Dark Knight*	April 4	53B0BB3	March 31, 1362
KATE HUDSON	Actress, *Almost Famous*	April 19	5300B09	March 27, 390
JAMES MCAVOY	Actor, *X-Men* franchise	April 21	5401B0A	July 12, 9143 BC
LANCE BASS	Singer, NSYNC	May 4	5401004	Before 10,000 BC
MARKUS PERSSON	Creator, *Minecraft*	June 1	5412124	June 9, 1934 BC
CHRIS PRATT	Actor, *Guardians of the Galaxy*	June 21	5412231	July 31, 6523 BC
JASON MOMOA	Actor, *Game of Thrones*	August 1	5424447	July 28, 1362
PINK	Singer, songwriter	September 8	5435550	August 27, 228
JOHN KRASINSKI	Actor, *The Office* (U.S.)	October 20	5546776	Before 10,000 BC
MICHAEL OWEN	English footballer	December 14	5558986	January 1, 2230 BC

It's awe-inspiring and humbling to consider that the configuration of the heavens on our birthday, or any given day, will almost certainly never repeat in our lifetime. Even the sum of human history has played out against a backdrop of just a small fraction of astrological possibilities. A horoscope in its best sense, then, can serve as a cosmic reminder of just how special each moment is. At least, that's how I like to look at them. Oh, and the poor fellow from the *Anthologies* who was thrown to the lions (Z-code: 3110BBB–7)? The next time anyone will be born with his unlucky horoscope will be March 30, 3328. Readers of the thirty-fourth century, take heed!

7

PATTERNS, PATTERNS, EVERYWHERE! MASHA'ALLAH'S ASTROLOGICAL HISTORY OF THE WORLD

Baghdad, 762

The location was perfect for a new capital city. There were, of course, the standard prophecies that a great metropolis was destined to arise here. Even more persuasive, perhaps, were the reports that of all the districts along the Tigris River, this site was said to be the least infested with mosquitoes. But the main reason the caliph Abu Jafar al-Mansur chose to build his capital at Baghdad was that, with the absorption of Persia into *Dar al-Islam*, the "abode of Islam" had spread far to the east, and Baghdad now lay right at its heart.

But what good is the right place if it's not also the right time? Accordingly, al-Mansur summoned his top astrologers—Nawbakht, a Persian, and Masha'allah, a Jew—to determine the optimal moment to inaugurate construction. Remarkably, the horoscope of Baghdad's foundation has been preserved in the writings of al-Biruni, one of the foremost astronomers of a few centuries later (plate 9). Baghdad's founding can therefore be dated with especially high confidence to the afternoon of July 30 in the year 762. A glance at figure 7.1 leaves no doubt as to why this moment was chosen. At that precise instant, Jupiter, the planet of kingdoms and dynasties, was rising in the east, while Mars, the planet of war, was setting in the west. Indeed, no horoscope could have been more appropriate for a city that al-Mansur insisted be called Madinat as-Salam, the "City of Peace."

A GOLDEN AGE?

The cosmic aspirations embedded in Baghdad's construction did not go unfulfilled, at least initially. Within a few decades after its horoscope was cast, Baghdad had grown into the single largest city on Earth. The commerce of the world—from India, China, Africa, and Europe—flowed into and out of its three concentric circular walls through four enormous iron gates. This was the Baghdad of the *Thousand Nights and a Night*, a city of wise caliphs and their clever viziers, of camel caravans and their Silk Road spices, of slender minarets soaring over booksellers' stalls, and teardrop archways lined with star-patterned tiles. And—what never fails to enkindle the modern imagination with romantic visions of medieval Baghdad—this was the city of the much-storied Bayt al-Hikma, the "House of Wisdom," where the caliphs of the Abbasid dynasty are supposed to have invited the world's greatest scholars to study, debate, and create anew all of the branches of earthly and celestial knowledge.

Whether the House of Wisdom ever existed as an actual research institute, like a modern university, or was simply one of several names for the royal library, there's no question that Baghdad was home to an extraordinary burst of intellectual energy. Beginning with al-Mansur, the Abbasid caliphs oversaw an ambitious and remarkably comprehensive program of translating Greek philosophical texts into Arabic. Under the caliph al-Mamun, the city's philosophic focus shifted increasingly to the natural sciences. Al-Mamun was patron to both al-Kindi, called by his contemporaries the "Philosopher of the Arabs," and the great mathematician al-Khwarizmi. It's al-Khwarizmi's Latin name, Algoritmi, that gives us the word "algorithm," and it's his book *Kitab al-Jabr wa-l-Muqabala* ("Book of Rectifying and Balancing") that gives

Figure 7.1: A Scheme of Heaven for Friday, July 30, 762
The Foundation of Baghdad

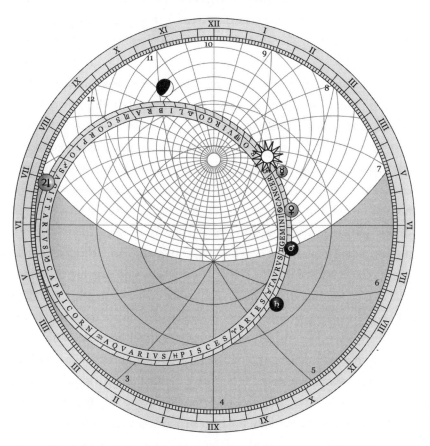

The Palace of the Golden Gate, Baghdad: 33°20'35"N, 44°21'14"E
JD: 1999588.98681
11:41 UT
ΔT: 3103s
Local Time: 2:34 PM
Local Apparent Sidereal Time: 11:23

		λ	β	RA J2000	Dec J2000	Az	El	House	
♄ Saturn	♉	1°25'	-2°32'	3ʰ 07ᵐ 33ˢ	15°03'	311°54'	-33°02'	⑤	18°50'
♃ Jupiter	♐	8°47'↓	0°14'	17ʰ 42ᵐ 41ˢ	-23°17'	115°28'	-1°02'	①	1°08'
♂ Mars	♊	6°16'	0°20'	5ʰ 31ᵐ 47ˢ	23°06'	296°31'	-1°15'	⑥	28°35'
☉ Sun	♌	9°49'	0°00'	9ʰ 57ᵐ 11ˢ	12°34'	255°37'	52°13'	⑧	23°06'
♀ Venus	♋	1°34'	-1°11'	7ʰ 20ᵐ 51ˢ	21°05'	283°47'	20°46'	⑦	21°19'
☿ Mercury	♋	27°03'↓	-3°02'	9ʰ 03ᵐ 32ˢ	13°43'	265°14'	40°52'	⑧	10°58'
☽ Moon	♎	14°28'	-5°36'	13ʰ 49ᵐ 51ˢ	-17°24'	152°57'	41°44'	⑩	26°59'

us the word "algebra." As a crowning monument to al-Mamun's enthusiasm for science, he ordered the construction of two astronomical observatories, one in Baghdad and a second near Damascus. To these he assigned the grand endeavors of updating the celestial and terrestrial data in Ptolemy's *Almagest* and *Geography*.

On account of the illustrious names associated with Abbasid Baghdad, the era is commonly referred to as the "golden age" of Islamic science. This is an awkward phrase, to say the least, and one that evidences the awkwardness Western histories often have when attempting to fit this period into narratives of the development of modern science. At a minimum, it makes more sense to speak about "Arabic science," which, it should be noted, is really a straightforward label about language, not ethnicity. Just as much of "Greek science" was the achievement of individuals like Archimedes, from Sicily, and Ptolemy, from Egypt, whose Greekness is, at the very least, debatable, a great deal of Arabic science was the work of individuals who may not have been Arab or even Muslim. In fact, many of the Abbasid-era luminaries, including al-Khwarizmi and al-Biruni, were proudly Persian. The notion of Arabic science, therefore, is meaningful expressly because among its multiethnic, multilingual, and multireligious practitioners, it was the Arabic language which provided a common framework of texts and terminology. This is the same unifying role that the Greek language played in the science of Roman times, and the same role that, increasingly, the English language plays in science today.

But beyond these pitfalls of basic terminology, historians of science looking for a shortcut between Rome and the Renaissance still find themselves forced to dance around two particularly thorny questions. Did Arabic science accomplish anything beyond merely preserving Greek science long enough for Europe to recover from its dark ages? And, if it did, why did the scientific revolution happen only in Europe, while the Islamic world sank back into a deep scientific slumber? Astrology can't avoid getting wrapped up in all this, since it was cultivated with particular enthusiasm at the time. But can advances in the theory and practice of astrology be counted as advances in science?

I find these questions about the achievements of Arabic science to be quite curious. Not on account of the issue itself—the scientific strides made during that era were enormous—but because they expose how we often focus on all the wrong things when thinking about what science actually is. And by wrong things, I mean that there's an unmistakable tendency to fixate on abstract, metaphysical ideas to the exclusion of everything else.

As a case in point, the assertion that the Earth revolves around the Sun and not the other way around is clearly an important statement about our universe. And yet, as we saw earlier, Aristarchus of Samos proposed a Sun-centered cosmos thousands of years before Copernicus. Evidently, a correct theoretical idea can't be the only ingredient needed for a scientific revolution. Nevertheless, the common perception seems to be that the technological and material advances of Renaissance Europe were somehow the result of Copernicus correctly recentering the cosmos, and not the other way around. Or, to phrase things in a way more in keeping with the themes of this book, we recognize in the history of science a correlation between a society's technological capabilities and its theoretical knowledge. I'd argue, however, that in almost every instance we get the causation exactly backward.

Which brings us back to Baghdad, a city that, under the Abbasids, made tremendous contributions to math and science and astronomy in particular. But since the Abbasid universe remained steadfastly geocentric, history books written as the triumph of ideas get stuck with the awkward conclusion that, however much Arabic science should be commended for its efforts, none of it actually mattered. I disagree with this wholeheartedly. Purely intellectual histories are, to be perfectly blunt, usually blind to the process by which even abstract ideas are facilitated, if not downright prompted, by the material and technological world of those who think them.

Consider, for instance, the lot of an astronomer in medieval Baghdad as compared to his predecessor in Greco-Roman Alexandria. Although both operated under the assumption that the Sun revolved around the Earth, our Baghdadi astronomer could consult significantly more accurate astronomical tables compiled from observations taken with larger and significantly more precise instruments. He was able to express his measurements using Hindu numerals—the digits 0 through 9—instead of the clunky Greek practice of using letters of the alphabet. His calculations could be performed by referencing tables of trigonometric functions, instead of having to rely on Ptolemy's tedious method of chords. And he could write on cheap and abundant paper—a trade secret smuggled out of China—instead of costly papyrus or parchment. More importantly, he worked in a milieu in which the shortcomings of Ptolemy's system were known and actively investigated, a tradition begun in earnest with Ibn al-Haytham's book *al-Shukuk ala Batlamyus* ("Doubts on Ptolemy"). And, to add an exclamation point to all this, the Arabic world offered access to that indispensable accelerant of scientific thought, coffee—an elixir entirely unknown to sleepy antiquity.

Copernicus, in his turn, was the beneficiary of each of these developments. (Except for coffee, which didn't really filter into Europe until the 1600s.) The point here is that while Copernicus's work truly was revolutionary, it's not as if he was sitting alone in a room with nothing but his thoughts and a copy of the *Almagest*. He was, as all scientists are, the inheritor of an oftentimes invisible intellectual infrastructure built piece by piece by those who had come before him.

NAMING THE STARS

For his part, Copernicus was never shy about acknowledging his debt to Arabic astronomers. In his famous *De revolutionibus*, he cited no fewer than five of them by name: al-Battani, al-Bitruji, al-Zarqali, Ibn Rushd (Averroes), and Thabit ibn Qurra. But the even more obvious evidence that Europe's scientific renaissance wasn't simply a reintroduction of Greek science, unmediated by a thousand years of technical refinements, can be seen in the stars themselves, or, rather, in their names. Of the top twenty brightest stars in the sky, ten are still called by names derived from Arabic. And when we consider the top 100, this number jumps to 72. This transmission into Europe came partly through paper and ink, as Arabic star catalogs such as al-Sufi's *Book of Constellations of the Fixed Stars* were transcribed and copied. But just as significantly, this transit of star names came also in metal, engraved on those instruments which provided a mechanical armature of sorts for the development of both astronomy and astrology: astrolabes.

Table 7.1: Name Origins of the 20 Brightest Stars

Visual Magnitude	Bayer Designation	Name	Origin	Meaning
–1.44	α Canis Majoris	Sirius	Greek	seirios, "scorcher"
–0.62	α Carinae	Canopus	Greek	kanobos, untranslated name
–0.05	α Boötis	Arcturus	Greek	arktouros, "bear-watcher"
–0.01	α Centauri	Rigil Kentaurus	Greco-Arabic	rijl qanturis, "centaur's foot"
0.03	α Lyrae	Vega	Arabic	al-nasr al-waqi, "the swooping eagle"
0.08	α Aurigae	Capella	Latin	capella, "she-goat"
0.18	β Orionis	Rigel	Arabic	rijl al-Jauza, "the foot of Jauza"
0.40	α Canis Minoris	Procyon	Greek	prokuon, "preceding the dog"
0.45	α Eridani	Achernar	Arabic	akhir al-nahr, "the river's end"
0.45	α Orionis	Betelgeuse	Arabic	yad al-Jauza, "the hand of Jauza"
0.61	β Centauri	Hadar	Arabic	hadari, untranslated name
0.76	α Aquilae	Altair	Arabic	al-nasr al-tair, "the flying eagle"
0.77	α Crucis	Acrux	Greco-Latin	a modern contraction of alpha crucis
0.87	α Tauri	Aldebaran	Arabic	al-dabaran, "the follower"
0.98	α Virginis	Spica	Latin	spica, "ear of grain"
1.06	α Scorpii	Antares	Greek	antares, "rival to Ares"
1.16	β Geminorum	Pollux	Greco-Latin	Poludeukes, mythological twin
1.17	α Piscis Austrini	Fomalhaut	Arabic	fam al-hut al-janubi, "mouth of the southern fish"
1.25	β Crucis	Mimosa	Greco-Latin	mimosa, "like an actor or mime"
1.25	α Cygni	Deneb	Arabic	dhanab al-dajaja, "the hen's tail"

Although the astrolabe is often held up as the iconic artifact of Arabic science, this is a bit misleading since, as discussed previously, the instrument's origins are indisputably Alexandrian. Nevertheless, the oldest surviving astrolabes, dating from around the year 900, are all creations of the Abbasid period. Over the course of several centuries of manufacture within the Islamic world, these instruments were refined to an absolutely exquisite level of elegant precision. Appropriately enough, the most dazzling way for an astrolabe maker to flaunt his artistry was in how he depicted the stars.

On an astrolabe, pointers to prominent stars are attached to a decorative framework called the *rete* in Latin or *shabaka* in Arabic; both words mean "net" (figure 7.2). Together with the ecliptic circle, the rete completes the stereographic map of the sky which, when rotated clockwise around the instrument, simulates the daily rotation of the heavens around the Earth. Although the positions of the star pointers are fixed by astronomy, the visual design of the rete is left entirely to the whim of the astrolabist. Arabic astrolabes sport retes that vary from simple geometric connectors to stunningly elaborate intertwinings of plant and animal shapes (plate 10).

But astrolabes weren't just a pretty way to model a cosmos frozen in time since Ptolemy's day. Successive generations of astrolabes incorporated many of the latest advances of Arabic science, such as Hindu numerals and diagrams for computing tangents and cotangents. Some even made accommodations for the slow motion of Earth's perihelion, a phenomenon completely unknown to Ptolemy. Thus, no less than by copying texts, European

Figure 7.2: On an astrolabe, pointers to prominent stars are attached to a decorative framework called the *rete*.

astronomers became aware of the latest advances of Arabic astronomy by copying Arabic astrolabes. And in carefully tracing out the star pointers of an Arabic rete, it's hardly surprising that the Arabic star names engraved by each one were carefully transcribed too.

PLANETS THAT PASS IN THE NIGHT

Yet what about the second of those two questions we introduced earlier? How could a city like Baghdad, which had ascended to the zenith of science, subsequently find itself so thoroughly eclipsed? And by Northern Europe of all places, a region which began that era still stuck in a state of semiliterate barbarity?

This is a question which rattles disquietingly even today, especially for those of us with a stake in the continued success of American science. What gives America its technological edge, and how long can it be kept? Quite clearly it's not because we're smarter. American students routinely perform abysmally in international assessments of math, science, and reading skills. But this was true when my dad was in school and the Russians were promising to bury us; this was true when I was in school and Japan, Inc., seemed unstoppable; and this remains true today, even though our national anxieties have shifted once again, this time onto China. Yet, somehow, in spite of it all, America continues to be the world's science and technology leader—at least, for now. So what is it, in the grand pageant of history, that permits a nation or people to claim the mantle of science, and what compels them to lay it down again once their time has passed? Curiously, in the case of Abbasid Baghdad, I think that both a modern and a medieval observer would come to the same, one-word conclusion: astrology.

Looking back at Baghdad's founding, there is a very strong case to be made that it was al-Mansur's personal obsession with astrology that was the not-so-secret impetus for his city's scientific pursuits. Certainly, the almost manic translation of Greek texts into Arabic appears a lot less eccentric if it's understood as part of a government initiative to harness the power of the stars. Wherever the truth may lie, it's undeniably the case that astrological texts were heavily represented among the earliest titles translated in Baghdad.

The caliph and his closest advisors would not, I think, have disagreed with this assessment. Prior to seizing the caliphate, al-Mansur had cultivated his power base among the conquered provinces of Persia. There, in return, he himself was influenced by a Persian tradition which saw the fall of Persia and the rise of the Arabs in explicitly astrological terms. Just as the planets rose and set in their allotted times, so too, it was said, did kingdoms, dynasties, and even religions. One of the earliest expositors of this idea was none other than Masha'allah, the astrologer hand-picked by the caliph to cast the horoscope for his new capital city.

Very little is known about Masha'allah's life except that he is usually described as a Jew. Given his name and his circumstances, however, it would not be surprising if he was, rather, a Jewish convert to Islam. Several centuries after his death, Masha'allah would become famous in medieval Europe as Messahala, the author of one of the most widely read treatises on the astrolabe. (In true medieval fashion, however, this was actually a Latin translation of someone else's Arabic astrolabe manual.) But Masha'allah's principal impact on history occurred during his stint at the court of the Abbasid caliphs. There he introduced a theory for understanding how history itself could be understood according to the cycles of astrology. The most important of these cycles, insofar as they were said to herald events of global significance, were the successive conjunctions of Jupiter and Saturn.

Saturn, the outermost planet visible to the naked eye, takes about thirty years to complete an orbit around the zodiac. Jupiter, the largest and the next most distant planet, takes about twelve years. As these two astral giants chase each other around the ecliptic, Jupiter will catch up to and pass Saturn roughly once every twenty years. The moment when these planets, or any two heavenly bodies, line up in ecliptic longitude is called a conjunction. And as a curious consequence of orbital mechanics, every conjunction of Jupiter and Saturn occurs almost exactly one third of the way around the zodiac from the spot of the previous conjunction. Thus, three successive Jupiter–Saturn conjunctions will trace out an almost perfect equilateral triangle in the sky.

To give an example: if Jupiter and Saturn come into conjunction in the zodiac sign of Aries, then, approximately twenty years later, their next conjunction can be expected to occur in Sagittarius; the following conjunction, twenty years after that, will be in Leo; and the conjunction after that, again some twenty years later, will cycle back to Aries. Recall that Aries, Sagittarius, and Leo are the three zodiac signs associated with the element of fire. Thus, in this example, the sequence of Jupiter–Saturn conjunctions occurred entirely within the triangle of fire signs, a pattern also known as the fiery trigon or triplicity.

Of course, the astral triangles traced out this way don't exactly overlap, and so after about ten conjunctions, or roughly two hundred years, the entire pattern ends up migrating to the next triplicity of signs. Over a period of about eight hundred years, therefore, the sequence of Jupiter–Saturn conjunctions will slowly cycle through all four triplicities: the fiery triplicity of Aries, Sagittarius, and Leo; the earthy triplicity of Taurus, Capricorn, and Virgo; the airy triplicity of Gemini, Aquarius, and Libra; and the watery triplicity of Cancer, Pisces, and Scorpio.

Masha'allah and his successors saw in this sequence of Jupiter–Saturn conjunctions an organizing principle for the entire history of the world. Local political changes, they suggested, were augured by the regular or "little conjunctions" that occur roughly once every twenty years. Larger shifts of kingdoms and dynasties, occurring about once every two hundred years, were heralded by "middle conjunctions," when the sequence migrates from one triplicity to another. Finally, the most momentous historical upheavals, such as the fall of empires or the rise of new religions, were portended by "great conjunctions." These occur only once in a millennium, when the sequence of conjunctions has completed a full cycle through all four zodiac triplicities: fire, earth, air, and water.

The conjunction theory of history is, without a doubt, the most significant addition to astrology since Roman times. It's believed to represent an infusion of several ideas from the ancient cosmologies of Persia and India. Indeed, Masha'allah's conjunction calculations have proven invaluable to historians wishing to reconstruct the lost parameters of Persian astronomy as it was practiced just prior to the Arab conquest.

The chronology Masha'allah developed with this theory places the creation of the universe in the year 8292 BC. Compared to the traditional Jewish creation date of 3761 BC, this is at least a little closer to modern astronomy's estimate for the age of the universe, albeit one that's still shy by about 14 billion years. Oddly, the planets in Masha'allah's universe remained completely motionless for the first 2,500 years, with the first conjunction of Jupiter and Saturn assigned to the year 5783 BC and occurring in the sign of Taurus.

Masha'allah then proceeds to hop through the history of the world, conjunction by conjunction, pausing only to comment on a select few whose horoscopes he deemed to be especially history-altering. First, there's the Great Flood, which he dates to 3361 BC and which occurred, naturally, during a watery triplicity. After leaping past several cycles of great conjunctions, he arrives at the year 26 BC, when the sequence of conjunctions shifted from a watery to a fiery triplicity. According to Masha'allah, this transfer heralded the birth of Christ and the advent of the Christian era. It also adds an interesting spin to John the Baptist's prophecy that, although he baptized with water, the one who followed him would baptize with fire.

Skipping ahead a half-millennium, Masha'allah next examines the conjunction of the year 571, which brought the sequence back to another watery triplicity. This transfer presaged the birth of Muhammad and the rise of the Arabs, whose sign, according to Masha'allah, was the watery sign of Scorpio.

Finally arriving at the events of his own day, Masha'allah regarded the conjunction of the year 769—a conjunction which ended that watery triplicity and began a new fiery triplicity—as an indicator of an ebb in Arab power and a reciprocal resurgence of Persia. This was the triplicity of the Abbasid caliphs who, both in their politics and their marriages, did indeed pursue a rapprochement of sorts with their Persian subjects. As for Masha'allah himself, it's believed that he died around the year 815. He did, however, extend his chronology a bit further into the future where he foresaw, entirely accurately although rather unimaginatively, continued political strife between Arabs and Persians.

CRACKING THE CODE

Table 7.2 re-creates Masha'allah's chronology of Jupiter–Saturn conjunctions using modern planetary data. It starts with the fiery triplicity of 26 BC and keeps going until the closest future fiery triplicity, slated to begin in the year 2338. The first thing this table reveals is that Masha'allah's approximations for the orbital periods of Jupiter and Saturn were actually pretty decent, since the years he gives for their conjunctions match the modern dates fairly well. The biggest difference is that, unlike in Masha'allah's scheme, there's not a sharp transition between one triplicity and the next. Instead, the sequence tends to dither a bit between triplicities before each shift is fully complete.

A more subtle difference arises from the fact that occasionally Jupiter, or Saturn, or both, will be in retrograde during a conjunction. This transforms what would otherwise be a straightforward single conjunction into a quick succession of three conjunctions as one or both of those planets' motions appears, from the vantage point of the Earth, to change direction. These little orbital do-si-do's typically take about six months to complete, so the dating of one of these Jupiter–Saturn conjunction triplets (shown in all caps) will sometimes span two adjacent calendar years.

Overall, though, the pattern of small, middle, and great conjunctions still stands out perfectly clearly in the modern data. It's a charmingly captivating system, and I'd think anyone with a knack for historical dates will have a hard time not getting engrossed by its narrative possibilities. Were the renewed conquests of Islam under the Ottomans due to the return of a watery triplicity? Conversely, is the Middle East more susceptible to European invasion, be it by crusaders or colonialists, when an earthy triplicity holds sway? Maybe, maybe not. And yet slicing up history into triplicities seems hardly more arbitrary than, say, the ancient, medieval, and Renaissance periods we're taught in school.

In fact, astrologically organized histories were considered quite scientific during the medieval period—or, if you prefer, during the seventh great conjunction cycle between the fiery triplicities of 769 and 1603. The most prominent popularizer of this approach was Abu Mashar, the preem-

Table 7.2: Chronology of Jupiter–Saturn Conjunctions using Modern Data

	Year	Sign	Triplicity		Year	Sign	Triplicity
Fiery Triplicity of Christianity	26 BC	♌	Fire	Fiery Triplicity of the Abbasids	769	♌	Fire
	7 BC	♓	WATER		789	♓	Water
	14	♐	Fire		809	♐	Fire
	34	♌	Fire		829	♌	Fire
	54	♓	Water		848	♓	Water
	74	♐	Fire		868	♐	Fire
	94	♌	Fire		888	♌	Fire
	114	♈	Fire		908	♈	Fire
	134	♐	Fire		928	♐	Fire
	154	♍	Earth		948	♌	Fire
	173	♈	Fire		967–8	♈	FIRE
	193	♐	Fire		988	♐	Fire
	213	♍	Earth		1007–8	♍	EARTH
	233	♈	Fire		1027	♈	Fire
	253	♑	Earth		1047	♑	Earth
	273	♍	Earth		1067	♍	Earth
	292	♉	Earth		1087	♉	Earth
	312	♑	Earth		1107	♑	Earth
	332–3	♎	AIR		1127	♍	Earth
	352	♉	Earth		1146	♉	Earth
	372	♑	Earth		1166	♑	Earth
	392	♎	Air		1186	♎	Air
	411–2	♊	AIR		1206	♉	Earth
	432	♑	Earth		1226	♒	Air
	452	♎	AIR		1246	♎	Air
	471	♊	Air		1265	♊	Air
	491	♒	Air		1286	♒	Air
	511	♎	Air		1305–6	♎	AIR
	531	♊	Air		1325	♊	Air
	551	♒	Air		1345	♒	Air
Watery Triplicity of the Arabs and Islam	571	♏	Water		1365	♏	Water
	590	♋	Water		1385	♊	Air
	610	♒	Air		1405	♒	Air
	630	♏	Water		1425	♏	WATER
	650	♋	Water		1444	♋	Water
	670	♒	Air		1464	♓	Water
	690	♏	Water		1484	♏	Water
	709–10	♋	WATER		1504	♋	Water
	729	♓	Water		1524	♓	Water
	749	♏	Water		1544	♏	Water
					1563	♋	Water
					1583	♓	Water

Year	Sign	Triplicity
1603	♐	Fire
1623	♌	Fire
1643	♓	Water
1663	♐	Fire
1682–3	♌	FIRE
1702	♈	Fire
1723	♐	Fire
1742	♌	Fire
1762	♈	Fire
1782	♐	Fire
1802	♍	Earth
1821	♈	Fire
1842	♑	Earth
1861	♍	Earth
1881	♉	Earth
1901	♑	Earth
1921	♍	Earth
1940–1	♉	EARTH
1961	♑	Earth
1981	♎	AIR
2000	♉	Earth
2020	♒	Air
2040	♎	Air
2060	♊	Air
2080	♒	Air
2100	♎	Air
2119	♊	Air
2140	♒	Air
2159	♏	Water
2179	♊	Air
2199	♒	Air
2219	♏	Water
2238–9	♋	WATER
2259	♓	Water
2279	♏	WATER
2298	♋	Water
2318	♓	Water
2338	♐	Fire

inent astrologer of Baghdad during the generation after Masha'allah. And among its notable proponents was Abraham ibn Ezra, medieval Spain's famed Jewish poet and philosopher, who inserted the theory into his commentary on Exodus.

Christian chronologists were similarly swept up. The dreaded return of the fiery triplicity in 1603, a year which saw the death of England's Queen Elizabeth I, was examined at length by no less an authority than the astronomer Johannes Kepler. Several history writers even went so far as to rely on the scheme for some pretty bold predictions and assessments. The German monk Johannes Trithemius, for example, writing around the year 1500, bluntly asserted that liberty would not be restored to the Jews prior to August 1880. In fact, this is more or less exactly when the first wave of Zionist settlers immigrated to Ottoman Palestine. The medical faculty of Paris blamed the Black Plague, which arrived in Europe in 1347, on a corruption of the atmosphere caused by the conjunction of Jupiter, Saturn, and Mars in the year 1345. But most notoriously of all, the French Catholic cardinal Pierre d'Ailly, writing around the year 1400, concluded his astrological history of the world with a warning that the Antichrist could be expected to arrive in the year 1789. Depending on how reactionary your views are regarding the French Revolution, this may strike you as a humorously prescient prediction.

With so many possible patterns correlating with so many historical storylines, what is one to make of the conjunction theory of history? Unlike with other astrological assertions, where an analysis might entail an elaborate hunt for the faintest hint of a correlation, here the correlations seem to leap out from everywhere. But are any of them genuine? This is roughly analogous to the engineering distinction between noise, where nothing looks like a signal, and clutter, where everything looks like a signal. Perhaps, though, an even better analogy can be made to cryptology: history, here, becomes like a secret code, and we want to know if astrology is its key.

The art of concealing a message in secret writing is called cryptography, and its practice is as old as writing itself. But to decipher a secret message without its key requires cryptanalysis, and this emerged as a science only

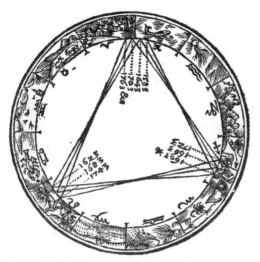

Figure 7.3: Johannes Kepler's diagram illustrating the progression of Jupiter–Saturn conjunctions during the "fiery trigon" which began in 1603. Johannes Kepler, *De stella nova* (Prague: 1606), 25. THE HUNTINGTON LIBRARY, SAN MARINO, CALIFORNIA.

in Islamic times, in Baghdad under the Abbasids. Within each of the three Abrahamic faiths—Judaism, Christianity, and Islam—there has long been a tradition that, side by side with the sacred scriptures, God's truth can also be read inscribed in the Book of Nature. And just as God's prophets often spoke in parables, so too is nature similarly enshrouded in mysteries and riddles. Accordingly, whoever would seek out the truth of the world must first learn to interpret its secret signs. It's fitting, therefore, that the father of cryptanalysis was a man who was both deeply devout and deeply mathematical. He was also, it should be no surprise to learn, deeply obsessed with astrology. This was Abu Yusuf Yaqub ibn Ishaq al-Kindi.

To the extent that the idea of Islam's golden age has any currency, it's al-Kindi's stamp that it bears. It was through his initiative that the headiest works of Greek philosophy were revived with such thoroughness and zeal. Beyond his own books on metaphysics, medicine, and music (to list just a few), al-Kindi also wrote extensively on astrology. On the empirical side, this included investigations into astrological weather forecasting. Meanwhile, on the more theoretical side, his treatise "On Rays" has to be history's most valiant attempt to give astrology—and magic—a firm, philosophical foundation. Here al-Kindi expands on the idea, implicit in earlier authors such as Ptolemy, that the physical reason why the stars and planets influence the Earth is because of their emission of cosmic rays. But al-Kindi takes this a step further by suggesting that these rays, although impossible to prevent, can be amplified or impeded by means of suitably chosen words, symbols, and images. And since words, symbols, and images are themselves propagated across time and space through rays of light and sound, al-Kindi presciently prefigures our modern age of advertising and agitprop by arguing that these too can be manipulated to bring about specific actions in those who receive them.

As al-Kindi recognized, the art of writing is really an act of magic. Its power is to transmit thoughts and emotions across vast distances using nothing more than a few squiggly symbols. By necessity, then, the efficacy of this magic will hinge upon the fitness of these symbols to their task. Nowhere is this more evident than in mathematics. (If you don't believe me, try adding the Roman numerals CXXXIX and DCXXIII together; or, even worse, the Greek numerals $\overline{\rho\lambda\theta}$ and $\overline{\chi\kappa\gamma}$.) Given al-Kindi's sensitivity to the power of symbols, it's altogether apt that he, together with his famous contemporary al-Khwarizmi, was instrumental in promoting the adoption of Hindu numerals. The magic of this system derives from the digit 0, which permits, through its use as a placeholder, every natural number to be expressed with just ten abstract characters. In their modern form, these are the familiar 0, 1, 2, 3, 4, 5, 6, 7, 8, and 9.

The Arabic word for the digit 0 is صفر, *sifr*. When this system was introduced into Europe by Fibonacci (he of the famous Fibonacci sequence), *sifr* was Latinized as *zephirum*, a transliteration that gave rise both to the word "zero" and the word "cipher." To medieval Europeans, who were used to seeing a quantity like one thousand, two hundred and two written as MCCII, the characters 1202 doubtless did look like a secret code, or cipher. In this, its modern sense, "cipher" signifies a special type of algorithm which maps symbols to symbols. For instance, using the cipher that shifts each letter three positions to the right in the English alphabet (a → d), the word ASTROLOGY gets enciphered as DVWURORJB.

Living in Baghdad, where transcription, translation, and interpretation rose to the level of a spiritual calling no less than an intellectual one, al-Kindi would have been well aware of the power of symbols to conceal. But through his magic of compelling symbols to reveal their secrets, al-Kindi outstripped all of his predecessors. His "Manuscript on Deciphering Cryptographic Messages" was the first to show that, so long as the statistical frequency of each letter in a language is known, simple ciphers like the one above can always be cracked. For example, the most common letter in English is "e." Therefore, with a sufficiently long sample of enciphered text, we should be able to recognize that the most frequently occurring symbol is really just "e" in disguise. This procedure, called frequency analysis, remains integral to the methods of mathematical cryptanalysis even today.

KNOWLEDGE IS POWER

And yet, not all of the universe's secrets are encrypted with a cipher. Therefore, not all of the universe's secrets are susceptible to the mathematical tricks of decipherment. Occasionally, some of the deepest secrets can be found hiding right before our eyes. The practice of concealing a message in plain sight, so to speak, is called steganography, from the Greek *stego* (στέγω), meaning "to cover," and *grapho* (γράφω), meaning "to write." Steganography is a much more devious craft than conventional cryptography since, while it's obvious that a text in cipher is concealing a secret message, however difficult it may be to decipher, the object of steganography is to deflect your suspicion that there's any secret at all.

Simply put, anything can, and most everything has, historically, been used to cloak secrets in settings that are otherwise perfectly public, be it poetry, music, botanical drawings, and even star charts. Could astrology likewise be used as a cover for secret communication? In fact, as recently as 1996, a hidden message was discovered to have been concealed in the astrological tables of a notorious occult manuscript from the 1500s. The mischievous monk who devised this scheme was Johannes Trithemius, whose astrological prediction concerning the political fortunes of the Jews we cited earlier. Remarkably, Trithemius even went so far as to write an entire book about steganography which, appropriately enough, he disguised to make it look like a book of magical spells for summoning spirits. (A pretty neat trick, don't you think?)

The ability to look at the world and see what others cannot is generally taken as a mark of genius. Of course, it only works out that way if what you're seeing turns out to be correct. But for every al-Kindi, Copernicus, or Einstein, there are thousands of others who insist on seeing connections that simply aren't there, or at least that others refuse to acknowledge. This, instead, is considered a sign of insanity. Astrology likes to hover on the boundary between the two, presenting endless layers of planetary patterns, many of which are perfectly real while others are positively paranoid.

Returning to our sequence of Jupiter–Saturn conjunctions, might they encode the secrets of history? Or is the semblance of any connection merely an illusion? With a traditional cipher, it's exhilaratingly obvious when you crack it: the correct key results in a perfectly readable message. An incorrect key, by contrast, gives you nothing but gibberish. With steganography, however, you can never quite rule everything out. Anyone who maintains that there's no correlation between the conjunctions of the planets and the events of world history ends up in the unenviable stance of having to prove a negative. So how do you determine if the pattern you've spotted is real? The mathematical procedures pioneered by al-Kindi, the original father of cryptology, are, alas, powerless here. We can, however, turn to the man who is rightly called the father of modern cryptology. This is William Friedman, who is best known for breaking the Japanese diplomatic ciphers—codenamed Purple—in the run-up to World War II.

Oddly humorous though it may be, it's nevertheless true that America's preeminent codebreaker during two world wars began his cryptologic career when he was hired, with no prior experience, to search for hidden messages in the plays and sonnets of William Shakespeare. Specifically, he was asked to verify the existence of certain ciphers, to use the term loosely, supposedly proving that the works of Shakespeare were actually authored by Francis Bacon, the essayist, philosopher of science, and onetime chancellor of England. Proponents of these ciphers claimed that individual letters in the early printings of Shakespeare's plays were marked in subtle but identifiable ways. With a generous eye and a suggestive mind, true believers had managed to combine these letters into startlingly elaborate confessions from beyond the grave that William Shakespeare was a fraud—a mere front for the genius of Francis Bacon. Friedman thought all of this was lunacy.

Later, during his retirement, Friedman was drawn back to this matter, and he determined to settle it once and for all. In this, he was joined by his wife, Elizabeth, whom he had first met as a fellow skeptic within the original Shakespeare cipher group. Like William, Elizabeth would become a distinguished cryptologist in her own right, leading, for example, the U.S. Treasury Department's efforts to decipher the codes of bootleggers and rum-runners during Prohibition. In 1957, this husband-and-wife cryptology team published *The Shakespearean Ciphers Examined* which took on the unglamorous but important task of demonstrating, one by one, that none of these so-called ciphers could stand up to careful scrutiny.

Operating according to the principles of an unbiased scientific inquiry (albeit with an oftentimes arch style of writing), the Friedmans' book demonstrates that there's no topic so low that we can't find in it something to learn, so long as we're willing to approach it with an open mind. And while an investigation into the authorship of Shakespeare's plays may seem far afield from the subject of astrology, it's actually directly relevant, because in their book, the Friedmans address head-on the question of how to determine if the signal, or pattern, or secret code you think you've discovered is real. (Or, alternatively, if you're just nuts.)

Generally speaking, there's no mathematical formula or algorithm that can solve a steganographic cipher. The Friedmans did, however, stipulate two general conditions that any such solution must satisfy in order to be considered valid. First, whatever decryption procedure is proposed must give a sensible result *when applied rigorously*. According to the Friedmans, the main problem with the so-called Baconian ciphers was that their "discoverers" were constantly inserting letters here or skipping letters there in order to make their systems work. Yet the very fact that such arbitrariness was necessary should, rather, be taken as an argument against these ciphers having been used in the first place. The conjunction theory of history exhibits a similarly ample amount of wiggle room, since the conjunctions themselves don't need to coincide with any historical date exactly. Instead, it's enough for a conjunction merely to foreshadow, in some vague way, an upcoming event or era. Thus the fiery triplicity said to presage the birth of Jesus is permitted to begin a full quarter-century before the birth itself.

Yet, to give a counterexample, if I told you that the first letter of each of the preceding paragraphs in this section, including this one, spells out ASTROLOGY ("And," Simply," … "Yet"), there should be no doubt that this message was placed there on purpose. The method is applied rigorously: no paragraphs are skipped and no letters are inserted. And, moreover, it can be shown that the probability of these nine letters occurring by chance at the beginning of nine consecutive paragraphs in an English-language document is impossibly small.

The second general condition stipulated by the Friedmans is that your solution must be unique. As they demonstrated so colorfully in their book, a decryption method which tells you that Francis Bacon was the true author of Shakespeare's plays can hardly be valid if the same method applied to the same texts can also be used to reveal that Theodore Roosevelt, Gertrude Stein, and even William Friedman himself were in on the plot. In other words, the significance of any one solution is diminished in accordance with how easy it is to produce competing, if not contradictory, solutions. As the Friedmans put it, "Just as there is only one valid solution to a scientific or mathematical problem, so there is only one valid solution to a cryptogram . . . to find two quite different but equally valid solutions would be an absurdity."

Thus, whatever you conclude about the conjunction theory of history should, properly, depend upon how uniquely you think it correlates with one sequence of historical dates and not any others. This, in turn, suggests a pattern-matching game. For instance, looking back at just the last two hundred years, we can note a remarkably strong correlation between the nine most recent Jupiter–Saturn conjunctions and the terms of U.S. presidents who either died in office, were assassinated, or survived a near-death mishap (table 7.3).

Table 7.3: Jupiter–Saturn Conjunctions as a Harbinger of Presidential Peril

Conjunction Year	President	Misfortune
1842	William Henry Harrison	Died in office (1841)
1861	Abraham Lincoln	Assassinated (1865)
1881	James A. Garfield	Assassinated (1881)
1901	William McKinley	Assassinated (1901)
1921	Warren G. Harding	Died in office (1923)
1941	Franklin D. Roosevelt	Died in office (1945)
1961	John F. Kennedy	Assassinated (1963)
1981	Ronald Reagan	Survived an assassination attempt (1981)
2000	George W. Bush	Nearly choked to death on a pretzel (2002)

And that's just for starters. We could, if we wish, also note an intriguing connection between these conjunctions and the development of space exploration: 1901—Orville and Wilber Wright experiment with powered flight; 1921—Robert Goddard experiments with liquid-fuel rocketry; 1941—Wernher von Braun begins development of the V-2 rocket; 1961—Yuri Gagarin is the first man in space; 1981—the maiden launch of *Columbia*, the first space shuttle; 2000—the initial manned mission arrives at the International Space Station.

And yet, maybe the true, cosmic significance of a Jupiter–Saturn conjunction is to ensure that the New York Yankees make it to the World Series, as, indeed, they have in every conjunction year since the game has been played: 1921, 1941, 1961, 1981, and 2000.

So, how many patterns can you pick out? But whatever you predict, get ready: The next Jupiter–Saturn conjunction is coming fast. It's scheduled for December 21, the exact date of the winter solstice, in the year 2020.

Figure 7.4: This photograph of U.S. Signal Corps officers taken in Aurora, IL, during World War I contains a hidden message. Can you see it? It says "Knowledge is Power." (Actually it says "Knowledge is Powe" since there weren't enough people.) The message is encoded according to whether each individual is facing forward (the A group) or to the side (the B group). Five individuals are needed to signify one letter of the alphabet: AAAAA is *a*, AAAAB is *b*, AAABA is *c*, and so on. This method of encryption, first described by Francis Bacon in the early 1600s, is an example of steganography, the art of concealing a message in plain sight. William Friedman (seated, right) and Elizebeth Friedman (seated, center) remained fascinated by steganography throughout their lives and stipulated conditions for determining whether a suspected secret code is real or illusory. IMAGE COURTESY OF THE GEORGE C. MARSHALL FOUNDATION, LEXINGTON, VA.

8

WHEN YOU WISH UPON A STAR, WHICH ALGORITHM SHOULD YOU USE? GUIDO BONATTI'S ASTROLOGICAL WHEEL OF FORTUNE

Mount Ventoux, France, 1336

"**B**ecause it's there." These three words were the only explanation the mountaineer George Mallory offered up when asked, "Why climb Mount Everest?" The Italian poet Petrarch gave much the same reason for why he ventured to the top of Mount Ventoux—the "windy mountain"—a bald limestone bluff overlooking the villages and countryside of southern France. He was, he said, "led solely by a desire to see the remarkable height of the place."

Petrarch, poet and patriot, believed that Italy's rebirth—its renaissance, if you wish—could only occur if its modes of expression, in Italian no less than in Latin, regained their capacity to speak the loftiest thoughts, as once they had for Virgil and Cicero fifteen hundred years before. In describing his little excursion, then, Petrarch can hardly be expected to have limited himself to Mallory's sphinx-like brevity. Instead, he treats us to one of the most delightful set pieces in all of medieval literature.

As Petrarch narrates it, he and his younger brother, Gherardo, set out in the early morning from the nearby village of Malaucène. They were accompanied on their trek by two unnamed servants, since, while it may be true, as the Renaissance humanists would insist, that "Man is the measure of all things," it's still nice to have someone to carry your stuff. After an earnest initial climb, Petrarch found himself repeatedly led astray by easier paths, which, however, all proved false. Recognizing the error of his ways, he returned to the straight but arduous track which alone could lead him to his hoped-for reward. At last attaining the mountain's peak, Petrarch was awed to see the clouds beneath him and, when they parted, the glorious sweep of creation below. Remembering that he had brought along a copy of Augustine's *Confessions*—what self-respecting medieval poet wouldn't?—he opened a random page and read:

> And men go to wonder at the heights of mountains, the huge swells of the sea, the rivers' wide falls, the ambit of the ocean, and the revolutions of the stars. But they forsake themselves.

Petrarch was thunderstruck. At a moment when his spiritual anxieties had converged with such intensity, it was as if those words had been addressed directly to him, reminding him that of all of God's wonders, the soul was the one most worthy of regard. If he had seen the stars at that moment, hidden though they were by the afternoon's daylight, he would have observed that they too had converged—into a quadruple conjunction of Jupiter, Mars, Mercury, and the Sun—with the full Moon perfectly positioned to receive their rays from directly across the zodiac.

Petrarch's experience on Mount Ventoux is often cited as a fourteenth-century example of the twentieth-century idea of synchronicity. This notion, devised by the Swiss psychoanalyst Carl Jung, expresses, as he put it, that "whatever is born or done this moment of time, has the qualities of this moment of time." In other words, encountering that passage from Augustine was no accident. The universe, and all of Petrarch's prior experiences, had primed him to receive that message at exactly that place and exactly that time.

Astrology similarly ascribes a distinct set of cosmic characteristics to

Figure 8.1: A Scheme of Heaven for Friday, April 26, 1336
Petrarch Reaches the Summit of Mount Ventoux

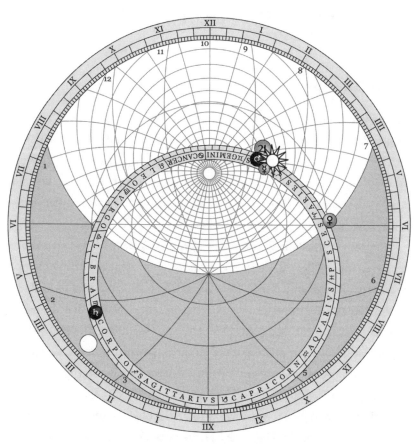

```
The Summit of Mount Ventoux, France: 44°10'26"N, 5°16'42"E
                    JD: 2209148.10764
                       14:35 UT
                       ΔT: 571s
                 Local Time: 3:00 PM
           Local Apparent Sidereal Time: 5:47
```

		λ	β	RA J2000	Dec J2000	Az	El	House
♄	Saturn	♏ 5°04'↓	2°39'	14ʰ 50ᵐ 39ˢ	-13°39'	70°27'	-33°40'	② 5°15'
♃	Jupiter	♉ 16°49'	0°48'	3ʰ 35ᵐ 47ˢ	18°33'	245°12'	44°50'	⑧ 17°36'
♂	Mars	♉ 19°18'	0°09'	3ʰ 45ᵐ 05ˢ	20°04'	244°33'	47°28'	⑧ 20°22'
☉	Sun	♉ 14°03'	0°00'	3ʰ 23ᵐ 40ˢ	18°40'	248°04'	42°51'	⑧ 15°00'
♀	Venus	♓ 28°29'	0°45'	0ʰ 29ᵐ 39ˢ	2°23'	267°28'	0°43'	⑦ 0°43'
☿	Mercury	♉ 21°16'	0°58'	3ʰ 52ᵐ 35ˢ	21°17'	244°02'	49°34'	⑧ 22°33'
☽	Moon	♏ 14°10'	-3°39'	15ʰ 20ᵐ 06ˢ	-22°14'	72°30'	-44°38'	② 15°59'

each moment, be it an age or the blink of an eye. And if the astrology of Petrarch's day had its own defining characteristic, it was in how its practitioners applied themselves to parsing each moment, and each moment's powers, with increasingly fine precision.

WANDERERS

The story of astrology which we've told so far has been one of cities and languages. Babylon, at the beginning, then Alexandria and Baghdad: each in its turn was the setting for the in-gathering, translation, synthesis, and dissemination of the scattered strands of the astral sciences. Many cultures contributed, but it was within these cities that astrology received its most significant and lasting expressions, first in Akkadian, then in Greek, and then in Arabic.

Astrology's handoff to Europe during the Middle Ages was the next link in this chain. As before, there was a dawning awareness of technological inferiority followed by a frantic translation effort—this time out of Arabic—with astrological texts conspicuously overrepresented. Names like Messahala (Masha'allah), Albumaser (Abu Mashar), and Alkindus (al-Kindi)—their strange Latin spellings making them all the more alien-sounding—became the new authorities of a new and cutting-edge science. But unlike the previous cycles of this sequence, there was never any one city that could claim, through its astrological preeminence, to be the obvious successor to Baghdad, Alexandria, or Babylon. Instead, in astrological expertise just as in everything else, the cities of medieval Europe vied with one another—a condition that doubtless contributed to the accelerating pace, once begun, of Europe's technological rise.

Even Latin, dominant though it was, did not go unchallenged as the language of European astrology. The first scientific textbook written in English, for instance, appeared as early as 1391; it's an astronomical and astrological manual on the use of the astrolabe written by none other than Geoffrey Chaucer (he of *Canterbury Tales* fame). Meanwhile, Europe's most prolific center of translation was Toledo, Spain, situated near the politically fluid frontier between Christianity and Islam. It was there that the great scientific books of the Muslim world—both Arabic originals and Arabic translations of Greek texts like the *Almagest*—were received into Europe. But with the arrival of King Alfonso the Wise onto the scene, around the year 1250, Toledo's translation efforts were redirected into producing books not in Latin but in Castilian Spanish. For his translation program, Alfonso relied heavily on a contingent of astronomically savvy Jews. Thus, although it may not be true in any specific instance, in principle it's possible for an astrological text to have been translated from Greek to Syriac to Arabic, and then from Arabic to Spanish by way of Hebrew before finally being converted from Spanish into Latin—with who knows what confusion introduced along the way!

Because no medieval city had a monopoly on scholarship, no single city had a monopoly on medieval scholars—who, instead, it seems, lived lives of ceaseless wandering. The newly created universities, such as at Paris, Oxford, and Bologna, might offer brief opportunities to study and teach, but they rarely provided a permanent home. Particularly charismatic thinkers—Peter Abelard springs to mind—might open up a school of their own, although in Abelard's case, he proved a bit too charismatic for his own good. His illicit love affair with his student Héloïse, and the scandal that ensued, led to some of history's most famously tragic love letters and, less well-known, the birth of a son whom Héloïse named (yes, it's true) Astrolabe.

For astrologers and poets alike, the most desirable employment was to be attached to the household of a noble patron. After nearly five decades of wandering across Europe, Petrarch was gratified to accept the patronage of the Visconti family, then the rulers of Milan. There he struck up an unlikely friendship with the Viscontis' court physician and astrologer—the two titles often went hand in hand—named Maino Maineri.

Petrarch, who viewed astrology as an affront to God's providence, used to tease Maineri about why his forecasts for events years into the future should be believed when Maineri couldn't even predict that week's weather. Maineri defended his art as best he could. But the backdrop to these conversations, as Petrarch makes plain in his letters, was the ever-present specter of the Black Death. This pestilence, which the University of Paris physicians had blamed on the triple conjunction of Jupiter, Saturn, and Mars in the year 1345, is estimated to have wiped out fully one-third of Europe's population before the close of the fourteenth century. With astrology looking increasingly helpless in its inability to predict when and where the next outbreak would occur, Petrarch's anti-astrological ribbings evidently touched a nerve one day, and he records Maineri's almost heartbreaking reply:

> My opinion about this is no different from yours, my friend, but this is how one must live here.

Knowing how fortunate I am to be able to use mathematics (and occasionally astronomy) in a job that actually pays me, I can sympathize with Maineri's professional compromise. Personally, I wonder how many other astrologers were persuaded to make the same bargain.

THE HEAVENS—AND HELL

On top of every other medieval vexation, there was still politics to contend with—a plague even less avoidable back then than it is today. Italy, in particular, spent most of the Middle Ages simmering in a slow-boiling civil war. With the origins of the conflict so obscure as to be largely forgotten—even to the combatants themselves—every Italian city and town was split into two warring camps: Guelphs on one side, Ghibellines on the other. This was the fractious setting in which Dante wrote that most political, but also most cosmological of all great poems, the *Divine Comedy*.

Dante, a partisan of the Guelph faction of his native Florence, began his metaphysical journey by descending down into the nine circles of Hell. There he conversed with prominent Ghibellines and Guelphs alike, their souls condemned to an eternity of torment for their various crimes. But led by Virgil, his poet guide, and spurred on by his love for the heavenly Beatrice, Dante was ushered up through the seven terraces of Purgatory. Then, leaving the Earth behind altogether, Dante continued his ascent through the celestial spheres of Paradise, each the abode of a planet in its geocentric order: the Moon, Mercury, Venus, the Sun, Mars, Jupiter, and Saturn. Passing beyond the stars and the radiant bounds of the universe itself, Dante was at last reunited with Beatrice in prayer, his soul turning as one with "the love that moves the Sun and the other stars."

Through his poetry, Dante was perhaps able to capture the divine rush which the astrologers felt too whenever they gazed at the starry sky. He certainly captured the political stakes—because, for all of its financial advantages, the obvious downside to having a patron was that you became wholly beholden to his political fortunes, not to mention his personality quirks. This relationship was particularly precarious for astrologers who, by dint of their profession, were often forced to deliver bad news or, even worse, explain why the good news they predicted failed to pan out. The astrologer Guido Bonatti witnessed these pitfalls firsthand when, in the first big break of his forecasting career, he was appointed court astrologer to a certain Ezzelino da Romano, endearingly nicknamed the "Tyrant of Verona."

Ezzelino was a Ghibelline warlord remembered chiefly for his violence— an impressive feat for the times. Dante placed him in the seventh circle of Hell, immersed in a river of boiling blood equal to the blood he had spilt while alive. For Bonatti, even worse than realizing that his new boss was a violent psychopath must have been discovering that Ezzelino's interest in the stars extended to arguing with his astrologers over the finer points of their craft. Bonatti recounts that his predecessor had always agreed with Ezzelino's astrological interpretations, even when he thought they were wrong, mainly out of a crippling sense of fear. Of course this fear becomes more understandable when, as Bonatti reminds us, Ezzelino held that astrologer's brother in leg irons under constant threat of execution.

Exactly how Bonatti fared so well under Ezzelino isn't something he chose to dwell on. Presumably, like Petrarch's astrologer friend Maineri, Bonatti did what he needed to do to make a living. After Ezzelino's predictably violent end, Bonatti served as court astrologer to a succession of Ghibelline princes. Whether Bonatti's own politics leaned that way or whether the networks of patronage were simply hardened along political lines is an open question. All the same, it's highly unlikely that Bonatti could ever have served at a Guelph court—certainly not after he chose the precise hour (or so he claimed) for the most smashing Ghibelline military victory of all. This was the Battle of Montaperti, fought on September 4, 1260, between the Florentine Guelphs and their hated Ghibelline rivals from Siena. The battle was a rout, resulting in a tremendous loss of life, the capture of Florence, and the expulsion of the leading Guelph families from the city.

Dante, although living a generation after the battle, was incensed even by its memory. He placed the Florentine leader he held responsible for the defeat in the ninth and deepest circle of Hell, a fate reserved only for history's

Figure 8.2: Giovanni Stradano, Illustration of Dante's *Inferno*, Canto XX, 8th Circle, 4th Bolgia: soothsayers and astrologers, ca. 1590. FLORENCE, BIBLIOTECA MEDICEA LAURENZIANA, MS. MED. PALAT. 75, F. 38R.

most abominable traitors. Whether Dante knew of Bonatti's self-professed role in the battle isn't clear, but he despised him all the same. He assigned Bonatti by name to Hell's eighth circle, the habitation of diviners, sooth-sayers, and astrologers. (To have been, as Bonatti was, both an astrologer and a Ghibelline could only have added insult to injury.) For his crime of attempting to see a future known only to God, Bonatti's punishment—one shared by all of his fellow fortune-tellers—was to have his head attached backward to his body.

> See how his shoulder-blades are now at his chest.
> Because he aspired to see too far ahead
> He looks behind and treads a backward path.

Even now, Bonatti is shuffling backward and weeping, a torment destined never to cease so long as Dante's undying words are read.

AN ALGORITHM FOR EVERY OCCASION

Notwithstanding his cameo appearance in Dante's *Inferno*, Bonatti's chief claim to fame is to have authored the most influential astrology book of the Middle Ages. This was the notorious *Ten Treatises on Astronomy* (*De astronomia tractatus x*) which, despite its name, had nothing to do with predicting the positions of the planets in the sky and everything to do with predicting the affairs of men on Earth. In fact, the *Ten Treatises on Astronomy* is about as astrological as you can get, insofar as the bulk of it is occupied with astrology's most unapologetically occult inner core—that branch of the discipline which for many centuries was known as judicial astrology.

The basic premise of judicial astrology is that you ask the stars a question—a question about pretty much anything—and the stars then reveal their judgment or, in Latin, *iudicium*. The astrologer's job is to interpret these judgments on your behalf. So far, so good. The odd thing about judicial astrology, however, was that for many questions, and especially the broad category of simple yes-or-no questions, the astrologer would determine the stars' judgment based on their positions in the sky at the moment your question was asked. In other words, the key celestial instant had nothing to do with the matter at hand. It was simply whenever you and your astrologer had managed to schedule an appointment.

This arrangement was undoubtedly convenient for the professional astrologer wishing to keep regular office hours. But I think I can speak for most twenty-first-century readers when I say that as a means of forecasting the future, it sounds totally nuts. What if you arrived at your astrological reading an hour late? The stars' coordinates could easily have rotated far enough for their judgment to become exactly the opposite of what it would have been had you arrived on time. True enough, but in the astrological universe, which was a universe governed entirely by Fate, this is all how it was meant to be. Your destiny has always been sealed, and it was always your destiny to ask the stars about your destiny at precisely that moment and not any other.

Yet however ho-hum this fatalistic outlook may have been during astrology's early days in Stoic ancient Rome, to deny the existence of free will was a decidedly and damnably heretical opinion in medieval Christian Europe. If there was no free will, then Adam and Eve could not be culpable for their original sin; and if there was no original sin, there was no need for salvation; and if there was no need for salvation, there was no need for the Church; and if there was no need for the Church . . . Well, that's the sort of thinking that could get you burned at the stake if you insisted on making a fuss about it. This was no idle threat. The astrologer Cecco d'Ascoli was condemned by the Inquisition on precisely these grounds and burned at the stake in Florence on September 16, 1327.

As was obvious to Dante, Petrarch, and many others, astrology—and especially judicial astrology—was fundamentally incompatible with Christian doctrine. Yet Bonatti's *Ten Treatises* remained in circulation for centuries, with several finely illustrated printings appearing as late as the 1500s. If Bonatti's popularity is anything to go by, there were plenty of otherwise pious readers who wagered that a little bit of sin was a small price to pay for a peek into the future.

And why not? The future promised by judicial astrology wasn't the ano-dyne drivel of a modern magazine horoscope. It was specific, precise, and mathematical. Would you like to know whether to buy that house or not, or if the woman you're thinking of marrying is a virgin, or how you're going to die? There was an astrological algorithm for that. In fact, Bonatti's *Ten Treatises* provided algorithms for determining the stars' judgments on hundreds of different questions. Taken together, they read like a laundry list of all the worries that might keep a medieval Italian prince awake at night. Some were deadly serious, such as whether to risk battle with an enemy. Some were more personal, such as whether an individual would recover from an illness. And some were so frivolous that there's nothing to do but laugh. I like to think that it was at the behest of Ezzelino da Romano, the Tyrant of Verona, that Bonatti included algorithms for the following sequence of vitally important questions: "If someone is invited to a banquet, should he go?" "What foods will be there?" "Will the banquet consist of multiple courses?" "What is the reason for the banquet?" "How long will the banquet last?" "Will a brawl break out among the dinner guests?" "When will the food be served at the banquet?" "Should one beware of the food at the banquet?" Yes, according to Bonatti, the stars in their majesty had answers for each and every one of these pressing concerns.

THE HOUSES OF HEAVEN

As a practical matter, computing the stars' judgments requires that last group of astrological elements which we've yet to properly introduce: the Houses of Heaven. These are astrology's system of local coordinates—the astrological analog to the modern-day quantities of azimuth and elevation. Very simply, the Houses of Heaven divide your local sky into twelve sectors. The First House is positioned at your eastern horizon; the Tenth House is directly above your head; the Seventh House is at your western horizon; and the Fourth House is the region of sky on the other side of the globe directly beneath your feet. The remaining eight Houses fill in the gaps. In our schemes of heaven, these twelve sectors are labeled with small numerals, 1 through 12.

I've refrained from describing the Houses of Heaven up until now mainly because astrology is complicated enough without them. But this shouldn't be taken to imply that they were less important to astrologers of earlier ages. On the contrary, the Houses of Heaven were integral to the earliest Greco-Roman astrological systems described by Marcus Manilius, Claudius Ptolemy, and Vettius Valens. More assertively, we can regard the Houses of Heaven as the defining elements of astrology itself, because, unlike the zodiac, the Houses of Heaven are not mentioned in the older Mesopotamian rites of celestial divination. And whatever the astral arts of ancient Babylon may have been, it's not strictly correct to call them astrology, since this is, properly, a Greek name for a Greek science.

The Houses of Heaven were more than just sectors of the sky. Each House was believed to be connected to specific aspects of human life, such as health, money, or children. As the sky's revolution carried the planets through each of the twelve Houses once per day, the nature of their significations thus changed hour by hour. Of the twelve Houses, the most powerful were at the four "cardinal" or "angular" points defined by your horizon: the First House (east); the Tenth House (up); the Seventh House (west); and the Fourth House (down). Next came Houses Two, Five, Eight, and Eleven; these were called "upcoming" or "succedent" Houses, since the sky's daily revolution would carry any celestial body within them into one of the angular Houses within the next hour or two. Houses Three, Six, Nine, and Twelve were called "falling" or "cadent" Houses. The bodies in these Houses had recently exited an angular House and, consequently, were seen as weak and unlucky.

Latin authors like Bonatti tended to refer to the Houses simply by their numbers, but in the older Greek tradition they were given mystically outlandish names. Of course, we're already familiar with one of them: the First House, in Greek, was the horoscope. The rest of the system is sketched out in table 8.1.

Table 8.1: The Houses of Heaven

House	Classical Name	Type	Signification
1st House	Horoscope	Angular	Birth, Life, Self
2nd House	Gate of Hades	Succedent	Wealth
3rd House	Goddess	Cadent	Siblings, Short Journeys
4th House	Lower Midheaven	Angular	Parents, Property
5th House	Good Fortune	Succedent	Children, Happiness
6th House	Bad Fortune	Cadent	Sickness
7th House	Occident	Angular	Marriage, Women
8th House	Beginning of Death	Succedent	Death, Misfortunes
9th House	God	Cadent	Religion, Learning, Voyages
10th House	Midheaven	Angular	Success, Honor, Power
11th House	Good Daemon	Succedent	Friends, Favors
12th House	Bad Daemon	Cadent	Enemies, Conspiracies

WILL IT BE A BOY OR A GIRL?

Their Greco-Roman antecedents notwithstanding, the cookbook-style algorithms of judicial astrology, in which the Houses of Heaven are the main ingredients, were the peculiar specialty of Arabic astrologers. Bonatti's *Ten Treatises*, in turn, was primarily a compilation of Arabic astrological methods repackaged for a European audience. Since Bonatti is not believed to have known Arabic himself, he would have relied on the Latin translations that were emerging from hubs like Toledo. By and large, Bonatti is conscientious about crediting the sources of the algorithms he recommends. To the roster of Arabic astrologers introduced earlier, we can add Alchabitius (al-Qabisi), Haly (Ali ibn Abi al-Rijal), and Zahel (Sahl ibn Bishr) as names Bonatti cites especially often.

What sort of procedures did Bonatti prescribe? Probably the best way to answer this is with an example. One of the simpler algorithms he relates is for determining the gender of an unborn child. Let's pretend that Petrarch, instead of turning to Saint Augustine for spiritual guidance at the summit of Mount Ventoux, had instead decided to ask the stars if he would become the father of a boy or girl—because while Petrarch is most famous for his love poetry to the aristocratic and unobtainable Laura, a rather more obtainable but otherwise unknown woman was at that moment pregnant with Petrarch's first child. Was it a son or a daughter?

According to Bonatti, in order to answer this question it's necessary to consider the Fifth House, since this signified children, and also the First House, since this signified the questioner himself. (This status made the First House a participant in every question.) Looking back at the scheme of heaven for Petrarch's ascent of Mount Ventoux, we see that the cusp of the Fifth House was in Capricorn, while the cusp of the First House (the horoscope) was in Virgo.

Judicial astrology, however, is a bit like a celestial shell game, where the signifier of the stars' judgment keeps moving around the zodiac until it seems to be both everywhere and nowhere at the same time. So, while we now know the signs of the First and Fifth Houses, what Bonatti next asks us to determine is the location of their lords. Using the standard system of sign rulership (table 5.2), we note that the lord of the Fifth House, Saturn, is in Scorpio. Meanwhile, the lord of the First House, Mercury, is in Taurus.

Since both Scorpio and Taurus are feminine signs (table 5.2), the judgment of the stars is that the child is a girl. Had the lords of the First and Fifth Houses been in masculine signs, the stars would have announced a boy. If the genders of the signs had been mixed, it would have become necessary to consult the Moon, and things get rather more complicated from there.

As it turned out, Petrarch's first child was a son, whom he named Giovanni. Sadly, at the age of only twenty-four, Giovanni became—as had Petrarch's poetic love, Laura, some years earlier—one of the many millions who succumbed to the plague.

CHEATING FATE

Amidst the whirl of Arabic texts translated in medieval Spain, one that proved weighty out of all proportion to its slender size was the *Kitab al-Jabr* by Muhammad ibn Musa al-Khwarizmi, the great mathematician of ninth-century Baghdad. This book is a short collection of easy-to-read, step-by-step instructions for solving certain types of algebraic equations. Its Latin translation, completed during the twelfth century, became so influential that, as mentioned previously, the book's title gave rise to the word "algebra," just as its author's name gave rise to the word "algorithm." The astrological procedures in Bonatti's *Ten Treatises* are presented in much the same step-by-step style, which is to say, with all due honor, that they're presented algorithmically.

Although quite a few of Bonatti's algorithms seem (to me, at least) ambiguous or difficult to follow, many others present no problem at all in their implementation. In fact, they read almost like the instructions of a computer program, a format to which they lend themselves with remarkable ease. But it's one thing to write a judicial astrology computer program; it's another thing altogether to wonder if the answers it spits back are any good. This is because, in judicial astrology, questions submitted for the stars' immediate judgment are supposed to be asked spontaneously. If I sit in front of my computer and click "query the stars" over and over again, it doesn't take long to figure out that certain configurations of the sky are more likely than others to give me the answer I want. Understandably, then, Bonatti insists that an astrologer must never cast a horoscope for his own questions. That would be a bit like cheating, wouldn't it? And yet, what's the point of a foreknowledge of the stars if you can't put it to good use?

I suspect that this line of thinking, or something very near it, was the inspiration for a complementary set of astrological algorithms called elections. The purpose of an astrological election was to look ahead to the planets' future configurations and then, with a knowledge of the relevant astrological considerations, to choose, or "elect," the most celestially auspicious moment to begin something. Bonatti devotes an entire treatise of his *Ten Treatises* to elections. It mirrors very closely the treatise he devotes to the judgment of direct questions; both sets of algorithms, for instance, are arranged according to the House of Heaven to which they pertain. So long as you could rephrase your direct interrogation as a "when" question, there was usually a corresponding election algorithm to tell you the optimal moment to get started.

Yet, however similar the two sets of algorithms appear on the surface, they are actually deeply incompatible. Whereas astral interrogations are predicated on the irrevocable decrees of Fate, astral elections require a future that hasn't yet been written. Otherwise, there could never be an optimal moment for anything. It's only in a cosmos in which the planets influence the Earth somewhat in analogy with the weather that astrological elections make any sense. If you see storm clouds gathering outside, you might minimize your chances of getting wet by choosing to stay indoors. Analogously, maybe it's equally prudent, if less immediately obvious, to avoid purchasing property when Mars is in the Fourth House. In both cases, there is at least the tacit premise of a physical cause and its effect. Conversely, if Fate really is running the show, then no amount of advance knowledge can help you avoid it or take advantage of it. That really would be cheating, and in a deeply metaphysical way.

Astrological elections allow us to keep our free will, and it's this quality which makes them seem, to our modern sensibilities, less philosophically troubling. But it was precisely this quality which, for much of astrology's history, made elections the more suspicious of the two sets of algorithms. Bonatti acknowledged this, but, ever the pragmatist, he recommended using both approaches just to be sure. If you were about to make a risky decision, wouldn't you want to have as many positive indicators as possible? Thus, when recounting his astrological triumph at the Battle of Montaperti, Bonatti explained that he first used a direct interrogation to ascertain that the Ghibellines would be victorious over their Florentine foes. Only then, with that judgment securely in hand, did he cast an election to determine the optimal moment for the Ghibellines to attack.

WHEN TO BUY AND SELL

Regardless of each system's metaphysical baggage, astral elections are, from an algorithmic perspective, significantly easier to implement. This is because elections are concerned with the timing of actual events, not something fuzzy such as when somebody asks a question about an event. Just as importantly, astral elections don't need to be perfect. Good weather, even if it isn't ideal, is still better than bad weather. Analogously, it's enough for an astrological election merely to ensure that the good planetary influences outweigh the bad. This is achieved by "accommodating" as many of the relevant "significators" as possible. Keeping the big picture in mind, Bonatti reassures us that "if you can't accommodate them all, accommodate those which you are able to accommodate, since you will not accommodate so few that there will be no benefit to your election, even if it's not as much as you would wish." And again, like an astrologer with a business to run, "for the most part we don't have time to wait [for the perfect moment], so we should elect for the time-frames we have and mix whatever good we can into our election."

All of this makes things especially convenient for the modern-day algorithm developer. Just as invitingly, since it's always possible to reconstruct the "astrological weather" at any time in the past, there are many ways for us to explore just how accurate Bonatti's election algorithms really are. How well, for instance, do they hold up to that most fickle of fortune's barometers, the stock market? This is a question we can meaningfully address, since Bonatti has given us matching algorithms for determining the best moments to buy and sell for the sole purpose of making a profit. (The thought that playing the markets was a pastime as far back as the thirteenth century caught me by surprise at first. But then again, who financed the Italian Renaissance if not the Italian banking families who made their fortunes right around this time?) Recall that we already have a list of every astrological state of the cosmos going back several thousand years; this is our list of Z-codes, which we compiled for chapter 6. Identifying the dates flagged by Bonatti's buy and sell algorithms therefore becomes, at least in principle, a reasonably straightforward affair.

When implementing an algorithm as a computer program, it's often helpful to first sketch it out in a format called pseudocode. This is a sort of half-human, half-robot style of writing whose purpose is to communicate the algorithm's basic steps in a way that's both easy to understand and also easy to convert into an actual programming language. Below is the pseudocode for my version of Bonatti's buy and sell algorithms. These are by no means the only implementations, especially since I have attempted to accommodate only those significators which seemed easiest to accommodate. But this should be forgivable since, following Bonatti's lead, we're not looking for the perfect algorithm, just one that shows itself to be even a tiny bit better than chance.

Table 8.2: Bonatti's Algorithms for When to Buy and Sell

Instruction	Pseudocode
Find buy dates such that:	Z-Codes where(
1. The Moon is not in Taurus, Cancer, Virgo, or Pisces	NOT(LUN in [TAU, CNC, VIR, PSC])
2. The Moon is not in conjunction, square, or opposition with Saturn	AND NOT(abs(LUN-SAT) in [0,3,6])
3. The Moon is not in conjunction, square, or opposition with Mars	AND NOT(abs(LUN-MAR) in [0,3,6])
4. The Moon is not combust by the Sun	AND LUN != SOL
5. Mercury is not in conjunction, square, or opposition with Saturn	AND NOT(abs(MER-SAT) in [0,3,6])
6. Mercury is not in conjunction, square, or opposition with Mars	AND NOT(abs(MER-MAR) in [0,3,6])
7. Mercury is not combust by the Sun	AND MER != SOL
8. The Moon is in conjunction, sextile, or trine with Mercury	AND abs(LUN-MER) in [0,2,4]
9. Mercury is in conjunction, sextile, or trine with Venus	AND abs(MER-VEN) in [0,2,4]
10. Mercury is not in retrograde	AND MER.retrograde == FALSE)

Instruction	Pseudocode
Find sell dates such that:	`Z-Codes where(`
1. The Moon is in Taurus, Cancer, Virgo, or Pisces	`LUN in [TAU, CNC, VIR, PSC])`
2. The Moon is not in conjunction, square, or opposition with Saturn	`AND NOT(abs(LUN-SAT) in [0,3,6])`
3. The Moon is not in conjunction, square, or opposition with Mars	`AND NOT(abs(LUN-MAR) in [0,3,6])`
4. The Moon is not combust by the Sun	`AND LUN != SOL`
5. The Moon is not in conjunction, sextile, or trine with Venus	`AND NOT(abs(LUN-VEN) in [0,2,4])`
6. The Moon is not in conjunction, sextile, or trine with Jupiter	`AND NOT(abs(LUN-JUP) in [0,2,4])`
7. The Moon is in sextile or trine with Saturn	`AND abs(LUN-SAT) in [2,4]`
8. The Moon is in sextile or trine with Mars	`AND abs(LUN-MAR) in [2,4] )`

Are these algorithms any good? One way to check this is by applying them to the Dow Jones Industrial Average, which is the longest-running and best-known U.S. stock market index. Suppose that in 1980 (the starting year is not terribly important) you had $1,000 to invest in the stock market. One option was simply to buy and hold in a fund that tracked the Dow. Another was to invest in what we can call the Bonatti Fund. The Bonatti Fund puts half of your money in the stock market and holds the remainder as cash. At every astrologically auspicious sell indicator, the fund manager, Guido Bonatti, sells off some fraction of your stock—let's say 20 percent—and converts it to cash; at every buy indicator, he takes the same fraction of your cash and invests it back in the market.

It all sounds promising enough. But as you can see in figure 8.3, whatever gains you may have realized by investing in the Bonatti Fund (cash and stock combined) are dwarfed by what you could have achieved simply by never selling. From 1980 to 2018, the Dow Jones Industrial Average has increased by an impressive 25 times, a rate of return that's proven very hard to beat. In

Figure 8.3: Guido Bonatti's Astrological Investment Fund

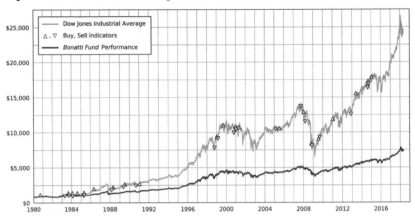

fact, it's estimated that in any given year, some two-thirds of managed funds fail to beat broad market indices like the Dow. Even worse, since any fund which beats the market in one year is just as unlikely to beat it the next, the odds of any one fund consistently outperforming the market over a multi-decade stretch of time is exceedingly small. Thus, whatever his shortcomings as a money manager may have been, Mr. Bonatti can hardly be said to lack for company.

WHEN TO TAKE A DRIVE

If you've been paying close attention, you may have noticed that, for all our talk about the Houses of Heaven, the previous example made no use of them at all. This is because the Houses of Heaven narrow the window of an algorithm's validity down from an entire day to just an hour or so, and from the whole globe to a much smaller geographic region—something closer in size to a city. That level of detail just isn't useful when looking at, say, large swings in the stock market over multiple decades. (A more technical argument is that since the entire sky rotates through all twelve Houses once per day, an auspicious day will generally also contain an auspicious hour.)

Nevertheless, there are many data sets where a specificity of both time and place is integral to the nature of the data itself. One example, which is remarkable, albeit grim, for both the quantity and meticulousness of its data, is the Fatality Analysis Reporting System (FARS) of the National Highway Traffic Safety Administration. FARS is a database of every fatal traffic accident that has occurred in the United States since 1975. Its tables record data in dozens of different categories, including the latitude, longitude, date, and time (to the nearest minute, where possible) of each and every fatal crash. This suggests that we have enough information to check another of Bonatti's astrological elections, namely, when to set out on a journey, because if there's any journey which can be said to have begun inauspiciously, it's one that is cut short by death.

Astrologically, travel is the bailiwick of both the Third House (short journeys) and the Ninth House (long journeys). The algorithms Bonatti gives for selecting the best times to set out are characteristically complex. Long journeys, for instance, ought to take into consideration the journey's purpose, the point of departure, the destination, and even the mode of travel. However, there's one basic consideration which Bonatti insists upon unambiguously: you should never begin a journey when the Moon is below the horizon. In other words, if you're planning to take a trip, make sure to begin it when the Moon is in Houses Seven through Twelve, and not in Houses One through Six.

Is there any merit to this advice? The FARS database, you will not be shocked to read, does not record the position of the Moon or any other celestial body. However, knowing the latitude, longitude, date, and time allows us to compute, with some effort, the lunar elevation at each crash site. (This is a seemingly simple computation made thoroughly un-simple by America's maddeningly local observance of time zone boundaries and Daylight Saving Time.) Keep in mind that the Moon can be above or below the horizon during the daytime just as well as during the night. So, at first glance, one wouldn't expect there to be any connection between the incidence of fatal traffic accidents and the position of the Moon. Expressed more statistically, we have a

49.6%
Moon Above the Horizon
Houses 7, 8, 9, 10, 11, 12
77,082 Fatal Crashes (2012-2016)

78,462 Fatal Crashes (2012-2016)
Houses 1, 2, 3, 4, 5, 6
Moon Below the Horizon
50.4%

Figure 8.4 : Fatal car crashes and the position of the Moon.

null hypothesis that the number of crashes when the Moon is above the horizon should be equal to the number of crashes when the Moon is below the horizon.

Is this correct? Figure 8.4 shows that for the last five years of complete statistics (2012–16), the results are extremely close to a 50–50 split. One may be tempted to dismiss the small discrepancy as just a bit of random noise. But it's not possible to ignore so easily the sheer number of crashes we're dealing with—well over 150,000. Beyond being a terrible reminder of just how many lives are lost this way, a sample size this large transforms otherwise coarse statistics into an extremely fine measuring tool. In fact, with a sample size of 150,000, even a difference of just 400 incidents, or 0.3 percent, can be meaningfully detected. Our data exhibit a discrepancy three times that size. Although the difference may seem small, it's extremely unlikely to be the result of random noise. All things being equal, the data indicate that you are slightly less likely to be involved in a fatal car crash when the Moon is above the horizon than when it is below.

I was, I admit, rather surprised by this. But with any statistical test, it's important to report the results whether they accord with expectations or not. To repeat a test until the "right" answer emerges serves only to exacerbate the widespread plague of confirmation bias in the sciences. But this need not be the end of the story—far from it. An unexpected outcome is always an invitation to investigate why.

Yet before embarking on an elaborate research program to get to the bottom of this mystery, it occurred to me that there's probably a very simple explanation. While the position of the Moon should have no effect on driving conditions during the day, this isn't really true at night. Especially on dark country roads, the difference in nighttime ambient light between a full Moon and a new Moon can be dramatic. And sure enough, it turns out that the measured discrepancy is contained entirely within the nighttime data.

Is this common-sense finding a vindication of the information encoded in Bonatti's astrological algorithm? Perhaps. But it strikes me as an even more emphatic vindication of the information contained in carefully collected data. With data, you can never quite predict exactly what you'll find. And this, it seems to me, makes its revelatory powers at least as exciting as anything promised by astrology.

DIVIDING THE HOUSES

The allure, during the Middle Ages, of increasingly sophisticated astrological algorithms raised the technical demands of the astrologer's craft considerably. With the movements of whole armies hinging upon the hourly shifts of the Houses of Heaven, the stakes could not possibly have been any higher. And yet, at that time, there wasn't any agreement about where one House ended and another began. Surprisingly, today, there still isn't.

Before I started writing this book, I didn't know all that much about the Houses of Heaven. (Or, if I thought I did, I was wrong.) What I did know was that modern astrologers still argue about where to place the dividing lines, or cusps, between the twelve Houses. This struck me as jarringly bizarre. How had this question not been settled two thousand years ago? More to the point, I didn't expect I'd need to worry much about it. I was excited by the idea of applying ancient astrological algorithms to modern data, but if my results depended on something as abstruse as using one set of House cusps over another, well, then, clearly I would have taken a wrong turn.

It's true that the precise boundaries of the Houses of Heaven can hardly hold the key to whether a horoscope is somehow right or wrong. But in a way that I had not anticipated, these boundaries do hold the key to the graphic design of a horoscope. This was the piece I hadn't recognized in horoscopes like the birth chart of King Henry VIII shown at the beginning of this book. The twelve compartments in that diagram are not fitted to the twelve signs of the zodiac, but rather to the twelve Houses of Heaven. Color plate 11 shows a manuscript illumination from King Henry's time that illustrates this setup beautifully. Very simply, you cannot draw a horoscope without committing

Figure 8.5: Stereographic Views of Several Common Methods of House Division

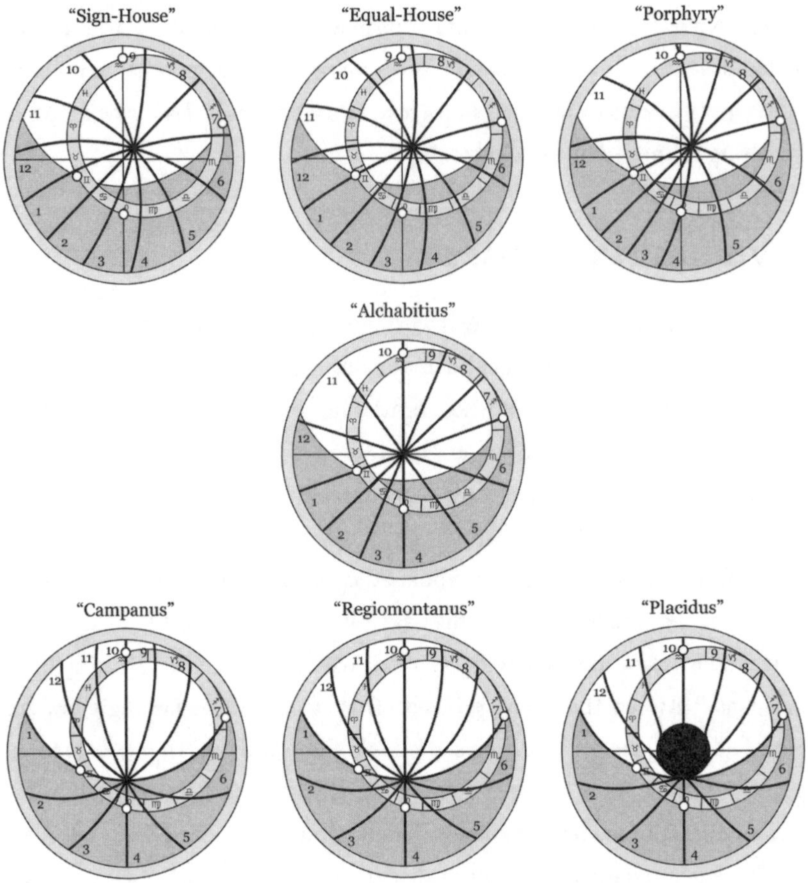

"Sign-House"   "Equal-House"   "Porphyry"

"Alchabitius"

"Campanus"   "Regiomontanus"   "Placidus"

to one of the various systems for dividing the Houses of Heaven. And once this dawned on me, I became determined to untangle the threads of this utterly obscure yet delightfully technical topic.

Now, if I may venture an opinion here, it seems that the continued confusion surrounding how best to position the Houses of Heaven derives from framing the problem in terms of how best to carve up the ecliptic circle. In fact, the problem is properly one of how best to carve up the larger celestial sphere. Fortunately, we already know a technique that can help us visualize the complicated contours of a three-dimensional sphere on a two-dimensional diagram:

the stereographic projection of an astrolabe. Figure 8.5, therefore, represents my contribution to this age-old astrological squabble. It shows several different versions of the Houses of Heaven extended over the whole celestial sphere and projected onto astrolabe-style maps. The geometric properties of each of these systems are summarized in table 8.3. Note that I've used the labels that are commonly found in modern astrology books, even if the individuals whose names they bear need not have been their original inventors.

Table 8.3: Geometric Properties of the Different House Systems

	Sign-House	Equal-House	Porphyry	Alchabitius	Campanus	Regiomontanus	Placidus
Reference Plane	Ecliptic	Ecliptic	Ecliptic	Equator	Horizon	Horizon	Horizon
First House cusp coincides with the ascendant	No	Yes	Yes	Yes	Yes	Yes	Yes
Tenth House cusp coincides with midheaven	No	No	Yes	Yes	Yes	Yes	Yes
Cusps do not wander during the day	No	No	No	No	Yes	Yes	Yes
Night Houses are fully divided from day Houses	No	No	No	No	Yes	Yes	Yes
Houses are all the same size	Yes	Yes	No	No	Yes	No	No
Cusps are arcs of circles	Yes	Yes	Yes	Yes	Yes	Yes	No
Houses fully cover the celestial sphere	Yes	Yes	Yes	Yes	Yes	Yes	No

In this book, we've already had occasion to encounter four of these systems. The oldest and simplest approach is the Sign–House system, which equates whole Houses to whole zodiac signs. This is what al-Biruni used for his horoscope of the foundation of Baghdad (plate 9). Meanwhile, Cardano's birth chart for King Henry VIII used the next simplest method, the Equal-House system. Here, 30-degree segments of the ecliptic are likewise apportioned to each House, but the cusp of the First House is placed at the exact location of the ascendant.

This is pretty much as sophisticated as things got until the 1400s, when the astronomer Regiomontanus was persuaded to try his hand. Regiomontanus was the mathematical boy genius of the Renaissance. In 1448, when he was only twelve, he computed a set of planetary tables that was more precise than any of the published almanacs for the year. By the time he was twenty-six, Regiomontanus had finished a complete reworking of Ptolemy's *Almagest* using all the newest trigonometric methods. His version immediately supplanted the twelfth-century Toledo translation of the *Almagest* as the chief astronomy manual in Europe, and it was used as a textbook by both Copernicus and Galileo. Thus, when a certain archbishop in Hungary demanded an improved system for determining the Houses of Heaven—in particular, one that would be more faithful to the vague instructions given by Ptolemy in his *Tetrabiblos*—there was only one person to ask.

Regiomontanus accepted the challenge. In a brash and masterly treatise, he surveyed the existing methods of House division, dismissed them all as inadequate, introduced an entirely new method, and provided tables for computing their boundaries at any latitude to the nearest minute of arc. Astrolabe makers in particular appreciated the geometric elegance of this method, and, if you look closely, you can see Regiomontanus-style cusps engraved on the astrolabe of Gerard Mercator (plate 1). This, then, is the third system of Houses of Heaven which appears in this book.

Regiomontanus's method ought, perhaps, to have been the final word on the matter. His mathematically rigorous system sliced the sky into sectors that have pretty much all of the attributes one could wish for in a system of Houses. And his tables made it possible for anyone to replicate his procedure. But in spite of their many advantages, Regiomontanus Houses have all but disappeared from astrology today. They've been usurped by Placidus Houses, named for Placidus de Titis, a seventeenth-century Italian astrologer who promoted their use.

Placidus Houses are, by a wide margin, the most popular system of Houses used by professional astrologers today. But from a mathematical perspective, they are also uniquely unsatisfying. This is because, alone among the systems for drawing the Houses of Heaven, Placidus Houses cannot be defined over the whole celestial sphere. This defect gets worse the further north or south you go until, at the Arctic and Antarctic circles, the system falls apart completely.

Of course, it's hardly my place to quibble with the astrologers over the application of their art. But nor can I refrain from pointing out that there is one system of Houses which actually embodies, or so it seems to me, the theoretical ideal. These are Houses which Regiomontanus attributed to Campanus of Novara, a thirteenth-century mathematician known for his Latin edition of Euclid's *Elements of Geometry*.

Regiomontanus argues, convincingly, that while Campanus may have conceived these Houses, he would not have had the mathematical tools to calculate them. He then goes on to argue, much less convincingly, that Ptolemy would have found them unacceptable. This is a weak gripe, and I find nothing in the *Tetrabiblos* to support it. Besides, I don't see how even the authority of Ptolemy here outweighs the compelling mathematical perfection of the Campanus system of Houses.

Visually, Campanus Houses are like the wedges of an orange whose central axis lies along your local north–south compass line. More technically, Campanus Houses are what would result if you rotated your azimuth–elevation coordinate system by 90 degrees so that its pole sat at the north point of your horizon. This relationship means that it's also possible to define a precise "House longitude"—not just a House number—for every point in the sky.

I've used Campanus Houses, along with this little innovation of House longitudes, in each of the schemes of heaven in this book, making it the fourth system to appear upon these pages. Might the superior precision of these Houses be the deciding factor in whether some astrological algorithm actually works? That seems most unlikely. But, speaking for myself, if I was going to wish upon a star, I'd still want all the mathematical precision I could get.

EX IIS UNAM CAVE: "BEWARE OF ONE OF THEM"

Beware of one of the hours, that is, for it will be your last. Disquieting little mementos like this about the fleetingness of life were often inscribed onto otherwise tranquil timepieces, such as sundials. During the plague years, however, no reminders were needed of time's lethal whimsy. Death came just as quickly to the young and the old, the strong and the weak, the righteous and the wicked. You were alive one moment, dead the next; exalted one instant, debased the next. The image of the universe ceased to be one of celestial order. In its place was a vision of all creation clinging desperately to the whirling Wheel of Fortune. Life had been reduced to being lived hour by hour.

A question, now, for your consideration: Do scientific revolutions occur from the top down or the bottom up? Do thinkers, writers, and individual

Figure 8.6: The Wheel of Fortune from Chrétien Legouais, *Ovide Moralisé* (fourteenth century). MS 1044 FOL.74 / BIBLIOTHÈQUE MUNICIPALE, ROUEN, FRANCE / BRIDGEMAN IMAGES.

men of genius advance society with their books and ideas, or are they merely expressing in words concepts already embodied in the technologies created by so many silent craftsmen? As a curious argument for the latter, consider that, during the 1300s, one of the most momentous technological upheavals in history transpired, one which has had a profound and irreversible impact on nearly every aspect of modern life. And although it occurred during the full wakefulness of history, it was accompanied by almost no written record whatsoever. I am referring, of course, to the development of the weight-driven mechanical clock. Who were its inventors? No one knows.

The mechanical clock most likely originated in northern Italy, perhaps a little before the year 1300. Charmingly enough, it's Dante who makes what may very well be the first mention of its mechanism, in the *Paradiso*, in a metaphor about the Sun. Yet if, in the year 1300, no one paid much attention to its small and awkward prototypes, by 1400 practically every major city in Europe had a large, public, mechanical clock to ring the hours.

The mechanization of time facilitated some fairly radical shifts in the perception of time. Previously, the twenty-four-hour day had been split into twelve daytime hours and twelve nighttime hours. This system of "unequal hours" meant that the length of an hour was different during the daytime than it was at night and, even worse, changed day by day according to the season and your latitude. From a modern perspective, this sounds horribly inconvenient, but it's really just a question of priorities. If you told me about an event which happened at 6 p.m., then, absent additional information, I have no way of knowing if it occurred during broad daylight or well after dark. Yet when the New Testament says that Jesus cried out at the ninth hour, everyone would have understood that this was during the middle of the day, halfway between noon (the sixth hour) and dusk (the twelfth hour).

The modern practice of dividing the day into twenty-four equal hours had long been preferred by astronomers. But for society as a whole to have embraced it is largely the result of mechanical expediency. A clock advances by equally spaced increments—it's the mechanical archetype for what Isaac Newton defined as "Absolute, true, and mathematical time [. . . which] without reference to anything external, flows uniformly and by another name

Figure 8.7: On this spring day (evident since the Sun is in Taurus), the Sun has advanced about halfway through the Eighth House of Heaven. This corresponds, roughly, to the ninth hour of the day. To convert from unequal hours to equal hours, look to where the "rule" or *index* of the astrolabe touches the outer rim. It's about 3 o'clock in the afternoon.

is called duration." By contrast, designing a clockwork mechanism around the system of unequal hours would have been complicated to the point of impracticality.

Yet in order for equal hours to become as intuitive as unequal hours had been, there needed to be a transition, and a way to translate between one system and the other. Luckily, a device already existed that was able to perform this translation visually: the astrolabe. This is why the earliest mechanical clocks, of which the one in Prague's old town square is the most magnificent example, had astrolabe-style faces (plate 12).

Illustrating how this translation was carried out gives us occasion to introduce the final component of an astrolabe. It's a simple pointer called the *index*, or "rule," and it functioned as the forerunner of the hour hand of a modern clock. By pointing the rule to the Sun's position on the ecliptic, both the unequal hour (indicated at the Sun's location) and the equal hour (indicated at the instrument's circumference) can be read at the same time.

That the development of the mechanical clock occurred precisely when the most intricate astrological algorithms were in vogue is a historical synchronicity too striking to ignore. Somehow astrologers and their patrons, no less than monks and metalsmiths, were responding to a world whose influences, they were convinced, needed to be tracked in finer and finer increments. In fact, the technological crossover between astrology and clock design was significant. The problem of drawing the unequal hour lines on an astrolabe-style clock turns out to be identical to the problem of dividing the Houses of Heaven. Indeed, what modern astrologers refer to as the Placidus method was the most common way of doing this, and Placidus-style cusps can be seen, albeit in a slightly modified form, as the hour lines on the astrolabe clock in Prague.

All of this extra complexity was considered necessary, at first, before people became comfortable with the much simpler design of a modern clock face. But traces of this transition can still be seen. For instance, it's expressly because clocks began as astrolabes that their hands rotate in the direction we now call clockwise. More subtly, life's inherent unpredictability ceases to be personified as Lady Luck spinning a wooden Wheel of Fortune, a visual trope whose roots reach back to the circular astrologers' boards of Roman times. I'm inclined to think this was because technology gave Fortune a much more compelling wheel to turn: the clock.

9

WHAT'S IN A NAME?
ASTRONOMERS, ASTROLOGERS,
AND MATHEMATICIANS

Herrevad Abbey, Denmark (now Sweden), 1572

The very first road and railway link joining Scandinavia to Western Europe was completed only recently, during the summer of the year 2000. It's a bridge and tunnel connecting Malmö, Sweden, on the eastern bank of the Øresund Sound, to Copenhagen, Denmark, roughly sixteen kilometers away on the western bank. Prior to the mid-1600s, however, both cities and both banks belonged to the kingdom of Denmark. Control of the Øresund allowed Denmark to regulate the lucrative trade of timber, furs, and amber shipped from the Hanseatic cities of the Baltic Sea to the North Sea harbors of England, the Low Countries, and points beyond. The kings of Denmark collected a tariff from all foreign ships passing through the Sound, upon penalty of being sunk by cannon fire. The most effective place to enforce these payments was, naturally, where the Sound was narrowest. This was a short distance north of Copenhagen, at the castle of Helsingør— or, as it's better known to the English-speaking world, Elsinore, the setting of Shakespeare's *Hamlet*.

The year 1572 saw Tycho Brahe back at the Danish court. Like Hamlet, he had been summoned home from his studies in Germany to attend upon the death of his father. Tycho (pronounced TEE-ko) was not, like Hamlet, the Prince of Denmark. But as the eldest son of one of Denmark's foremost feudal lords, Tycho was heir to a tremendous fortune, vast landholdings, and, along with his noble rank, an expectation that he would serve at the highest levels of state. Yet by all accounts, Tycho wanted nothing to do with Denmark's administration, its wars, its politics, or its pageantry.

For a nobleman like Tycho, the purpose of a university education was not to obtain a degree—that would have been unthinkably déclassé—but merely to pick up a little worldly polish of the sort that might prove serviceable in war and diplomacy. In this respect, Tycho's education backfired spectacularly. He returned from Germany utterly captivated by the latest advances in alchemy, astronomy, and astrology. He also returned missing most of his nose. One of the other Danish aristocrats at his university had hacked it off in a duel. The underlying grievance, it's said, was the mockery Tycho received for his astrological prediction of the Sultan of Turkey's death. (Embarrassingly for Tycho, it turned out that the sultan, Suleiman the Magnificent, had died several months beforehand.) For the rest of his life, Tycho would wear a metal prosthetic nose affixed to his face with salves and ointments. Whether it was of gold or silver or copper, the sources vary, and quite possibly he had different noses for different occasions. Far from a badge of dishonor, though, getting disfigured in a duel was probably the most socially acceptable thing Tycho did while at university. Certainly it would have been more understandable to his noble peers than his reputation for constructing clever astronomical instruments.

Returning home to Denmark seems to have exacerbated Tycho's naturally melancholic disposition. He did his best to avoid palace life altogether, taking up residence instead in a small, abandoned monastery on his family's land. (Just as in Henry VIII's England, the Protestant Reformation in Denmark entailed the dissolution of the monasteries and the confiscation of their property.) The remains of the old monastery, called Herrevad Abbey, can still be visited across the Sound from Helsingør, a short distance inland on the side that now belongs to Sweden.

At Herrevad Abbey, Tycho, then twenty-five years old, found a welcome seclusion to wrestle with the overriding worry of his young life: what was to become of him? Was it his duty to serve the Danish crown like his father and his father's father before him? Or could he follow the inclination of his heart and devote himself to the secrets of nature? To be, or not to be, an astronomer: that was Tycho's question. Whether Tycho was looking for a sign or not, one appeared to him all the same. It would change not only his conception of his own place in the universe, but science's conception of just what sort of place the universe really is.

As Tycho tells the story, it was a little before dinner when he went to check on some alchemy experiments he had left running in a house near the monastery. On his walk back, he took the opportunity, as he generally did, to observe the night sky. But that evening—it was the eleventh of November, 1572—he was surprised to see something shining overhead near the stars of the constellation Cassiopeia. And he didn't have to squint, either. Whatever it was, it glowed as brightly as the planet Venus, the brightest object in the night sky after the Moon. This was a most strange eruption, as Tycho noted in his characteristically intimidating style:

And since from boyhood I had known all of the stars in the sky perfectly (for there is no great difficulty in knowing this) it was obvious enough that no star had ever existed in that part of the sky before, not even a minuscule one, and certainly none of such conspicuous clarity.

What was it? What name could Tycho use to describe what he was seeing? According to the science of his day, any transitory phenomenon in the sky— and this included comets—had to be a "meteor." And by their very definition, meteors were atmospheric effects occurring somewhere between the Earth and the Moon. That such a phenomenon might occur beyond the Moon was an impossibility, for reasons that Tycho reviewed:

For it is established among all the philosophers, and the thing speaks for itself not unclearly, that in the ethereal region of the celestial universe, no change can occur by generation or decay. Instead, the heavens and the ethereal bodies contained within them neither increase nor decrease nor vary in number or size or brightness or by any other account. They remain forever the same, and similar to themselves in every respect, with the years scraping nothing away.

It's a humbling reminder of just how infrequently people look up at the stars that the only record Tycho could find of a similar observation was from Hipparchus, two thousand years earlier. And so unthinkable was the idea that the heavens could undergo any sort of alteration that subsequent astronomers were willing to dismiss even the great Hipparchus's testimony as merely a misidentified comet. Much closer to Tycho's time, during the eleventh and twelfth centuries, Chinese and Arabic astronomers had recorded three such cosmic apparitions, two of which were said to be so bright that they could be seen even during the day. Somehow, the astronomers of Europe had managed not to notice. Be that as it may, on this occasion there was nowhere in the world a more careful witness than Tycho Brahe.

Tycho immediately set about taking detailed astronomical observations using an instrument of his own design. He continued to do so until the object finally became too faint to see, some sixteen months later. Yet just those first few nights of observation were enough to convince Tycho of what he was looking at. This was no meteor. The complete absence of any measurable parallax meant that the object had to be situated far beyond the Moon. With supreme self-confidence, Tycho named it a *nova stella*—a new star.

In his enthusiasm, Tycho proclaimed that his star was a miracle of the sort not seen since Joshua's prayers had halted the Sun, or the darkening of the sky at Christ's crucifixion. In fact, systematic observation of the heavens would show that new stars, or novas, appear in the sky fairly regularly. Indeed, Johannes Kepler, Tycho's sometime assistant and collaborator, would spot another one in 1604.

In the 1930s, the astronomers Fritz Zwicky and Walter Baade recognized that phenomena of the sort observed by Tycho and Kepler were fundamentally different from other, less energetic types of novas, and so they

Figure 9.1: A Scheme of Heaven for Tuesday, November 11, 1572
Tycho Brahe Discovers a New Star

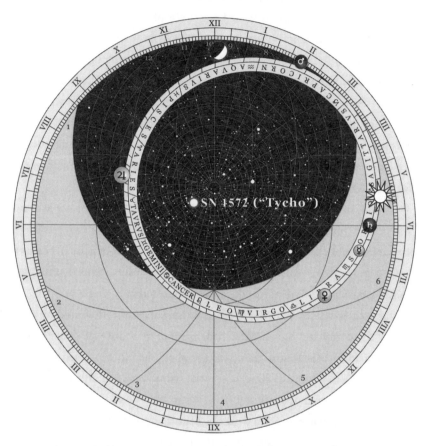

Herrevad Abbey, Denmark (now Sweden): 56°05'14"N, 13°14'00"E
JD: 2295546.17708
16:15 UT
ΔT: 134s
Local Time: 5:21 PM
Local Apparent Sidereal Time: 21:10

	λ	β	RA J2000	Dec J2000	Az	El	House
♄ Saturn	♏ 19°37'	2°00'	15ʰ 34ᵐ 59ˢ	-17°15'	260°58'	-12°57'	⑥ 16°53'
♃ Jupiter	♈ 21°03'↓	-1°28'	1ʰ 42ᵐ 25ˢ	9°04'	109°42'	20°51'	⑫ 7°57'
♂ Mars	♑ 17°27'	-1°23'	19ʰ 42ᵐ 11ˢ	-22°49'	206°04'	6°35'	⑦ 14°43'
☉ Sun	♏ 29°30'	0°00'	16ʰ 14ᵐ 12ˢ	-21°16'	250°47'	-11°21'	⑥ 17°59'
♀ Venus	♎ 16°55'	1°07'	13ʰ 26ᵐ 21ˢ	-7°53'	294°01'	-21°51'	⑥ 6°17'
☿ Mercury	♏ 9°43'	2°17'	14ʰ 55ᵐ 36ˢ	-14°22'	270°46'	-15°44'	⑥ 14°15'
☽ Moon	♒ 12°48'	-3°23'	21ʰ 29ᵐ 16ˢ	-18°26'	181°16'	13°39'	⑨ 24°47'

coined a new name: supernova. And as recently as 2008, astronomers finally confirmed that Tycho's new star was, more specifically, a Type Ia supernova. Thus, what Tycho witnessed wasn't the birth of a new star, but the ultra-violent death of an ancient star some 9,000 light-years away. It had most likely begun as one half of a binary star system. Then, after burning brightly for billions of years, it ran out of fuel and collapsed in on itself, becoming a super-dense white dwarf, perhaps no bigger in size than the Earth. At that stage, it began to feed upon its companion star until, reaching a critical pressure, the whole system detonated in a spectacular thermonuclear explosion that, for a few months at least, made it the brightest star in the Earth's night sky.

Today, supernovas and their remnants (plate 13) serve as cosmic beacons that help astronomers piece together a coherent story of the universe's age, size, and rate of expansion. Given the billions of trillions of stars in the universe, supernovas are quite rare, but, with modern observational techniques, it's not unusual for several hundred to be detected in a single year. In star catalogs, their names bear the prefix SN (for supernova) followed by their year of discovery and then a letter-code if more than one was detected in a given year. Thus, the official name for the phenomenon witnessed by Tycho is SN 1572. Considering its fame, however, astronomers usually call it Tycho's supernova or, even more casually, just "Tycho."

Tycho's supernova is of tremendous historical importance because it was the first detailed observation which the old cosmological framework simply could not explain away. Something was rotten in the state of astronomy indeed. Tycho's new star was a small crack in what had previously been considered a pristine crystalline firmament. There would be others—so many, in fact, that the entire system would soon collapse and shatter. It wasn't just the heavens which had proven themselves mutable. A revolution was underway, and science, philosophy, astronomy—and astrology—would never be the same.

A STAGE FOR ALL THE WORLD

Forget our own, comparatively languid times, or even the tumultuous twentieth century; when it comes to truly radical disruption, I'm not sure that any era can compare with the 1500s. Within a single fifty-year span, Columbus returned from the New World, Luther instigated the Protestant Reformation, and Copernicus published his argument that the Earth orbits the Sun. Suddenly it seemed possible to reimagine everything—new forms of government, new types of religion, even new arrangements of the universe itself. And all of this was amplified, as never before, by the recent invention of the printing press.

In gauging the impact of these new ideas, it's not unreasonable to look first to the era's most prominent voices. Shakespeare stands out in this regard not only for his fame but, even more pertinently here, because his plays contain spoken parts for an astounding 1,100-plus unique characters. Shakespeare is like a voice of voices, an almost one-man statistical sampling of the whole of Renaissance society. Indeed, as one of his most memorable characters, Hamlet, put it, the power of a good play is

> to hold, as 'twere, the mirror up to nature, to show virtue her own feature, scorn her own image, and the very age and body of the time his form and pressure.

The age and time inhabited by Shakespeare's characters was, to take them at their words, one brimming with astrology. Some characters seem trapped by the heavens' decrees, like those famously "star-cross'd lovers," Romeo and Juliet. Others rebel against the idea of a cosmic destiny, as when Cassius exhorts, "The fault, dear Brutus, is not in our stars, / But in ourselves." Yet whatever their words, and whatever their actions, Shakespeare's characters, from the roguish Ned Poins to the regal King Lear, know enough about astrology to pick up on their author's allusions. And so, presumably, would Shakespeare's audiences.

But did Shakespeare, or his personae, have anything to say about the revolution in astronomy which occurred during his lifetime? Certainly not directly. Yet in using astronomical terms such as "conjunctive," "opposition," and "retrograde," Shakespeare seems to have infused *Hamlet*, more so than any of his other plays, with cosmological overtones. Take, for instance, Hamlet's exclamation, "O God, I could be bounded in a nut shell and count myself a king of infinite space." It's difficult not to read in this a wink toward the idea, espoused by Copernicans like Giordano Bruno in Italy and Thomas Digges in England, that if the cosmos wasn't enclosed by a celestial sphere, then perhaps it extended infinitely outward. An even more arresting reference to the new astronomy is woven into Hamlet's love letter to Ophelia:

Doubt thou the stars are fire,
Doubt that the sun doth move,
Doubt truth to be a liar,
But never doubt I love.

Yet the most eyebrow-raising association of all isn't one of words but of names, because on a contemporary portrait of Tycho Brahe, two of the heraldic shields which proclaim his noble pedigree carry names that are shared by Hamlet's famously hapless schoolmates, Rosencrantz and Guildenstern (figure 9.2).

With all of these astral allusions, might there be more to the play than merely what it seems? One modern commentator has connected the drama's dots in such a way as to claim that the entire play is actually an elaborate astronomical allegory. (And who better to represent the false, geocentric universe of Claudius Ptolemy than Hamlet's uncle, the usurping King Claudius?) I enjoy this reading quite a bit, even if I don't find it very persuasive. Shakespeare was typically omnivorous in his influences, so a handful of astronomical references hardly amounts to a cosmological conspiracy. Besides, even if Shakespeare really did turn to Tycho's well-known portrait, maybe it was for no other reason than to find some good Danish-sounding names. But what higher praise can there be of the deeply layered nuance of Shake-

Figure 9.2: Jacques de Gheyn, portrait of the astronomer Tycho Brahe at the age of 40, 1586, copperplate engraving. In this portrait you can see the faint outline of Tycho's nasal prosthesis and two family names, Rosenkrans and Guldensteren, which may hint at a connection with Shakespeare's *Hamlet*. SMITHSONIAN INSTITUTION.

speare's prose than that—to a degree matched only by the complex orbits of the planets themselves—people have never stopped finding secret storylines hidden within it?

Hamlet was first performed on stage around the year 1600. It may seem surprising, then, for cosmological questions to play any role at all in the drama, given that Copernicus's book *On the Revolutions of the Heavenly*

Spheres (*De revolutionibus orbium coelestium*) had been in circulation for nearly sixty years at that point. In fact, it took several generations before Copernicus's heliocentric universe convincingly displaced its older, geocentric rival. Copernicus had worked out a mathematical model of a Sun-centered cosmos but, as a philosophical proposition, he hadn't advanced the argument much further than where it stood when Archimedes noted it in the third century BC.

Placing the Sun at the center of the universe offers an elegant solution to why the planets occasionally exhibit a backward, or retrograde, motion when viewed from the Earth. But Copernicus had no better answer than Ptolemy as to why the planets perform their forward motions with such uneven speeds. Nor could he explain why, if the Earth really was moving in a giant circle around the Sun, the shapes of the constellations didn't change with the seasons (that is, there was no observable stellar parallax). Most alarmingly of all, there still wasn't a halfway plausible explanation for why, if the Earth was whirling at incredible speeds around the Sun (once per year) and its own axis (once per day), everything that wasn't bolted down to the ground didn't get hurled off into space. Convincing answers to these questions would need to await Tycho's more accurate planetary observations (compiled by Kepler as the *Rudolphine Tables* in 1627), Kepler's realization that the orbits of the planets are ellipses, not circles (*Astronomia Nova*, 1609), Galileo's development of the laws of motion and inertia (*Two New Sciences*, 1638), and Newton's grand synthesis of physics and astronomy based on the law of universal gravitation (*Principia Mathematica*, 1687). Incredibly, there were no instruments precise enough to measure stellar parallax until Friedrich Bessel's observations of the star 61 Cygni in 1838.

In the meantime, people were left to wonder precisely where they stood, because the fundamental question was never about the Earth or the Sun but, rather, whether *man* was at the center of the universe. Tycho, who held radical positions on most of the issues of his day, nevertheless championed the spiritual traditions of Christian metaphysics when he penned this impassioned credo:

That this universal and most ample theater of the whole cosmic machine, O men of renown—the heavens, the Earth, the seas and what is contained within them: the Sun, the Moon, the stars, the animals, plants, and minerals—that these were created by the wisdom of the divine spirit, and established for the benefit and necessity not of Himself, but for man, whom He fashioned in likeness to His image, no one who is wise can object . . . [And man] He therefore placed on the Earth, at the center of the entire universe, so that from there he might contemplate, as if in a mirror, the composition and nature of the universal orb. And in this way he might, through bodies visible and created, recognize to some extent in this mortal life the majesty and wisdom of the invisible and incorporeal God.

Clearly Tycho's commitment to a geocentric cosmos ran much deeper than astronomical arguments alone. In fact, so central was the Earth's fixity to Tycho's philosophy that he proposed a compromise cosmology, one in which Mercury, Venus, Mars, Jupiter, and Saturn orbited the Sun, as in the Copernican system, but the Sun and Moon orbited the Earth, as in the Ptolemaic system. It sounds ungainly, and Tycho may have been the only person who ever thought otherwise, but the alternative was truly terrifying. If Copernicus was correct, and the Earth was just another planet like Mercury or Mars, to what extent could man be certain that he really was central to the act of creation? It's a melancholy thought, if ever there was one.

Today we are taught from childhood that the Earth is not the center of the universe, so it's difficult, if not impossible, to imagine just how dislocating it would be to learn this as an adult. Shakespeare's generation, however, would have had to deal with the psychological fallout of man's demoted status firsthand. If there's any cosmological subtext to be found in *Hamlet*, I think it is this. Look again at Tycho's declaration of man's place in the cosmos. It provides an almost perfect foil for Hamlet's famous lament to Rosencrantz and Guildenstern:

this goodly frame, the Earth, seems to me a sterile promontory; this most excellent canopy, the air, look you, this brave o'erhanging firmament, this majestical roof, fretted with golden fire—why, it appeareth nothing to me but a foul and pestilent congregation of vapors. What a piece of work is a man, how noble in reason, how infinite in faculties, in form and moving how express and admirable; in action how like an angel, in apprehension how like a god: the beauty of the world, the paragon of animals—and yet, to me, what is this quintessence of dust? Man delights not me, no, nor woman neither . . .

Whether by design or not, this speech could just as well express the gloom of an entire age bewildered at the loss of the old cosmic harmony. Yet however intriguing the suggestion, this may be as much as Shakespeare or any of his characters ever has to say about the matter.

WORDS, WORDS, WORDS

With regard to the opinions of his time, Shakespeare will never be more than an imperfect witness. He is, however, an impeccable source for its words. And a great many things can be learned about an idea simply from its words. This is especially true with astrology, which also happens to be the source for many of the most colorfully cosmic words and phrases in the English language, and many other languages too.

Even words as mundane as "consider" and "desire" are thought to have an astral origin—from the Latin word *sidus*, meaning "star." If so, then any honest consideration (*consideratio*) should properly entail a consultation of the stars, just as every true desire (*desideratio*) is really a wish upon a star. Whatever the etymologies of these words, it's undeniably the case that the Roman emperors, following the lead of Julius Caesar, had great desires of "becoming a star."

It was similarly during Roman times that the mixing of Hellenistic cosmology with Judaism colored, quite likely, the Talmudic notion of the seven heavens. These heavens, in turn, participated in a mystical, tenfold hierarchy of angels. Filtered through Islamic writers, this notion found its way into Dante's *Paradiso*, where to be in "seventh heaven"—that is, the sphere of Saturn—was a bliss reserved only for the most contemplative of souls.

Since, by the late Roman Empire, astrology had become the settled science of its day, the Talmudists frequently had cause to reference it. The technical term they adopted for a ruling planet or zodiac sign was *mazal*. Thus the expression "Mazal tov!" meaning "Congratulations!" literally translates to "Good zodiac sign!" with the sense of "May the ruling zodiac sign be favorable!" Of course, the alternative to having a good mazal is to have a bad mazal, which would make you a "schlimazl," a Yiddish word one occasionally sees in English. This condition was formerly known as being "starstruck," although today that term seems to be reserved solely for the shock of meeting a celebrity.

Yet for all the good that might come from a "lucky star" or "the stars aligning," the bad from a bad star was incomparably worse. It was literally a disaster (from Greek, *dys*, "bad" + *aster*, "star"), a word that appears quite ancient but is actually unattested before the Middle Ages. The disastrous influences of evil stars were to be avoided at all costs, not least because they were believed to corrupt the atmosphere, giving rise to the bad airs or "malarias" that caused diseases like the Black Plague. One especially nasty influence (or, to use the Italian word, *influenza*) was considered responsible for an outbreak of the influenza we now call the flu.

The influences of the stars gave each moment its characteristic, but fleeting qualities. Yet these same influences could leave a permanent mark on your personality if you received them at particularly critical moments, such as the moment you were born or, even more powerfully, the moment you were conceived. It was Saturn and its cosmic rays that made you "saturnine"; Jupiter made you "jovial"; Mars made you "martial"; Venus made you "venereal"; Mercury made you "mercurial"; and the Moon made you a "lunatic."

The words "martial"—having to do with war—and "venereal"—having to do with sex—are close enough to their namesake deities, Mars and Venus, to still align with their classical, pre-astrological meanings. Lunacy, or being "moonstruck," is likewise an ancient malady whose symptoms encompassed madness and, most characteristically, epilepsy. The other planetary adjectives, however, owe their meanings mainly to astrology. To an ancient Roman, for instance, similes involving Saturn were reserved for the Saturnian golden age or the merriment of their winter solstice festival, the Saturnalia—in other words, the exact opposite of the melancholy gloom conveyed by our modern, astrologically-influenced word "saturnine."

Melancholy was the acknowledged cause of Hamlet's moodiness, although he disguised it by pretending a "turbulent and dangerous lunacy." Hamlet, however, is hardly the only character whom Shakespeare describes in planetary terms. Shakespeare's plays are filled with astrological references, and so too are they filled with astrological words. Yet, surprisingly, there is one word that never appears anywhere in the entire corpus of Shakespeare's writings: "astrology." Shakespeare preferred the more poetic "star," "starry," "stars," and their variants, which occur nearly 150 times in his sonnets and plays. He does, however, make use of the word "astronomy," whose variants appear on four occasions: "astronomer" (*Cymbeline*, 3.2); "astronomers" (*Troilus and Cressida*, V.1); "astronomical" (*King Lear*, I.2); and in sonnet 14, which begins, "Not from the stars do I my judgment pluck; / And yet methinks I have astronomy . . ."

Shakespeare's meaning in each of these four instances is unambiguously astrological. In other words, every time Shakespeare says "astronomy," what he really means is "astrology." We saw much the same thing with Guido Bonatti's astrological *Ten Treatises on Astronomy* (*De astronomia tractatus x*). Were these careless slip-ups? An embarrassing case of mistaken identity? From a modern perspective, it can be quite disorienting to see how fluid and interchangeable these words used to be, especially since, today, we tend to picture the word "astronomy" standing in defiant opposition to the word "astrology," their different spellings proclaiming starkly different views about the universe and what makes it tick. And yet to look back, as in table 9.1, at the sources we've encountered in this book (together with a few others added in for good measure), it's clear that the histories of these two words are so tightly intertwined that neither can be fully untangled from the other.

Table 9.1: "Astronomy" and "Astrology" Through the Ages

		Source	Astrology	Astronomy	Astrologer(s)	Astronomer(s)
700 BC	cuneiform tablets		ṭupšarrūtu Enūma Anu Enlil		ṭupšar Enūma Anu Enlil	
550 BC	Isaiah	Hebrew Bible			hovrei shamayim	
380 BC	Plato	Republic		astronomy		astronomers
330 BC	Aristotle	Physics, Metaphysics On the Heavens		astrology		
220 BC	Archimedes	Sand Reckoner				astrologers
150 BC	Isaiah	Septuagint			astrologers	
44 BC	Cicero	On Divination	astrology		astrologers Chaldeans	
15	Manilius	Astronomica	astronomy			
60	Petronius	Satyricon		astronomy	mathematician	
100	Matthew	Gospel			magi	
150	Ptolemy	Almagest		mathematics		mathematicians
150	Ptolemy	Tetrabiblos	astronomy, mathematics genethlialogy		astrologers, mathematicians genethlialoger	
150	Ptolemy	Geography		meteoroscopy mathematics		
175	Vettius Valens	Anthologies	astronomy		astrologers	
600	Isidore	Etymologies	astrology	astronomy	astrologers, genethliacs, mathematicians, magi, horoscopes	
950	Ibn Hibinta	Fragment of Masha'allah's Astrological History	sena'at al-nujoom		al-monajjem	
1260	Albertus Magnus	Mirror of Astronomy	judicial astronomy	astronomy	astrologers	
1275	Bonatti	Ten Treatises on Astronomy	astronomy		astrologers	
1400	Chaucer	Canterbury Tales	astrology, astronomy		astrologer	
1543	Copernicus	On the Revolutions of the Heavenly Spheres		mathematics		mathematicians
1573	Tycho Brahe	On the New Star	astrology	mathematics astronomy	astrologers	mathematicians astronomers
1600	Shakespeare	Cymbeline, Lear, Troilus, sonnet 14	astronomy		astronomers	
1627	Kepler	Rudolphine Tables	astrology	astronomy	astrologers, genethliacs	astronomers

THE PITH AND MARROW OF ITS ATTRIBUTE

There's no question that the trajectories of these two words through time often overlapped. But does this really mean, as is so often claimed, that there was no difference at all between the words "astronomy" and "astrology" in the run-up to the scientific revolution? In many cases, it certainly seems that way. In Chaucer's *Canterbury Tales*, for example, the words "astronomy" and "astrology" each appear three times, with no obvious distinction between them.

To answer this question properly, though, it would be nice to know more about how often, and in what contexts, these two words were used at the time. Unfortunately, although an impressive number of medieval and Renaissance texts have now been photographically digitized, the optical character recognition on older documents remains quite poor, such that, in general, it's not possible to perform simple computerized word searches. (Incidentally, this is a problem that today's artificial vision algorithms can certainly handle, and presumably will over the next decade or so.) Nevertheless, if you're a fan of mathematical games and puzzles, then you've probably heard the mathematician George Polya's famous advice: If you can't solve a problem, then there is an easier problem you can solve—find it.

Allow me, then, to propose an easier problem. In place of the vague category of texts written prior to the scientific revolution, we can examine, instead, the well-defined category of books printed on a printing press before the year 1500. These special books are called *incunabula*, a Latin word which loosely translates to "cradle books." They're called this because they represent the earliest infancy of the publishing industry in the decades following Johannes Gutenberg's introduction of the printing press around the year 1450. Because of their historical significance, efforts to track down and catalog *incunabula* have been especially thorough. The Incunabula Short Title Catalogue (ISTC) of the British Library, for example, maintains a database of 30,518 editions, which, they claim, "records nearly every item printed from movable type before 1501."

Unfortunately, a global search for variants of the words "astronomy" and "astrology" in these texts is currently not feasible. As a cheap substitute, though, we can search through just the titles. The drawbacks to this are fairly obvious. For starters, a number of significant books will be excluded by this approach. Thus, neither Regiomontanus's *Epitome of the Almagest*, which was the most important astronomy book of the 1400s, nor his *Tables of Directions*, where he introduced his new system of astrological Houses, will be included in our sample, since neither has the correct key word in its title. On the flip side, however, this approach will include important works like Manilius's *Astronomica*. The first printed edition of this poem was published in 1473 by, of all people, Regiomontanus, who, as a side venture, set up the world's first scientific press in Nuremberg, Germany.

A more subtle problem with using just a title search is that the "short title" entries in the ISTC database often do not correspond with the full title of the work (some of which even interchange "astronomy" and "astrology"). For this reason, I've limited the sample to only those titles—still the majority—that can be verified by consulting a digitized facsimile or, in a few special cases, a physical copy. This results in a pared-down sample of twenty-eight titles, which, however, still presents a fascinating snapshot of astral writings from the late Middle Ages and early Renaissance.

To display how frequently our two classes of book title—"astronomy" vs. "astrology"—coincide with our two classes of subject matter—astronomy vs. astrology—these twenty-eight titles can be arranged into what's called a contingency table. Of course, some amount of subjectivity is unavoidable in deciding which book goes into which bin, but for the most part this proved to be surprisingly straightforward. My best effort to identify and sort a sample of titles is shown in table 9.2.

The first thing that jumps out from the contingency table is that there are a lot more books about astrology than astronomy (twenty-three vs. five). In this respect, maybe not much has changed over the last six hundred years. But unlike today, the astrology books are split right down the middle with respect to their titles: eleven "astronomy" vs. twelve "astrology." This certainly supports the contention that the words "astronomy" and "astrology" were indeed interchangeable, at least when it came to books about astrology. But the story looks quite different for the astronomy books. Here the split is

Table 9.2: Astronomy–Astrology Contingency Table for Fifteenth-Century Printed Books

	Subject Matter: *Astronomy*	Subject Matter: *Astrology*
Title Contains: Astronomy	Hyginus, *Poeticon astronomicon* (1482) • Alphonsus Rex Castellae, *Tabulae astronomicae* (1492) • Alfraganus, *Brevis compilatio totum id continens quod ad rudimenta astronomica est opportunum* (1493) • Petrus Cracoviensis, *Computus novus totius fere astronomiae fundamentum pulcerrimum continens* (1499) N = 4	Marcus Manilius, *Astronomicon* (1473) • Johannes de Brugis, *De veritate astronomiae* (1486) • Albumasar, *Introductorium in astronomiam* (1489) • Petrus de Aliaco, *Tractatus de legibus et sectis contra superstitiosos astronomos* (1489) • Petrus de Aliaco, *Concordantia astronomiae cum theologia* (1490) • Petrus de Aliaco, *Concordantia astronomiae cum hystorica narratione* (1490) • Guido Bonatus, *Decem tractatus astronomiae* (1491) • Albertus Magnus, *Liber de duabus sapientiis et de recapitulatione omnium librorum astronomiae* (1493) • Petrus Bonus Advogarius, *Astronomicon anni gratiae Mcccciiii* (1494) • Valerius Superchius, *De laudibus astronomiae oratio* (1498) • Firmicus Maternus, *Astronomicorum libri octo* (1499) N = 11
Title Contains: Astrology	Bonetus de Latis, *Anuli per eum compositi super astrologiam utilitates* (1492) N = 1	Johannes Gerson, *Trigilogium astrologiae theologistate* (1477) • Firminus de Bellavalle, *Opusculum repertorii pronosticon in mutationes aeris tam via astrologica quam metheorologica* (1485) • Hippocrates-Pseudo, *Libellus de medicorum astrologia* (1485) • Albumasar, *Tractatus florum astrologiae* (1488) • Johannes Eschuid, *Summa anglicana de astrologiae prognosticationibus* (1489) • Benedictus Ellwanger, *Iudicia vel prognostica astrologorum superstitiosa* (1490) • Johannes Baptista Abiosus, *Dialogus in astrologiae defensionem* (1494) • Johannes Picus Mirandulae, *Disputationum adversus astrologiam divinatricem* (1496) • Hieronymus Torrella, *Opus praeclarum de imaginibus astrologicis* (1496) • Hieronymo Savonarola, *Tractato contra li astrologi* (1497) • Lucius Bellantius, *De astrologica veritate* (1498) • Thomas Murner, *Invectiva contra astrologos* (1499) N = 12

four to one in favor of titles containing the word "astronomy." This suggests an added nuance, namely, that the word-swapping worked mainly one way, and that for purely astronomical topics, the term "astronomy" was predominant even during the 1400s.

This is an intriguing observation, and it may even be true. Unfortunately, from a statistics point of view, it's not possible to draw this conclusion confidently. Regardless of which statistical test you use, the number of books in our sample is just too small. Our scenario is roughly equivalent to flipping a coin five times and getting four heads and one tails. It's a result that may make you feel lucky, but it's not quite enough to convince you that your coin is special. If anything, you'll probably want to flip the coin some more times to see what happens next—which is exactly our case. To bring any sort of clarity to this question, we would need to add more examples to our table. Alas, absent the ability to search through these texts more thoroughly, we must leave the question as tantalizingly inconclusive as when we found it.

THE TIME IS OUT OF JOINT

Whatever the finer-grained subtleties, there's no denying that the boundary between the words "astronomy" and "astrology" was pretty blurry in the run-up to the scientific revolution. But why is this interesting? Most importantly, it's a reminder that the boundaries between the actual people involved, the individual astronomers and astrologers, remained every bit as blurry.

At the University of Bologna, for example, where Copernicus went to continue his studies, it was the responsibility of the professor of *astronomia* to publish, at the start of every year, an unabashedly astrological forecast called the *prognosticon*. These pamphlets outlined major celestial happenings, such as upcoming conjunctions and eclipses, alongside predictions about the weather, politics, the economy, plagues, and various social trends. In 1487, for instance, women were predicted to be particularly frisky due to the influence of the planet Venus.

Astrological *prognostica*, which are the ancestors of our modern-day almanacs, quickly became a staple of the early printing houses. Indeed, astrology and the Bible have been the two constants of the publishing indus-try ever since its inception. The more astronomical counterpart to the *prog-nosticon*, and often authored by the same university astronomer–astrologers, was a publication called the *computus*, meaning "the computation." These booklets provided tables and algorithms for computing the cycles of the Sun and Moon, specifically as they pertained to determining the dates of Easter and the other "moveable feasts" of the year.

The major factor that kept these competing *computi* in print was that, by the fifteenth century, the rules for computing Easter had become increas-ingly confusing. The problem was that the Julian calendar year of 365.25 days is slightly longer than the actual solar year, as measured from equinox to equinox. Thus, year by year, the astronomical spring equinox was sneaking further and further ahead of March 21, which was the Church-sanctioned equinox date used for selecting Easter Sunday.

Addressing this mismatch was always more of a political problem than an astronomical one, and it wasn't until the 1570s that a compelling com-promise was put forward. This proposal, drafted by a certain Aloysius Lilius, was circulated in a document addressed in bold letters: "To the Expert Math-ematicians" (*PERITIS MATHEMATICIS*). Elsewhere in his proposal, Lilius referred to these same savants as the "expert astrologers" (*peritis astrologis*).

After some debate, Lilius's plan was adopted by the Catholic Church, and so, by the decree of Pope Gregory XIII, Thursday, October 4, 1582, was immediately followed by Friday, October 15, 1582. The intervening ten days simply never happened. This disruptive beginning to the new "Gregorian" calendar, named for its papal patron, was a one-time fix meant to bring the spring equinox back to its nominal date of March 21. Then, moving forward, the length of the Gregorian year would be shortened by the following scheme: every fourth year is a leap year, unless that year is divisible by 100, unless that year is also divisible by 400. Thus 1900 wasn't a leap year, and 2100 won't be a leap year but, as those of us who experienced the calendrical confusion of the millennium may recall, the year 2000 *was* a leap year.

The effect of having only ninety-seven leap years every four hundred years is to reduce the length of the average year to $365 + (97/400) = 365.2425$ days, or

365 days, 5 hours, 49 minutes, and 12 seconds. How close is this to the actual length of the year? Well, it turns out that it's not possible to assign a definitive length to the year in terms of days, since the Earth's rotation is gradually but unevenly slowing down, which means the length of a day is gradually but unevenly getting longer. Duly noting this, the average duration from spring equinox to spring equinox is currently about 365.242374 days, or 365 days, 5 hours, 49 minutes, and 1 second. We can all rest easy, then, knowing that the Gregorian calendar is not expected to gain or lose a day with respect to the astronomical spring equinox for several thousand more years.

Today, the Gregorian calendar is recognized as the standard civil calendar the world over. However, because it was initially conceived within the Roman Catholic Church, the non-Catholic countries at first resisted it, in some cases for an extraordinarily long time. Britain and her colonies didn't switch over until 1752, at which point the Gregorian–Julian discrepancy had grown to eleven days. Most of Eastern Europe, meanwhile, remained on the Julian calendar well into the twentieth century. This is why, for example, as far as the Western world is concerned, Russia's "October Revolution" of 1917 actually occurred in November.

Copernicus cited the prospect of a more accurate calendar as one reason why he hoped (quite wrongly) that his new, Sun-centered theory of the universe might be well received by the Church. In the meantime, it was expressly to avoid any calendrical confusion that Copernicus, following the example of Ptolemy's *Almagest*, used the ancient Egyptian year of a clean 365 days—and no fractions—for his calculations.

For this same reason, modern astronomers also use a simplified calendar for long-term orbit computations. It involves nothing more than tallying the days from a (mostly) arbitrary start date of Monday, January 1, 4713 BC. This day-count is called the Julian Day, denoted JD. It's an unfortunate name, since it's easily confused with the Julian calendar, from which it was derived. However, the Julian Day and Julian calendar exist independently from each other. This scheme and its strange start date were originally proposed, albeit in a slightly altered form, by Joseph Scaliger in 1583 in a book entitled *On the Emendation of Times* (*De emendatione temporum*). To give an example of its use, January 1, 2000, is JD 2451545—a nice reminder that all of recorded history consists of not much more than two million days. Minus a small correction for changes in the Earth's rotation (denoted ΔT), the Julian Day is the only temporal input needed to compute the schemes of heaven which appear in this book.

Employing the ancient Egyptian calendar wasn't the only way in which Copernicus consciously modeled his *De revolutionibus* after Ptolemy's *Almagest*. He consistently eschewed words like "astronomy" and "astronomer" in favor of the Ptolemaic terms "mathematics" and "mathematician." Thus his famous line, often translated as "Astronomy is written for astronomers," is more accurately rendered as "Mathematics is written for mathematicians" (*Mathemata mathematicis scribuntur*). Whatever its translation, this little quip was hardly enough to deflect the theological and cosmological uproar Copernicus knew his book would incite. Instead, Copernicus adopted a more definitive strategy of conflict avoidance, which was to delay publication until 1543, the same year he died peacefully of old age.

It's easy to overlook, but the appearance of the *De revolutionibus* didn't mark the end of the controversy about whether the Earth orbits the Sun. On the contrary, it signaled the beginning. And just as with the old and new calendars, the old astronomy and its lingo lingered on with the new for much longer than one might otherwise suppose. For example, Tycho's account of the supernova of 1572 consisted only partly of an astronomical analysis, or what he called a "mathematical contemplation" (*contemplatio mathematica*). Appended to it was an "astrological judgment" (*astrologicum iudicium*), in which Tycho forecast worldwide upheavals of the sort not seen since Christ's birth and the rise of the Roman Empire.

In fact, many of the most forward-looking thinkers of the 1500s and 1600s mixed their astronomy, astrology, and mathematics together. And many believed that astrology, stripped of the superstitious algorithms of judicial astrology, could be recast as a respectable science. Tycho, who often referred to "both astrologies"—a reference to Ptolemy's distinction between "general" and "genethlialogical" astrology—proposed a detailed scheme for correlating planetary and weather observations. Johannes Kepler suggested that astrology should be reduced to solely a consideration of planetary aspects. And Girolamo Cardano, who is best known today as a mathematician, compiled a list of horoscopic case studies, much like Vettius Valens before him.

Even the *Rudolphine Tables*, Kepler's monumental astronomical tables based on Tycho's observations and his own newly discovered laws of planetary motion, included a section on how to cast horoscopes. Incredibly, for a work that is today regarded as one of the crowning achievements of the scientific revolution, Kepler acknowledged that astrology was likely the only reason why most people would consult his *Tables* at all!

Kepler had reason to know. Following Tycho's death in 1601, Kepler succeeded his sometime patron, sometime collaborator, and sometime rival as Imperial Mathematician to the Holy Roman Emperor Rudolph II in Prague (the emperor for whom the *Rudolphine Tables* are named). Of course, the role of the Imperial Mathematician wasn't to solve math problems. "The job of a *mathematicus*," as Kepler noted, ". . . is to write the annual *prognostica*"— which, indeed, Kepler did for many years.

Did Kepler believe in astrology? His private papers contain a mind-boggling collection of over one thousand horoscopes cast with his own hand. And as a younger man, he scrutinized the horoscope of his newborn son with all sincerity. Yet by the time he completed the *Rudolphine Tables* in 1627, just a few years before his death, his exasperation with the "dreams and nonsense of horoscopic predictions" appears to be total. Johannes Kepler, the genius who discovered the three laws of planetary motion in Tycho's scattered data, was unable to find any pattern at all in all the horoscopes he cast. It wasn't for lack of trying.

Despite its relatively late publication, the *Rudolphine Tables* may also be the first major work to explicitly differentiate "astronomy" and "astrology" along the lines we know them by today. Kepler states that both were originally known by one name, *astrologia*, but that they were now separate enterprises deserving of the separate names which "later usage" had given them. Yet, while Kepler is clear that astronomy had finally outgrown its astrological infancy, he insists that astronomy cannot deny its astrological origins any more than a daughter can deny her own mother. Their relationship is too obvious in the observations, instruments, and calculations which the one has passed down to the other. For Kepler, therefore, setting aside a section of his astronomical *Tables* for astrology was simply an act of filial devotion. Otherwise, mother astrology might "complain that she has been abandoned and scorned by her ungrateful and arrogant daughter," astronomy. Coming from Kepler, this is an especially poignant metaphor. He wrote those words shortly after spending six agonizing years defending his own mother in court against a capital charge of witchcraft.

The *Rudolphine Tables* illustrate that even as late as the 1620s, astronomy and astrology were just beginning to go their separate ways. Professionally, the differences would hardly have been noticeable. Take a look, for example, at Johannes Vermeer's famous painting *The Astronomer* (plate 14). The sitter's profession is indicated by two instruments: a celestial globe and, lying flat on the table, an astrolabe. The portrait was painted in 1668—nearly forty years after Kepler's death—but these are the same two instruments that would have signified any astronomer–astrologer from the time of Ptolemy. What's conspicuously not present is the recently invented telescope. If, as many have argued, Vermeer used lenses and mirrors while painting, then we have to acknowledge the historical irony that even well into the seventeenth century, a painter might employ more advanced optics than an astronomer.

The development of the telescope as an instrument to investigate the heavens is due, of course, to Galileo (who, like Kepler, was astrologically curious enough to cast horoscopes for his own children). The telescope rightly symbolizes astronomy's emancipation from astrology. It embodies both the new questions astronomy was asking and the new approaches being used to answer them. Hamlet was right: there are more things in heaven and Earth than had been dreamt of in anyone's philosophy. And it was through the telescope that the truth of these words became visible, at last, to anyone who cared to look.

10

BIG ASTROLOGY

Mare Tranquillitatis, the Moon, 1969

Opening the forward hatch of Apollo 11's lunar module, commander Neil Armstrong descended the ladder to a dusty patch within a large, featureless region of the Moon's surface called *Mare Tranquillitatis*, "The Sea of Tranquility." At mission timestamp 109:24:15—corresponding, in Eastern Daylight Time, to Sunday, July 20, 10:56 p.m. and fifteen seconds—Armstrong's boot made contact with the Moon. For the very first time in the history of our species, a human being had set foot on another world. "That's one small step for man, one giant leap for mankind." Armstrong's words at that moment left nothing unsaid.

The Apollo 11 Moon landing answered the hopes of a thousand generations of stargazers and cosmic dreamers. It was a voyage which astronomy and astrology had begun together. For millennia, astrology had provided the primary motivation for improving the accuracy of planetary observations. But, like the first stage of the Apollo spacecraft's Saturn V rocket, once its contribution was spent, it became a dead weight that needed to be jettisoned in order to enable any further ascent.

And what an ascent it was. Apollo 11 will forever be remembered as a marvel of engineering, organization, and vision. And its success demonstrated that sophisticated astronomical models were capable of predicting certain types of future events, like the positions and forces between the Earth and the Moon, to an almost unbelievable level of precision. Meanwhile, back on Earth, astrology was riding the crest of a popular revival, so much so that its global appeal at that moment was likely greater than it had ever been at any time in the past. Who could have predicted that?

OCCULTATION

In astronomical observations, it sometimes happens that your line of sight to a star, planet, or satellite gets blocked by the passage of another celestial body. This is called occultation. In an analogous fashion, the rise of the new astronomy during the 1600s, and the increasing brilliance of each new telescopic discovery, caused astrology to dim by comparison. It wasn't that astrology was inherently incompatible with these new developments. At a much more basic level, astrology was exhausted. Despite centuries of earnest searching, seventeenth-century astrologers could not point to a single unequivocal correlation between the planets' positions and anyone's personal destiny. Meanwhile, for the very first time, those who loved numbers had options. The burgeoning professions of surveying, cartography, banking, insurance, and, of course, astronomy all needed mathematicians. Petrarch's friend, the reluctant astrologer Maino Maineri, could only have sighed in envy.

Even the astrological almanac trade, which had been astrology's most public medium, likewise culminated during the 1600s. At mid-century, the astrologer William Lilly had become a meteoric publishing sensation by seeming to predict—and encourage—the victories of Parliament during the English Civil War. (Recall that it's through Lilly's lively writing that a horoscope can become, more grandly, a "scheme of heaven.") But politics, in the long run, has a way of making fools of its forecasters, be they seventeenth-century astrologers casting horoscopes or twenty-first-century analysts running sophisticated statistical models.

As discord turned to revolution, revolution led to regicide, regicide inaugurated a republic, and the republic reverted to one-man rule, Lilly's alma-

Figure 10.1: A Scheme of Heaven for Sunday, July 20, 1969
Neil Armstrong Sets Foot on the Moon

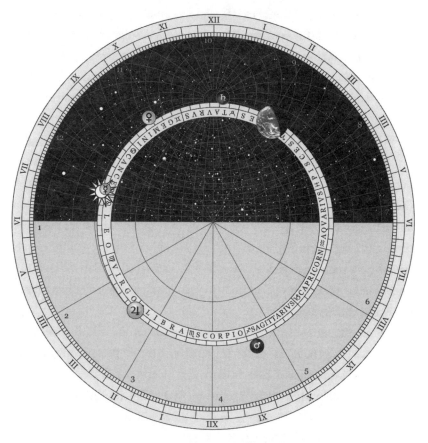

Mare Tranquillitatis, The Moon: 0°41'15"N, 23°26'00"E
JD: 2440423.62240
2:56:15 UTC
ΔT: 40s
Eastern Daylight Time: 10:56:15 PM
Local Apparent Sidereal Time: 2:52

		λ	β	RA J2000	Dec J2000	Az	El	House	
♄ Saturn	♉	8°31'	-2°25'	2ʰ 27ᵐ 47ˢ	12°02'	242°40'	85°31'	⑨	26°01'
♃ Jupiter	♎	1°12'	1°13'	12ʰ 06ᵐ 22ˢ	0°38'	87°36'	-48°39'	②	18°40'
♂ Mars	♐	3°26'	-3°23'	16ʰ 02ᵐ 49ˢ	-24°10'	258°22'	-68°45'	④	20°50'
☉ Sun	♋	28°27'	0°00'	8ʰ 02ᵐ 19ˢ	20°28'	88°50'	14°05'	⑫	15°54'
♀ Venus	♊	15°37'	-2°25'	4ʰ 58ᵐ 43ˢ	20°14'	92°43'	56°52'	⑪	3°06'
☿ Mercury	♋	26°45'	1°29'	7ʰ 56ᵐ 23ˢ	22°16'	87°16'	15°46'	⑫	14°12'
⊕ Earth	♈	11°42'	1°40'	0ʰ 40ᵐ 25ˢ	6°10'	272°57'	59°05'	⑧	29°07'

nacs somehow managed to stay one step ahead. Yet the subsequent turn of events—the collapse of the Protectorate and the restoration of King Charles II in 1660—was something that Lilly simply could not or would not foresee. The magnitude of this epoch-making episode was so great, Lilly protested, that no one could have predicted it. It had been an act "above nature." Sales of Lilly's almanac, which had peaked at 30,000 copies per year during the 1650s, quickly slumped and never recovered. At least the seventeenth-century public, it can be said to their credit, didn't hesitate to dump their underperforming political prognosticators.

Whether regarded as a high-minded endeavor or merely as a platform for popular superstition, astrology's visibility diminished significantly during the eighteenth and nineteenth centuries. But a celestial body in occultation doesn't cease to exist. It's still there, ready to reappear whenever the object that's blocking it gets displaced. And sure enough, by the turn of the twentieth century, there were plenty of people who had grown dissatisfied with the unchecked advances of science, industry, and that new breed of know-it-alls known by the newly coined name of "scientist."

Of all the anti-science movements to emerge, the one that seems to me to have been the most successful, in no small part because its influence remains so poorly known, held its inaugural meeting on November 17, 1875, in a lecture hall at 64 Madison Avenue in New York City. This was the birth of the Theosophical Society, the brainchild of a Russian-born spiritualist named Helena Petrovna Blavatsky.

Like previous mystic groups, the theosophists claimed that all of the world's religions, and all of science's recent discoveries, were merely the superficial expressions of an ancient wisdom whose deeper truths had been purposefully kept hidden from an unready world. What made theosophy new and different, however, was that into the usual stew of Kabbalistic, Pythagorean, and Neoplatonist teachings, Blavatsky added a heaping spoonful of Hindu and Buddhist notions, which had only recently been introduced to the West. But how to make sense of it all? Miraculously, Blavatsky claimed to have access to a secret book written in a secret language which revealed, at long last, the hidden connections between man and the cosmos. It thus became Blavatsky's calling, and the calling of the Theosophical Society, to reconstitute these ancient truths and to prepare the world for the "Dawn of the New Cycle," which, she prophesied, would begin sometime in the early twentieth century.

Theosophy's message was timely. Given the choice between the soulless, machinelike universe of Western science and the dogmatic certainties of Western religion, many people increasingly opted for neither. Theosophy promised an appealing way out: science and spirituality could be reconciled, but the path for doing so led to the East. To the theosophists, therefore, the Christian literalists were just as blinkered as the scientists who insisted that the universe was nothing more than matter in motion, and that man was nothing more than a Darwinian descendant of apes. In her magnum opus, *The Secret Doctrine: The Synthesis of Science, Religion, and Philosophy*, Blavatsky neatly summarized her assumptions:

> The aim of this work may be thus stated: to show that Nature is not "a fortuitous concurrence of atoms," and to assign to man his rightful place in the scheme of the Universe; to rescue from degradation the archaic truths which are the basis of all religions; and to uncover, to some extent, the fundamental unity from which they all spring; finally, to show that the occult side of Nature has never been approached by the Science of modern civilization.

Prominent among the "archaic truths" which Blavatsky wished to "rescue from degradation," there was one whose practice in both India and the West seemed, at least to Blavatsky, to offer evidence not of the cultural exchange of ideas, but rather of a shared primordial heritage: astrology. And whether Blavatsky could foresee it or not, mixing theosophy and astrology together would precipitate a radical transmutation of astrology's character, reshaping it into the form we recognize today. The individual most responsible for this change was an English astrologer and theosophist named William Frederick Allan—or, to use the zodiacal pen name by which he's chiefly known, Alan Leo.

It was Leo who, more than anyone, shifted astrology's focus away from predictions in the material world and toward an elucidation of an individual's changing states of consciousness. Moreover, according to Leo, the best way to forecast how someone's inner cosmos would respond to changes in the outer universe was to examine that person's "Sun sign." This is your zodiac sign as you know it today, meaning the zodiac sign of the Sun on your birthday. Traditionally, as we've discussed throughout this book, the Sun sign was only one quantity among many that went into a birth horoscope, and by no means the most important. All of this changed with Alan Leo. As Nicholas Campion, a historian of astrology and formerly the astrologer for the U.K.'s *Daily Mail*, writes, Alan Leo "embarked on a programme of deliberate invention without which modern astrology would be simply unrecognizable."

From Alan Leo's astrological improvisations, it was a quick progression to today's familiar format. There were two major milestones along the way, the first of which is well established. On August 24, 1930, the *Sunday Express* in London became the first modern newspaper to publish a horoscope. It was a birth chart for the newborn Princess Margaret (younger sister to Queen Elizabeth), cast by the astrologer Richard Harold Naylor.

There's always an exhilarating instant of surprise whenever predictions, however vague, appear to be vindicated by subsequent events, however charitably selected. Thus, no account of Margaret's horoscope can ever omit the following premonition: "Events of tremendous importance to the Royal Family and the nation will come about near her seventh year (1937), and these events will indirectly affect her own fortunes." Sure enough, Margaret's uncle, Edward VIII, abdicated the throne in 1936, which made Margaret's father King George VI, Margaret's sister, Elizabeth, heir to the throne, and Margaret herself second in line. As for Naylor's other specific predictions—"In the course of life there will probably be some minor injury to the face or head," and, "She will marry rather suddenly, about the twenty-fourth or twenty-sixth year, but as the result of an attachment of long standing"—well, now, who wants to ruin the fun by bringing these up?

Naylor's forecast proved popular enough for the *Sunday Express* to reward him with a regular column. Yet however trend-setting his horoscope was, Naylor's accompanying, hand-sketched scheme remained remarkably old-fashioned. Just like Cardano's horoscope for King Henry VIII, Naylor's birth chart for Princess Margaret displayed the configuration of the planets and zodiac signs within the twelve Houses of Heaven at the precise time and place of her birth. But this highly personalized format was hardly suited for a mass readership. Royal babies notwithstanding, there would simply never be enough celebrity infants to fill up a weekly column this way. The solution to this problem, and the final milestone on the road to today's astrology, was the development of the popular twelve-paragraph horoscope arranged according to zodiac sign.

It's not entirely clear who first invented this format. Nicholas Campion traces it to a Detroit-based magazine of the 1930s called *Modern Astrology* and the influence of the theosophically inspired "transpersonal astrologer" Dane Rudhyar. Whatever its origins, the format spread rapidly, and newspaper astrologers had begun incorporating it into their columns by the end of the decade.

For the publishing industry, the twelve-paragraph horoscope was an instant classic. The simplified format proved a perfect fit for print-based mass media, striking just the right balance between specificity and generality. It's fascinating to consider, but a single blanket prediction addressed to the whole world would surely have been rejected by readers as too impersonal. Yet splitting humanity up into just twelve factions is, apparently, enough to establish an enduring sense of group identity. Would seven groups have worked? Or fifty? Who knows? But the stunning success of the twelve-sign system speaks for itself. No matter how silly or how serious you think it is, unless you've been living under a rock your whole life, you almost certainly know your zodiac sign. From a marketing perspective, therefore, the simple switch to Sun signs has made astrology's brand-awareness practically total.

But the introduction of a new and popular format does not, by itself, fully account for why astrology became so popular during the twentieth century. A more complete explanation, I believe, would note that astrology was merely one star among many within a larger and tremendously popular constellation: the rejection of materialism. By materialism, I don't mean the idea that we buy too much stuff (however true this may be), but rather the metaphysical stance, in the tradition of thinkers like Lucretius, that the universe consists of nothing more than matter in motion and is devoid of spiritual causes and effects. Or, to spell out the implications of materialism more bluntly, that there is no God, or gods, or goddesses, in whatever form you may imagine He, She, It, or They to be.

The usual opponent of materialism had always been organized religion. But the serious rattling religion received during the nineteenth century created a void into which new ideas, as well as old ideas repackaged in new forms, could emerge. Off to one side, movements like Marxism doubled down on a radically materialist stance. Meanwhile, there's a strong case to be made that the earliest, the best organized, and the most influential movement to rally the misfit strands of spirituality outside of organized religion was theosophy.

Figure 10.2: Seal of the Theosophical Society. *The Theosophist* 29, 1908.

Although the original Theosophical Society of Madame Blavatsky splintered after her death in 1891, it's difficult to overstate the influence her followers have had on the intellectual currents of the twentieth and twenty-first centuries. Most immediately, the theosophists were at the forefront of popularizing Buddhism and Eastern meditation practices in the West. Less directly, and in a much more sinister vein, Blavatsky's fixation with the spiritual destiny of the "Aryan fifth root-race" (descendants, she claimed, of the inhabitants of Atlantis) exerted an undeniable influence via occultist groups like the Thule Society on the ideology of Nazism.

But far and away the most significant legacy of theosophy was to implant the idea that a spiritual revolution was imminent, one that would overthrow the materialist understanding of the world and usher in a New

Age in which the mystic intuitions of antiquity—astrology included—would be vindicated by a new and spiritual science. This was a sentiment which galvanized more than just daydreamers and soul-searchers. Artists especially felt called to form the vanguard of this uprising. No less a painter than Wassily Kandinsky, for instance, speaks in explicitly these terms and praises the Theosophical Society by name in his modernist manifesto, *Concerning the Spiritual in Art.*

In sympathy with modernism's wild spasms of color, the vision of a New Age is a proposition that either compels, or fails to compel, holistically. Its broad and provocative brushstrokes are the message. The content of any individual detail, viewed up close, is irrelevant. In this regard, astrology might be true, or it might be false, but symbolically it serves as a shorthand for acknowledging a nonmaterial plane of existence. And insofar as many twentieth-century artists did not feel obligated to respect a strict correspondence between symbols and their literal meanings—indeed, just the opposite—astrology can pop up, perhaps for no fixed reason at all, in a sculpture by Max Ernst, a poem by Sylvia Plath, or the jazz of John Coltrane.

Whatever such artists may have wanted to say with astrology, the cumulative effect of their creations has been to deepen astrology's resonances in our culture. My own favorite example of this is Gustav Holst's *The Planets.* Holst conceived the musical sweep of this composition in a burst of enthusiasm after a friend introduced him to astrology. He even purchased a copy of Alan Leo's *What Is a Horoscope and How Is It Cast?* for psychological insights into each planet's character. And although one less-than-impressed critic has described the resulting music as "a banal thumpety-thump 1916 ooze orgy," the suite is still widely performed, widely recorded, and also widely referenced in modern movie scores. Most famously of all, the ostinato, or "thumpety-thump," in "Mars, the Bringer of War," echoes throughout John Williams' soundtrack to the *Star Wars* films. In fact, a few bars can be heard almost note for note in the opening minutes of the original 1977 movie.

OH THE WEATHER OUTSIDE IS . . . RADIOACTIVE?

New Age influences in pop culture are pretty easy to find, once you know where to look. But New Age influences in science? Madame Blavatsky threw down the gauntlet when she wrote, "the occult side of Nature has never been approached by the Science of modern civilization." Would anyone rise to the challenge?

In fact, throughout the twentieth century, plenty of scientists set out to soberly examine occult phenomena such as telekinesis, precognition, and extra-sensory perception (ESP). And quite a few of these studies were pursued at the world's most prestigious research universities. Remarkably, one of the last redoubts of this type of work, the Princeton Engineering Anomalies Research laboratory, or PEAR, only closed up shop in 2007.

But so long as science based its findings on the measurable universe only, why should its conclusions have any validity in the unmeasurable universe beyond? The proper guide to the New Age cosmos, therefore, could never be the scientist. It had to be someone more spiritually sensitive—someone much more like a shaman.

Not surprisingly, there were not many professional scientists eager to abandon a hard-won allegiance to skepticism, empiricism, and objectivity in favor of what was, essentially, a vision of science as séance. I say "not many," however, since there were certainly some who proved all too happy to affect an otherworldly persona. Yet I can think of only one whose scientific prestige, such as it was, could be said to derive expressly from his excursions into the occult. This was the Swiss psychoanalyst Carl Jung, whose blurring of the boundaries between science and shamanism left a legacy of encouraging, and to some extent legitimizing, the ideals of the New Age within the scientific mainstream.

Jung had been fascinated by spiritualism even before he began his medical practice. But to the horror of his sometime mentor Sigmund Freud, Jung started to see occult traditions like astrology as holding the key to unlocking the unconscious mind. In a letter to Freud dated June 12, 1911, Jung laid bare his thinking:

My evenings are taken up very largely with astrology. I make horoscopic calculations in order to find a clue to the core of psychological truth. Some remarkable things have turned up which will certainly appear incredible to you . . . I dare say that we shall one day discover in astrology a good deal of knowledge that has been intuitively projected into the heavens. For instance, it appears that the signs of the zodiac are character pictures, in other words libido symbols which depict the typical qualities of the libido at a given moment.

This is essentially a restatement of Alan Leo's psychological astrology, albeit couched in more sophisticated language. Yet, far from a youthful extravagance, Jung's enthusiasm for astrology only deepened during his career, influencing his theory of synchronicity and buttressing his later conviction that "astrology represents the summation of all the psychological knowledge of antiquity."

Taken at face value, Jung's astrological writings would seem to suggest that nobody can become a competent psychoanalyst without first becoming an expert astrologer. I very much doubt that this is a widely held opinion among professional therapists today. Yet the converse opinion—that every good astrologer must also be a good psychoanalyst—is pretty much the default among modern astrologers and their clients alike. For the professional astrologer, this represents a tremendous job promotion. A classical astrologer was, first and foremost, a human calculator, one whose most important qualification was his ability to solve long and tedious mathematical equations. By contrast, the modern astrologer is billed as a full-fledged spiritual guide, one whose chief professional claim is a heightened intuition into the psychic vibrations of the cosmos.

Modern astrology, which is profoundly influenced by Jung, took the hint that in order to thrive in the New Age, it had an opportunity to reinvent itself as a spiritual science. The physical sciences, meanwhile, never did find any use for their would-be shamans. On the contrary, it was through the traditional methods of careful observation and testing that science was opening up new and unimagined vistas into the unknown. Or, to put it another way, twentieth-century science was getting weird enough on its own without having to channel the occult. Leading the way was physics. The dual developments of relativity and quantum mechanics forced a radical rethinking of space, time, matter, and measurement. And, to top it all off, there was the serendipitous discovery which needed both relativity and quantum mechanics to explain, and which, to a remarkable degree, has determined the direction of physics research ever since. This was the discovery of ionizing radiation, meaning radiation that is powerful enough to break apart matter.

Nothing like it had ever been seen before—that much scientists could agree upon. The Nobel Committee of 1901, therefore, didn't have to think too hard about who should receive their very first prize in physics; it went to Wilhelm Roentgen for his discovery of X-rays and their supernatural-seeming ability to image his bones straight through his skin. In quick succession, Henri Becquerel, and then Marie and Pierre Curie, found a similar but spontaneous behavior in uranium, radium, polonium, and other exotic elements hauled up from the mines. Yet it's not down into the Earth, but up toward the heavens that our story will take us. Because no matter how diligently these researchers shielded their radioactive sources, some amount of ionizing radiation could always be measured. Where was it coming from?

A surprising answer arrived in 1912, via hot-air balloon, and courtesy of an Austrian physicist named Victor Hess. Contrary to all expectations, Hess detected higher and higher radiation levels the higher he and his balloon ascended. Thunderstorms and other atmospheric processes were quickly ruled out. Whatever this anomalous radiation was, it wasn't coming from the Earth. A new name soon summed up all that was known at the time: Earth was being bombarded by "cosmic rays."

The discovery of cosmic rays was only the latest and strangest indication that space was a lot less empty—and a lot more violent—than had once been believed. Starting with Tycho's supernova in 1572, astronomers had been crowding the cosmos with an ever-expanding cast of unexpected entities. Most dramatically of all, two enormous and entirely new planets were detected beyond Saturn: Uranus, in 1781, and Neptune, in 1846.

An additional gas giant named Planet X was, for a time, hypothesized to account for some quirks in the orbits of Neptune and Uranus. When Pluto was discovered in 1930, it was initially assumed to be this predicted, large, ninth planet. Subsequent observations, however, revealed that Pluto wasn't massive at all. In fact, it's smaller than its fellow Kuiper belt object Eris, and only about fourteen times heavier than Ceres, the largest of the asteroids. And so, in 2006, the International Astronomical Union voted to demote Pluto to a "dwarf planet," making it merely the second largest (after Eris) of the nearly one million cataloged "minor planets" which orbit the Sun.

Yet for every never-before-seen space oddity attracting the attention of astronomers, the old, familiar celestial bodies still had plenty of wonders of their own in store. Almost as soon as Galileo turned his telescope to the heavens, astronomers discovered that Jupiter has moons, Saturn has rings, and the Sun has—well, there really isn't any better name for it—the Sun has spots. These dark sunspots appear and disappear on the Sun's surface, and rotate together with the rest of the Sun around the Sun's internal axis about once every twenty-five days.

In the mid-1800s, a German astronomer named Heinrich Schwabe realized that the number and intensity of these sunspots increased and decreased over a fairly regular, eleven-year cycle (figure 10.3). Impressed by this finding, Rudolf Wolf in Zurich, Switzerland, began the modern era of systematic, daily sunspot counts. Using historical records, Wolf was able to extend his sunspot series back to the year 1749, with 1755 marking the beginning of what is now called Solar Cycle 1. It's possible to extend the sunspot record all the way back to the first telescopic observations of the Sun in 1610, although, not surprisingly, these data are less consistent than those from later periods.

Sunspots provide an external, visual clue to the Sun's internal rumblings. The rise and fall of the sunspot count during each eleven-year solar cycle corresponds to a rise and fall in overall solar activity. Here on Earth, this is manifested primarily through increased geomagnetic disturbances, interference in certain radio signals, and an increase in the vibrancy and range of the northern and southern auroras (plate 16). The total sunlight

Figure 10.3: The 11-Year Solar Cycle

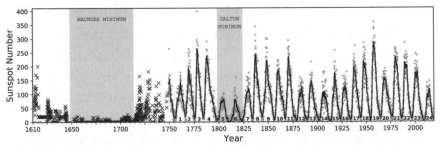

Sunspots are the most visible indicator of the Sun's approximately 11-year cycle of activity. Monthly mean sunspot numbers are plotted from 1749 to the present, with the solar cycle's name (1–24) displayed at the base of each peak. Data prior to Solar Cycle 1 are the scaled, revised, monthly mean group numbers (see notes). DATA SOURCE: WDC–SILSO, ROYAL OBSERVATORY OF BELGIUM, BRUSSELS.

emitted by the Sun also peaks with the solar cycle, although the variation amounts to only a small fraction—about 0.1 percent—of the Sun's baseline heating power.

Like the medieval chronologists who organized the history of the world according to the twenty-year conjunction cycle of Jupiter and Saturn, scientists have looked for correlations between the eleven-year solar cycle and various happenings here on Earth. William Herschel, who is chiefly famous for the discovery of Uranus, tried to correlate sunspot counts with the wheat prices published in Adam Smith's *Wealth of Nations*. Herschel's basic idea was that more sunspots meant warmer weather and therefore higher wheat yields and lower wheat prices. More adventurously, the Soviet scientist Alexander Chizhevsky suggested that mass uprisings, like riots and revolutions, all marched to a sunspot rhythm.

The correlation that has received the most scientific support (even if the link remains speculative) is that the two recorded periods of extended, below-average sunspot numbers—the Maunder Minimum and the Dalton Minimum—line up with known periods of extended cold weather. In particular, the Maunder Minimum, which overlaps almost perfectly with the reign of the French king Louis XIV, is thought to be connected with a climatological cooling event known as the Little Ice Age. Whether this represents a real effect or merely a coincidence, we can still make the perfectly factual observation that France's so-called Sun King presided, ironically, over a period of unusually low solar activity.

As of 2019, we have arrived at the tail end of Solar Cycle 24. It was a comparatively weak solar cycle and part of a tentative trend, starting with Solar Cycle 22, of diminishing sunspot counts. Whether Solar Cycle 25 will be strong or weak, and whether this will have any implications for the Earth's climate, remains anybody's guess.

This uncertainty about our nearest stellar neighbor is fairly typical. In fact, some of the Sun's most remarkable features remained entirely unknown right up until the dawn of the space age. For instance, during the 1950s, the American astrophysicist Eugene Parker was trying to understand why comet tails always point away from the Sun. His explanation completely upended the concept of "empty space." The Sun, Parker theorized, was emitting not just light and heat, but also a supersonic stream of charged and magnetized particles which spread out and fill up the solar system. The existence of this outflow, now called the solar wind, was decisively confirmed by satellite measurements in the late 1950s and early 1960s.

Thus, far from the stainless golden disc of myth, the Sun turns out to be more like a roaring, smoking, spinning bonfire. Its heat (the solar irradiance) and smoke (the solar wind) peak every eleven years or so, accompanied by increased crackling (sunspots), bright flashes (solar flares), tongues of flame (solar prominences), and even the occasional hurling of a burning log (a coronal mass ejection). For the most part, the Earth's atmosphere and magnetic field keep us well protected from the Sun's stormy temperament. But satellites and spacecraft remain very much exposed. This is why the spacefaring nations maintain facilities dedicated to monitoring and, to the limited extent possible, predicting "space weather."

But back to our earlier mystery: cosmic rays. All of these discoveries point to the Sun as their source, right? Surprisingly, no. (Although the Sun does contribute some of the weaker rays.) The relationship is actually the reverse: cosmic radiation *decreases* with increasing solar activity. The solar wind, it turns out, provides an extra layer of shielding which, at its most intense, significantly reduces the amount of cosmic radiation reaching the Earth. Thus, to further stretch an already overextended metaphor, cosmic rays are like a constant swarm of mosquitoes which can be repelled, at least somewhat, by the smoke from our solar bonfire.

Yet if the Sun isn't the main source of cosmic rays, then what is? This has been one of the great detective stories of modern astrophysics. But with increasing conviction, scientists keep coming back to the same suspects: supernovas. Not all supernovas, mind you; mainly supernovas, like Tycho's, whose remnants are located within our own Milky Way galaxy. These spectacular stellar explosions have all the requisite violence to account for the bulk of the cosmic rays we receive on Earth. In fact, one of the earliest and most revealing clues was that these so-called "rays" are actually made up of charged particles: protons mainly (about 90 percent), some helium nuclei (about 9 percent), and a sprinkling of the innards of every other element of the periodic table, all accelerated across the galaxy at close to the speed of light.

This last point turns out to be vital, because in the early universe, right after the Big Bang, the only elements which had been created were hydrogen and helium. Every other element had to be forged, over billions of years, in the nuclear furnace of a star. Thus, supernovas are not merely the memorials to long-dead stars. Their destructive violence also seeds the cosmos with all the materials needed for the next generation of stars, planets, and even life itself. This is a process which the astronomer Carl Sagan described so unforgettably in his wonderful 1980 television series, *Cosmos*:

> Our Sun is probably a third-generation star. Except for hydrogen and helium, every atom in the Sun and the Earth was synthesized in other stars. The silicon in the rocks, the oxygen in the air, the carbon in our DNA, the gold in our banks, the uranium in our arsenals were all made thousands of light-years away and billions of years ago. Our planet, our society, and we ourselves are built of star stuff.

Supernovas have given us the "star stuff" out of which we're made. Supernovas also shower us in the cosmic radiation that is an invisible but constant accompaniment to life on Earth. In fact, cosmic rays deliver, on average, about 0.3 millisieverts per person per year, or about 10 percent of the natural ionizing radiation we're subjected to at all times simply by being alive. (Radon in the air we breathe accounts for much of the rest.) For the most part, the human body is pretty good at repairing this type of low-level damage. But it's inescapable that some cosmic rays will induce mutations in our cells, both benign and not so benign. And when you consider that cosmic rays have been bombarding the Earth for the entirety of its 4.5-billion-year history, and that their intensity ebbs and flows according to cosmic cycles of which we're only dimly aware, the implications suddenly become startling. Have the stars been modulating the tempo of our biological evolution all along? We are made from the stars, and perhaps, ever so subtly, we are shaped by the stars as well. Once again, it was Sagan who said it best: "The evolution of life on Earth is driven in part through mutations by the deaths of distant stars. We are, in a very deep sense, tied to the cosmos."

The discovery of the interplay between supernovas, the solar cycle, and cosmic rays has taught us that Earth is not a planetary bubble, untouched by the faraway stars. Today, we recognize that we are, and we have always been, creatures of the cosmos. This awareness—that our lives are influenced by events in the wider universe—has been the basic intuition of astrology from the beginning. Modern science, it must be admitted, has vindicated this intuition—even if, as so often happens, not at all in the way it was originally imagined.

As we now know, it's not the planets which generate the cosmic rays that subtly influence our lives, but the radioactive remnants of supernovas in the far corners of the galaxy. Astronomers would love to be able to trace these rays back to specific sources in the sky, like Tycho's supernova remnant in the constellation Cassiopeia, or the Crab Nebula, which is the remnant of the supernova of 1054, in the constellation Taurus. Unfortunately, the magnetic fields of the Earth, Sun, and interstellar space scramble the directions of these rays before they enter our atmosphere. This is what makes pinpointing their origin so difficult. Yet, for this same reason, how crazy is it to imagine a scenario in which the two planets in our solar system with the largest magnetic fields—Jupiter and Saturn—subtly modulate the incoming flux of cosmic rays according to their positions relative to the Earth and the Sun? Might it be possible, therefore, for these planets to exert a small but critical influence on, say, some particular weather pattern here on Earth? This scenario is, admittedly, far-fetched. And yet it says something about our knowledge of the world that a scenario which today is merely far-fetched would have been altogether inconceivable one hundred years ago but perfectly believable one thousand years ago. Perhaps certain cosmological ideas have cycles of their own, and, like the skies they seek to explain, are destined to rise, set, and rise again for as long as we keep watching the stars.

WE ARE LIVING IN AN EMPIRICAL WORLD

Against all odds, modern astrology has managed to make itself comfortably at home in modern astronomy's strange and rapidly expanding universe. In fact, when it comes to all of astronomy's newfound cosmic objects, it's the more the merrier, since each new heavenly body multiplies the total number of astrological possibilities to consider. A typical modern-day birth horoscope, for instance, will include not only the seven naked-eye "planets," but also Uranus, Neptune, Pluto, and possibly even a few small solar system bodies such as Chiron or Ceres.

How do I know this? I went out and got my horoscope read, naturally. When I began this book, one of the things I became most curious to see was what a state-of-the-art professional horoscope looks like these days. And so, on a trip back to my home state of Arizona, I made sure to swing by the beautiful little town of Sedona, whose striking red rock vistas and, so they say, "natural energy vortices" inspire a thriving New Age community of crystal healers, aura readers, astrologers, and spiritual teachers of every persuasion. But for all of Sedona's natural beauty, this is the twenty-first century, and so I wasn't terribly surprised to discover that today's deluxe astrological reading begins indoors, on a computer.

Astrologers today have a whole galaxy of professional software packages to choose from, with celestially flashy names like Kepler, Sirius, and Solar Fire. All of these programs can compute and display the positions of the planets and other heavenly bodies. Quite a few can also generate fully automated reports and interpretations. Thus, the only information my astral guide for that afternoon needed from me was the day, time, and city of my birth, along with my name, my gender, and my sexual orientation. A few minutes later, I was handed a slick-looking, personalized, thirty-page astrological report.

On the cover of my report is a full-page diagram of my horoscope. Modern astrology programs provide multiple options for the visual look and feel of a horoscope, but the go-to style is the chart-wheel, which is also what you'll find on most astrology websites. Mine shows a large circle evenly divided by the twelve signs of the zodiac, and unevenly divided by the twelve, Placidus-style Houses of Heaven labeled 1 through 12. The planets are appropriately positioned near the outer rim of the wheel, with lines and symbols indicating their aspects to one another (figure 10.4).

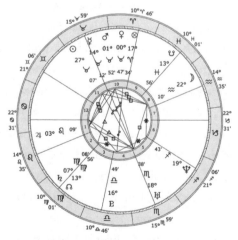

Figure 10.4: Birth horoscope of the author, displayed in the chart-wheel format typical of modern horoscopes.

Incidentally, although chart-wheel horoscopes occupy two dimensions on a piece of paper, they convey only one dimension of information: ecliptic longitude. In principle, therefore, they could be drawn as just ticks on a straight line. This is why, for all of the schemes of heaven in this book, I've preferred the stereographic projection of an astrolabe, which generates a proper mathematical map of both dimensions of the celestial sphere.

The remainder of my astrological report explained what the configuration of the heavens at my birth had to say about my personality. For such a lengthy document, I was impressed at how artfully vague each pronouncement was, such that there were very few sentences in which I could not recognize at least some aspect of myself. This experience has been called the Barnum Effect. For instance, since I'm a Taurus, I "feel at home with people who prove to be friendly, affectionate, and gentle." Why, yes, I do. And since Jupiter was ruling in the First House, I am "very attracted to traveling and . . . have a great desire to discover every part of the world; this impulse could lead to frequent travels or many changes of residence." Hey, not bad!

Of course, these reports are meant to serve merely as conversation starters. An intuitive interlocutor would have no trouble zeroing in on the topics that are most relevant to me and proceeding from there. And a birth chart can be just the beginning. I could have stayed to hear the various chapters of my life analyzed in terms of astrological "transits" and "progressions." But I was more interested in the mechanics of how the ancient craft of horoscope-casting had been carried into the computer age. Therefore, in addition to my own birth report, I purchased one for Olivia Koski (born eight minutes after me), then another one for myself had I been born eight minutes later (it was identical to my original one, not surprisingly), and then a few more, just for fun, to give to friends and loved ones. And though the costs of these reports can add up quickly, nonetheless, I left the lovely little town of Sedona feeling richer in spirit than when I arrived.

As perusing page after page of these astrological reports makes clear, astrology today is best regarded as a flavor of self-help, one focused primarily on personal and spiritual growth. This is all fine and good, and certainly one big advantage of making purely subjective pronouncements is that they can never really be "wrong." But astrology occupies the spiritual high ground only at the high cost of abandoning its original domain of expertise, namely, making objective predictions about objective events. Astrology's abdication doesn't mean, however, that the forecasting field has now been left vacant. Far from it. The notion that formulaic algorithms should explain not just some things, but most things in our lives, remains as seductive as ever. Who needs the stars and planets, anyway? Maybe, like in a good magic trick, they were just a form of misdirection all along.

These days, almost all of astrology's prognosticatory products have been replaced by newer, and more "scientific" substitutes. In many cases, however, it's not altogether clear that these replacements are any better, or even all that different from what astrology had to offer. For example, who hasn't encountered the ubiquitous Myers–Briggs Type Indicators, which diagnose personality type? In place of the twelve zodiac signs, Myers–Briggs posits a system of four psychological processes, each with two opposing preferences: Introversion/Extroversion, Sensing/Intuition, Thinking/Feeling, and Judgment/Perception. This gives a total of $2 \times 2 \times 2 \times 2 = 16$ personality types, which are denoted by their initial letter codes, for instance ISTJ or ENFP. The Myers–Briggs Type Indicator was developed in 1943 as an explicit application of Carl Jung's fourfold theory of personality types. And Jung himself explicitly acknowledged that this fourfold division could trace its lineage back to the ancient theory of the four elements, the four humors, and the four astrological triplicities associated with them. Thus, while the Myers–Briggs test isn't exactly astrology in disguise, as many of its detractors like to joke, it isn't so far removed, either.

The situation is similar for politics, economics, and the weather. Just because astrology has fallen out of favor doesn't mean people won't still pay top dollar for what they hope to be a winning predictive formula. But you don't need to have an especially long memory to appreciate that even the latest and greatest forecasts in these fields can still be spectacularly wrong. Hence the oft-quoted quip by the economist Ezra Solomon: "The only function of economic forecasting is to make astrology look respectable."

Have we gotten any better at characterizing large, complex, and highly random systems? Unfortunately, the old saying remains as true today as ever: "It's tough to make predictions—especially about the future." So why, then, is astrology singled out as uniquely not "respectable"? Having a poor track record for accuracy can't be all there is; if it was, quite a few modern forecasting operations should have been shut down a long time ago. Or are we to believe that only astrology has attracted its share of swindlers and crooks? Several centuries of financial scandals would seem to argue otherwise. No, astrology has been the butt of scientific ridicule because it uses algorithms which seem completely arbitrary, and which take as their inputs data that have no apparent connection to the effects being predicted and which cannot be justified from a scientific understanding of the underlying phenomena. (See, for instance, Bonatti, Guido.) Funnily enough, however, this describes pretty well the sort of algorithms increasingly being used in modern forecasting models today.

In general, a predictive model can be constrained by the laws of a larger theory, or it can be purely empirical. A physics-based weather model, for instance, must respect the laws of thermodynamics and fluid mechanics. By contrast, a purely empirical model simply hunts around for the best algorithm to relate the input data to the output data, whatever those data may be. An empirical rain model, for example, might consist of nothing more than a best-fit curve to historical precipitation data, without any assumptions of an underlying mechanism.

Outside of some specialized cases in the physical sciences, however, there's rarely ever much theory with which to build a model. These days, though, there tends to be plenty of data. The easy availability of vast computerized records about pretty much anything—what's usually called "big data"—and the rise of machine-learning algorithms to sift through it all is radically reshaping the entire enterprise of scientific modeling. We are exiting, it seems, a brief age of triumphant theories. With big data and machine-learning, what we "know" about the world, and about ourselves, is increasingly whatever our empirical models tell us.

Astrology can likewise be approached as a purely empirical problem. Forget all the ancient theories and superstitions: are there earthly data sets which correlate with the planets, or aren't there? During the twentieth century, several astrologers equipped with the newly developed tests and techniques of statistics set out to examine this question in precisely this way. The most provocative finding came from a French psychologist named Michel Gauquelin. Beginning in 1955, Gauquelin claimed to have detected a small but statistically significant incidence of key planets appearing in key Houses in the horoscopes of eminent professionals. For athletes, it was Mars; for scientists, Saturn; and for actors, Jupiter. This observation, known as the Mars Effect, would become astrology's last and most valiant bid for scientific legitimacy. Controversy over the claim dragged on for decades. One commentator in the 1970s summed up the stakes:

> Both those who are for and against astrology (in the broadest sense) as a serious field for study recognize the importance of Gauquelin's work. It is probably not putting it too strongly to say that everything hangs on it.

To the great disappointment of its promoters, however, the most recent attempts to replicate Gauquelin's findings—and particularly with data sets independent of Gauquelin's original sample—have failed to find any evidence of a Mars Effect.

Meanwhile, in the United States, astrological correlation chasers were looking to prove their point not with statistics, but with cold, hard cash—by beating the stock market. Speculators like the mercurial W. D. Gann in the early part of the twentieth century claimed to have uncovered complex numerological and astrological patterns behind the fluctuations of the financial markets. Sidestepping his more esoteric assertions, one thing Gann did demonstrate was that even if you can't quite beat the market, you might still be able to make a small fortune selling books and instructional courses teaching others how to do it.

Today, there's no need to root and rummage for incidental correlations. Modern machine-learning algorithms are correlation monsters. They can make pretty much any signal correlate with any other. To illustrate this, we can update financial astrology for a task that's a bit more twenty-first-century: predicting the price of Bitcoin. Using a machine-learning algorithm called a neural network, it's possible to devise a model that perfectly mimics Bitcoin's

Figure 10.5: Planetary Prediction of the Price of Bitcoin

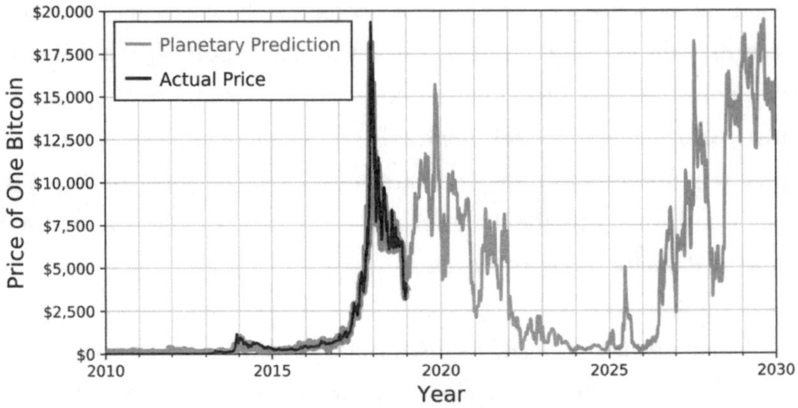

Space junk in, space junk out. Modern machine-learning algorithms can "learn" to correlate almost any signal with any other. This chart shows an algorithm that mimics, and then predicts, the daily price of Bitcoin using only the planets' zodiac signs as input.

price history and that takes, as its input data, nothing more than the zodiac signs of the planets on any given day (figure 10.5).

Does the close correlation surprise you? Well, I'll admit there's a little sleight-of-hand here. The model we've trained is so big—meaning that it has so many free parameters—that it's essentially able to learn a separate relationship for each individual data-point without discovering any meaningful underlying pattern. (Imagine connecting two data points with an overly complicated curve instead of a simple, straight line and you'll have the basic idea.) The machine-learning term for this is "overfitting." It's entirely equivalent to the concept of a spurious correlation. In both phrases, what's implied is that if we were to sample more data—for instance, next year's prices—the correlation would quickly fall apart. Of course, the only way to really know how prescient this model is (or isn't) is to wait and see. In the meantime, though, I'd suggest that the standard financial disclaimer—"past performance is no guarantee of future results"—can be prudently assumed to extend to the zodiac, too.

The ability of modern machine-learning algorithms to generate convincing-looking correlations so easily makes it critical for all of us, as data consumers, to remain wary of what these models are really telling us. This is especially true given the tendency of media outlets to blur the differences between, on the one hand, a simulation or model prediction and, on the other, a real measurement of a real thing in the real world. Purely empirical models, no differently than the algorithms of medieval astrology, provide no justification for how or why they're supposed to work. The risk, then, of relying on these models, absent any deeper understanding, is that you can't be certain whether the correlations they're based on are genuine or not. And yet no special powers of clairvoyance are needed to foresee that our interaction with these sorts of increasingly opaque machine-learning models is only set to accelerate.

We've already outsourced to algorithms judgments about what mortgage we're eligible for from the bank, and how long we're expected to live and at what cost. With big data and machine-learning, our algorithms are becoming ever more personal, recognizing our faces, deciphering our voices, finishing our sentences, answering our questions, and ascertaining our shopping, reading, dining, and voting preferences.

Today, there's a bit of a gold rush to find new data sets that can be "learned" and turned into viable applications. Whenever my colleagues or I come across (or, worse, create) a predictive model that seems especially dubious, it's not uncommon for us to describe it as "basically astrology." This is never meant as a compliment. And yet, I confess, it was in reflecting upon this insult that I began to feel a real sympathy for those hoary old astrologers of ages past. It's a sympathy that has led, in part, to this book. Day in and day out, astrologers struggled to interpret the meanings of complex mathematical models centuries before the statistical tools were developed to assess whether those models meant anything at all. Hundreds of years from now, will our own age be similarly mocked, or perhaps merely pitied, for our feeble attempts to predict the future?

Or, just maybe, will our new breed of algorithms finally succeed where astrology has failed? How prepared are we to live in a world in which each of us has become dispiritingly predictable? What would it mean for our sense of self, not to mention our sense of justice, to conclude that nature, not nurture, was driving our actions? On the plus side, I suppose there's a lot of unnecessary suffering we'd be able to avoid. Looking back at my own life, I can think of many times I would have appreciated an algorithm to warn me which of my plans was destined to fail, or which of my relationships was never meant to be. And yet, had I been told from the beginning the path I was meant to follow, how could I have even set foot upon it without the experience of all my previous missteps? No, to err is human, and I don't foresee an algorithm ever truly learning what that means.

SKEPTICISM AND WONDER

The really breathtaking thing about our civilization's collective knowledge is that, every now and again, those who have come before us have managed to link arguments and evidence together into chains of reasoning which are so compelling that they can convince even the most hardened skeptic of a fact that seems utterly and completely counterintuitive. In Plato's dialogue *Meno*, Socrates draws a diagram in the sand to convince a slave—one who knows absolutely nothing about geometry—that a square's area can be doubled by, counterintuitively, drawing a new square upon the diagonal of the old one. During the scientific revolution, astronomers and physicists toiled for generations to demonstrate convincingly what was, and perhaps always will be, history's most outrageously counterintuitive claim: that the Earth is not fixed, but hurtling rapidly through space in an orbit around the Sun.

For many people today, modern astrology's basic claim—that people's personalities can be meaningfully grouped according to their zodiac sign—appears to be borne out by day-to-day experience. The counterclaim, that these groupings have no actual meaning, is therefore the counterintuitive one. The persistence of astrology shows how tenacious our pattern-matching tendencies can be. Once the suggestion of a pattern has been made—in this case, a suggestion first put forward thousands of years ago—it can be very difficult not to see evidence for it everywhere. Yet astrology's persistence tells us something else, too, something that many seem unwilling to acknowledge: the arguments against astrology are, evidently, not nearly as compelling as

Socrates' argument about how to double a square, or even the argument that the Earth revolves around the Sun. Why not?

First of all, it should be noted that no direct evidence of the Earth's motion was observed until the nineteenth century, when telescopes finally became powerful enough to measure stellar parallax. A conflict is settled, however, when opposition ceases. In this case, the religious institutions which were the primary opponents of a heliocentric cosmos had already conceded the argument during the 1600s. What this sequence implies is that, at a popular level, no one much cares whether the Earth is moving or not. Otherwise, this debate might have lingered on at least through the nineteenth century, if not well into the space age.

Yet people do care about astrology. Its system of explaining our personalities and our compatibilities has proven enduringly popular. It's really not surprising, then, and certainly not unreasonable, that those who find astrology compelling would require something a bit stronger than the old, mostly theoretical arguments against it to convince them otherwise. But just as it was quite late before the Earth's motion could be measured directly, the statistical tests which furnish the most direct evidence against astrology were developed only very recently, during the twentieth century. And the large data sets which give these tests their persuasive power are only just now becoming readily accessible.

Today there are reference surveys, such as *Tests of Astrology: A Critical Review of Hundreds of Studies*, which document decades' worth of investigations, all of them arguing against the claims of astrology and astrologers. Yet it remains the case that most of these tests are indirect. They demonstrate primarily that professional astrologers can't do what they say they can do, not so much that astrology itself is invalid. In order to directly test astrology's core assertions, what's needed most of all are large data sets of births recorded to the minute, or at least to the hour—the kind of data that Michel Gauquelin attempted to compile. Unfortunately, that sort of data, even today, remains difficult to come by. But it is out there. And it's my belief that as more to-the-minute birth data becomes available online, perhaps on websites devoted expressly to this purpose, it will become easier for people to examine astrology's claims for themselves. And who knows? Maybe with the benefit of larger data sets—and using tests not unlike the ones we've applied throughout this book—the results may one day even be as clear as a geometric proof.

In the meantime, though, astrology appears to be enjoying one of its small periodic revivals, especially as savvier astrologers have learned to adapt the art to the internet. But I very much doubt that today's astrology will regain anything like the appeal it held even as recently as the 1970s. That was a decade when statistical methods were being applied (and misapplied) in medicine and the social sciences in a major way, and when sensationalized interpretations of equivocal results could be reported in scientific journals just as glibly as on the nightly news. Dubious findings, such as Gauquelin's Mars Effect, seemed to argue either that astrology was legitimate or, more disturbingly, that the methods being used in the sciences were somehow deeply unreliable. Not coincidentally, this was also a period when institutional science, caught off guard, found itself challenged as never before to justify its exalted role in society. Was there even such a thing as science, objective truth, and a scientific method, or was the whole edifice nothing more than an expression of power?

One small episode from that decade saw several of these trends come into conjunction. In 1975, the September/October edition of *The Humanist* magazine published a declaration entitled "Objections to Astrology: A Statement by 186 Leading Scientists." It began:

> Scientists in a variety of fields have become concerned about the increased acceptance of astrology in many parts of the world. We, the undersigned—astronomers, astrophysicists, and scientists in other fields—wish to caution the public against the unquestioning acceptance of the predictions and advice given privately and publicly by astrologers. Those who wish to believe in astrology should realize that there is no scientific foundation for its tenets.

Appended to the full statement were the names and affiliations of 186 scientists, beginning with eighteen Nobel Prize winners; these included Francis Crick, the co-discoverer of DNA's double helix, and Hans Bethe, who first worked out how the Sun and other stars synthesize heavier elements through nuclear fusion. The lead author was the Dutch-American astronomer Bart J. Bok. Previously a president of the American Astronomical Society, Bok was at that time a professor at the University of Arizona in Tucson where, not quite four years later, Olivia Koski and I would be born.

The article, with its impressive list of signatories, conveys an important and powerful message. And yet, today, it is mainly remembered not for who signed it, but for who didn't. Astronomy's most well-loved public ambassador, although personally asked to endorse the statement, reluctantly determined he could not. This was Carl Sagan. Sagan was a vociferous critic of astrology, but he objected to the "Objection" for several reasons. First, because "the tone of the statement was authoritarian." Indeed, the philosopher Paul Feyerabend, at that time a professor at Berkeley, made a similar observation and mocked the scientists' statement for how closely it matched the wording of the Catholic Church's fifteenth-century condemnation of witchcraft.

More substantively, Sagan objected to the statement's emphasis that there was "no mechanism by which astrology could work." As Sagan noted, this point, by itself, is meaningless. The theory of continental drift, he offered by way of example, had been dismissed for exactly the same reason, and yet it subsequently became one of the fundamental pillars of modern geophysics.

But I suspect that Sagan also intuited how counterproductive and silly the statement would seem to those to whom it was nominally addressed. Sagan recognized that what motivates those who turn to astrology is, deep down, a sense of curiosity and wonder. He recognized this because it was the same curiosity and wonder he experienced whenever he looked up at the stars. This basic human empathy was a big part of what made him such a gifted communicator.

Sagan pursued science as an expression of his wonder. And he never made any secret of the fact that, as a child, his wonder had been sparked in part by reading science fiction novels, like the *John Carter of Mars* series, with their exotic tales of extraterrestrial beings. Until the day he died, Sagan never stopped dreaming of making contact with intelligent extraterrestrial life. But it was precisely this point of reference that made Sagan eager to share with everyone what he had long ago learned: that the wonders of science's universe were so much more amazing than whatever fictions pseudoscience might invent.

That Carl Sagan, the great evangelist of scientific wonder, was also one of the twentieth century's great proponents of skepticism is no contradiction. Personally, it's this paradoxical quality that I've long admired most in him. To borrow a New Age notion, wonder and skepticism are like yin and yang, two seeming opposites that must balance each other in creative conflict—because, if we're so quick to be deceived by falsehoods, how will we recognize true wonder when we see it? Conversely, what is the purpose of skepticism if not to prepare our wonder when, against all challenges, what seemed impossible actually proves true?

For all of these reasons, it's no mystery to me why astrology provokes such sharp emotions. At stake is not so much which truth is true, but where we should seek our wonder. To acknowledge science as a source of wonder is to acknowledge, implicitly, a profound debt to history, and also a profound responsibility—for if we cannot faithfully preserve the knowledge which previous generations have hewed out of bleakest ignorance, then we will squander that wonder for the generations to follow. Nevertheless, and however well-meaning the motives, those who would amputate astrology from science's history, or set it apart for ridicule, do nothing to preserve science or its history. On the contrary, they are being deeply unfaithful to both. To tell a messier story of *how* we know is not to diminish *what* we know, but rather to appreciate it all the more as something at once more astonishing and more humbling.

THE FINAL FRONTIER?

Astrology is an inseparable part of science's past. And insofar as it still serves as a caution against the careless application of modern pattern-matching methods, astrology remains very much a part of science's present. But can astrology possibly coexist with science's future? If that future is anything like what Sagan and other visionaries imagined, then it's only a matter of time before our species leaves the Earth to inhabit other worlds. Will we be bringing our astrology with us?

Computing the aspects of the stars and planets from other locations in the universe does not, by itself, pose any great challenges. In fact, Johannes Kepler worked through this problem in detail as far back as the 1600s. In an early work of science fiction called *Somnium* (*A Dream*), Kepler examined what the heavens would look like to an observer on the Moon. (By an incredible coincidence, this book, as announced on its title page, was printed in Sagan, a city in what's now Poland.) Charmingly, Kepler wove his calculations into a story about a young boy from the island of Thule whose mother, a sorceress, in a fit of anger sells her son to a passing ship captain. That captain, in turn, deposits the boy in Denmark with Tycho Brahe, from whom he learns the art of astronomy. Years later, upon his return to Thule, the boy and his mother are joyfully reunited. Delighted by her son's mastery of Earth-bound astronomy, she uses her magic to summon a *daemon*, or spirit, from the Moon to teach her son the deeper mysteries of lunar astronomy.

The stated purpose of Kepler's *Dream* was to show that the hypothesis of a moving Earth presented no obstacle to astronomy. Indeed, the appearances of the heavens could be computed just as well, albeit with different results, for an observer on the moving Moon. Kepler's investigations with the newly invented telescope had convinced him that there was probably intelligent life on the Moon. He believed that the dark regions of the lunar surface, such as the Sea of Tranquility, were watery seas like those on Earth. But for the Moon's inhabitants, whom Kepler surmised must be giants, the skies would look very different. A lunar day and a lunar night, for instance, together last an entire Earth-month. Meanwhile, the precession of the equinoxes, a cycle which on Earth lasts 26,000 years, takes only about nineteen years on the Moon.

Today we know that, contrary to Kepler's *Dream*, the Moon is sadly dry and lifeless. But the basic premise of Kepler's lunar astronomy remains perfectly sound. Updated versions of Kepler's lunar calculations can be used, for instance, to determine the precise arrangement of the heavens from Neil Armstrong's vantage point at the instant he set foot on the Moon. These data can even be displayed as an astrolabe-style lunar scheme of heaven, as in figure 10.1. Compared with the other schemes of heaven in this book, however, there are several important differences. For starters, the location of the Apollo 11 landing site is given in terms of selenographic coordinates (from *selene*, the Greek word for the Moon), which are determined with reference to the Moon's axis of rotation. Additionally, the ecliptic circle is seen to cling more closely to the lunar equator. This is because the obliquity of the ecliptic on the Moon is only about 1.5 degrees, as compared with 23.4 degrees on Earth.

But the biggest difference is that there's now an entirely new heavenly body in the sky: the Earth! What does it mean, astrologically speaking, for the Earth to have been in Aries at that moment? This isn't a question astrologers have ever had to deal with before. To make things even more confusing, it's generally the case that observers on different planets will, at one and the same instant, perceive the different celestial bodies at different locations in the sky. Thus, an Aquarius on Earth, determined according to the Sun, might be a Gemini on Jupiter, a Virgo on Venus, and a Sagittarius on Saturn. How would anyone know which horoscope to read? Still, at least within our own solar system, the concept of a zodiac system based on solstices and equinoxes might conceivably be salvaged. But what happens when we finally venture to stars beyond our Sun? How could astrology possibly function?

Astrology, it is worth remembering, has faced two such crises before: first, when Hipparchus discovered the precession of the equinoxes, and second, when Copernicus and his successors dismantled the Earth-centered cosmos. In each instance, astrology not only adapted and survived but thrived. Such is our stubborn insistence on seeing a correlation between the stars and ourselves. Similarly, I suppose, the rules of a truly extraterrestrial astrology might, in principle, be worked out. But will they? What future stargazer will devote the time and effort, with so many new cosmic wonders to explore? Personally, I'd be pretty surprised if astrology ever accompanies us beyond Earth's orbit. But considering astrology's history, maybe the only reading I can give is that astrology's destiny, whatever it may be, is one which hasn't yet been written.

UPON THE WORDS
OF NO ONE

With names like Isaac Newton, Charles Darwin, and Stephen Hawking among its list of fellows, there's really no other scientific institution with a history as illustrious as London's Royal Society. In the mid-1600s, when the group was granted its royal charter, the founding members chose for their motto a Latin phrase: *Nullius in verba*. It's a verse from the Roman poet Horace and it means "Upon the words of no one." What this motto signified was that the new science was to be based on careful and reproducible experiments. Hearsay would no longer substitute for firsthand evidence. And the words "Trust me, I'm an expert" could no longer suffice as scientific proof.

As a maxim for scientific knowledge, *Nullius in verba* is a bit aspirational. If everyone had to prove every fact for themselves, no one would live long enough to learn what had already been learned, let alone contribute anything new. Out of pure, practical necessity, all of us, and scientists especially, have to rely on the expertise of others. But the skeptical contrarianism conveyed by *Nullius in verba* still animates the grand enterprise of science. Each link in the chain of knowledge remains accessible for examination, questioning, and doubt. I know that you know the Earth revolves around the Sun. But how do you know? How could you prove it? What if, in a fit of contrarianism, you decided that just because everyone says something is true isn't enough for you? Gratifyingly, this stance isn't just tolerated in science; it's encouraged. All of the arguments have been preserved for inspection. All of the measurements are ready to be taken anew. Nor is it the case, with science subdividing into increasingly specialized silos of expertise—and its claims subjected to the scrutiny of fewer and fewer independent eyes—that *Nullius in verba* has grown less relevant for our times. On the contrary, as an ideal, it remains as vital as ever.

Astrology is one of those topics on which everyone seems to have an opinion—often a very strong one—and under which bookshelves groan with the expositions of experts both for and against. And yet nowhere was I able to find answers to many of my own seemingly simple questions. No matter. *Nullius in verba.* I recognized that the resources were at my disposal to answer most of my questions for myself. All of the data used in this book is publicly available, starting with the extraordinarily precise astronomical data from NASA's Jet Propulsion Laboratory. All of the most important primary sources, from Ptolemy to Bonatti to Kepler, are digitized and accessible online. Even the Python programming language, which I used to run all of my analyses and to generate all of my figures, is completely free and open-source. To be sure, it takes a bit of skill and commitment to weave these threads together. But fundamentally, I've said nothing in this book which cannot be checked, challenged, or expanded upon by anyone reading at home. Why take my word for it? *Nullius in verba.*

Invoking the rallying cry of science for a book about astrology, the arch-pseudoscience, may come across as a little preposterous. Perhaps it is. Yet it strikes me that the prerogative to ask honest questions about a topic ought to be insisted upon all the more wherever asking those questions is most discouraged. Because, and let's be honest, it's not as if writing a book like this is entirely without risk. My aim has been only to explore astrology, certainly not to endorse it. And I trust that this book will be received in the spirit of curiosity and openness with which it was written. But there's still a panic-inducing scenario where this nuance gets lost and things go terribly pear-shaped for me, even to the point where I'm no longer able to work in a technical field. Such is astrology's taboo, even today.

Otto Neugebauer, the historian of science who single-handedly did more than anyone to reconstruct the history of ancient mathematical astronomy, had to deal with similar sideways glances whenever his research touched upon astrology. In a powerful 1951 essay called "The Study of Wretched Subjects," Neugebauer defended those who were painstakingly piecing together the writings of science's also-rans, like Vettius Valens, against the slights of scholars who studied more respectable topics. Those wretched writers, Neugebauer noted, "may one day furnish the missing link in the transmission of doctrines which have left their imprint in almost all phases of Mediaeval learning, Medicine, Botany, Chemistry, etc."

Neugebauer's essay resonates very strongly with me. I would only add that, for me, the history of astrology has a value all its own, apart from whatever relevance it may or may not have to other strands of history. And I certainly wouldn't describe the time I've spent researching this subject as in any way "wretched." I consider the opportunity to write about astrology to have been both a privilege and a joy. This book has given me a delightful excuse to connect my love of history with my love of numbers in a way that few other topics could. But what has consistently amazed me throughout is astrology's almost magical ability to connect not just these, but practically any subject with any other. It may not be "cosmic sympathy," but there is an undeniable power in astrology to reveal the surprising ways in which everything, and all of us, are connected to each other across time and space. These little reminders, as unexpected as they are wonderful, have more than rewarded my efforts in writing this. For your efforts, patient reader, I hope that somewhere among these pages, you too were given something to wonder about.

ACKNOWLEDGMENTS

My first thanks go to Rachel Vogel (♓), originally of the Waxman Leavell Literary Agency, for suggesting that now is the right moment for a new book about astrology, and to Olivia Koski (♉), my zodiac twin, for suggesting that I may be just the right person to write it. To my great delight, Quynh Do (♑) of Norton, and Ed Lake (♌) of Profile Books, agreed to turn this idea into an actual book, assisted by the tremendously helpful Norton team, including Joe Lops (♈), Sarahmay Wilkinson (♊), Allegra Huston (♍), Lauren Abbate (♐), Drew Weitman (♐), and Susan Sanfrey (♒).

I'd especially like to thank my good friend Justace Clutter (♌) and his unmatched data-wrangling wizardry. Justace was indispensable in helping me draw up the early outlines of this project and scope out some of its more adventurous calculations. Color plate 8, showing arcs to every zodiac ancestor for 1979, is his creation.

The wonderful zodiac illustrations appearing throughout this book are the original work of James Evans (♓) (jamesevansgraphicdesign.com). The photographs from museums and collections across the globe, so vital to the story I wanted to tell, are reproduced here thanks to the tireless efforts of Elyse Rieder (♋).

For assorted facts and insights, whether cosmological, historical, etymological, statistical, or purely weird and whimsical, I'd like to thank: Ben Cash (♈), Guido Festuccia (♋), Loren Goldman (♌), E. R. Truitt (♌), Aous Abdo (♍), Thomas A. Brady (♍), Daniel Starza Smith (♎), Ferdinando Buscema (♏), Charles Chuman (♐), Joseph de Feo (♓), Shay Deutsch (♓), Allen Dickerson (♓), Brian Lang (♓), and Ben Sugerman (♓).

The faults of this book, dear reader, are not in its stars, but in myself.

NOTES

INTRODUCTION

Girolamo Cardano, *Libelli Quinque* (Nuremberg: Johannes Petreius, 1547), geniture XLVI, 148v. Nearly the identical figure (and almost, but not quite, the identical interpretation) appears in an earlier edition of 1543. The 1547 illustration was chosen for its superior detail.

William Lilly, *Christian Astrology* (London: Thomas Brudenell, 1647). Lilly's phrase "a Scheam [*sic*] of Heaven" appears prominently on the title page, while the equivalent phrase, "a Figure of Heaven," appears more generally throughout the body of the work, e.g., I.33.

All of the planetary data in this book is from the HORIZONS online solar system data service provided by NASA's Jet Propulsion Laboratory. J. D. Giorgini and JPL Solar System Dynamics Group, "NASA/JPL Horizons On-Line Ephemeris System," http://ssd.jpl.nasa.gov/?horizons.

1: TO EVERYTHING THERE IS A SEASON

Torah Nevi'im u-Khetuvim: The Holy Scriptures According to the Masoretic Text (Philadelphia: Jewish Publication Society of America, 5677–1917).

The Strangeness of Seeing

ESA, 1997, The Hipparcos and Tycho Catalogues, ESA SP-1200. As a point of comparison, the Bright Star Catalog, 5th revised edition (BSC5), edited by Dorrit Hoffleit and Carlos Jaschek (New Haven: Yale University Observatory, 1991), lists 5,080 stars with a visible magnitude of 6.00 or less.

George A. Davis, Jr., "The Origin of Ursa Major," *Popular Astronomy* 54 (April 1946): 111–15.

The DeepDream algorithm was introduced (although not by name) in Alexander Mordvintsev, Christopher Olah, and Mike Tyka, "Inceptionism: Going Deeper into Neural Networks," Google AI Blog, June 17, 2015, https://research.googleblog.com/2015/06/inceptionism-going-deeper-into-neural.html, accessed July 24, 2017.

The International Astronomical Union (IAU) boundaries of the 88 modern constellations can be found at https://www.iau.org/public/themes/constellations. The portion of the celestial sphere covered by each constellation can be computed using, for example, Monte Carlo integration. The constellations Perseus, Andromeda, Cassiopeia, Cepheus, and Cetus cover approximately 9.1% of the sky. If Pegasus, a much later addition to the legend, is included, the coverage jumps to 11.8%.

The principal anisotropy in the distribution of stars in the night sky is the Milky Way, a feature which indeed provides a vital clue about the structure of the cosmos. For a similar discussion on how randomly distributed dots give the illusion of structure, see Stephen Jay Gould, "Glow, Big Glowworm," in *Bully for Brontosaurus: Reflections in Natural History* (New York: W. W. Norton, 1991), 255–68.

Keeping Count

A typical roulette wheel has 38 pockets, so your chances of losing are 37/38 = 97.4%. There are 40 non-facecards in a 52-card deck, so the chances of choosing one are 40/52 = 76.9%. The probability of flipping a coin twice in a row and getting heads both times is ½ × ½ = 25%. The probability of flipping a coin six times in a row and getting heads each time is ½ × ½ × ½ × ½ × ½ × ½ = 1.6%.

Ronald A. Fisher, *The Design of Experiments* (Edinburgh and London: Oliver and Boyd, 1935), chap. 2. For a nonmathematical account, as well as the claim that all eight cups were sorted correctly, see David Salsburg, *The Lady Tasting Tea: How Statistics Revolutionized Science in the Twentieth Century* (New York: W. H. Freeman, 2001), chap. 1.

In many areas of research, the threshold for statistical significance in published findings is 5%, or 1 out of 20. Taken at face value, this would imply that one out of every twenty such findings is expected to be random noise, and not the effect the authors claim. See, for example, John P. A. Ioannides, "Why Most Published Research Findings are False," *PLoS Med* (2005): e124. The situation is exacerbated when researchers repeat an experiment until a "significant" result is obtained. In particle physics, by contrast, the threshold for significance is 5 sigma, or roughly 1 in 3.5 million.

Time's Petty Tyrants

Compare Shakespeare, *As You Like It*, 2.7, and Ptolemy, *Tetrabiblos*, 4.10.

The Astrological Origins of the Week

The planetary hour scheme is described by Cassius Dio, *Historiae Romanae*, 37.18–19. Dio, who wrote around the year 200, notes that "The custom . . . is now found among all mankind, though its adoption has been comparatively recent." *Dio's Roman History*, with an English translation by Earnest Cary, Ph.D., on the basis of the version by Herbert Baldwin Foster, Ph.D., 9 vols. (London: W. Heinemann; New York: The Macmillan Co., 1914-27), 3:128–31. For a fascinating discussion of the origins of the week and its social impact, see Eviatar Zerubavel, *The Seven Day Circle: The History and Meaning of the Week* (Chicago: University of Chicago Press, 1989, c1985).

The Age of Aquarius

The discovery of the precession of the equinoxes is recounted in Ptolemy *Almagest*, 7.2–3. Ptolemy, writing around the year 150 of the Common Era, records that Hipparchus (ca. 150 BC) had access to the even earlier observations of Timocharis (ca. 300 BC) and was able to compare these against his own. See Claudius Ptolemy, *Ptolemy's Almagest*, translated and annotated by G.J. Toomer, rev. ed. (Princeton: Princeton University Press, 1998), 327–29.

For two early mentions of the Age of Aquarius, see "A New Cycle of Progress," *The Esoteric: A Magazine of Advanced and Practical Esoteric Thought* 1, no. 1 (July 1887): 1–5, and "A Few Points of the Koreshan System," *The Flaming Sword* 3, no. 12 (March 1892): 10–11. No doubt earlier examples can be found. However, the fact that both of H. P. Blavatsky's influential tomes, *Isis Unveiled* (1877) and *The Secret Doctrine* (1888), mention precession but not the Age of Aquarius suggests that the idea is unlikely to have arisen much earlier. The notion of a "New Age" is very ancient. The phrase *Novus ordo seclorum*, for instance, adopted as part of the Seal of the United States in 1782, is itself an echo of Virgil's Fourth Eclogue.

The official reference systems and models used to compute the precession quantities are set forth in "International Earth Rotation and Reference System Service (IERS) Conventions (2010)," edited by Gérard Petit and Brian Luzum (IERS Technical Note no. 36). These standards adopt the P03 Precession Theory and Definition of the Ecliptic detailed in N. Capitaine et al., "Expressions for IAU 2000 Precession Quantities," *Astronomy and Astrophysics* 412 (2003). The new precession equations, which are fifth-order in time, supersede the third-order equations given, for example, in Jean Meeus, *Astronomical Algorithms*, 2nd ed. (Richmond, VA: Willmann–Bell, 1998), 134–37. In our application, the third-order and fifth-order precession formulas yield results which differ by eight days.

"Aquarius" from *Hair*. Lyrics by James Rado and Gerome Ragni, music by Galt MacDermot, © 1966, 1967, 1968, 1970 (copyrights renewed) James Rado, Gerome Ragni, Galt MacDermot, Nat Shapiro, and EMI U Catalog, Inc.

2: FROM OBSCURE BEGINNINGS

Fred Espenak and Jean Meeus, "Five Millennium Catalog of Solar Eclipses: –1999 to +3000 (2000 BCE to 3000 CE) Revised," NASA Technical Publication TP-2009-214174 (Greenbelt, MD: NASA, 2009), Catalog Number 1571, Canon Plate 079.

Sigmund Freud, *Moses and Monotheism*, translated by Katherine Jones (Mansfield Centre, CT: Martino, 2010).

That Amarna was located within the path of totality is derived from the eclipse predictions of Fred Espenak and Chris O'Byrne, NASA Goddard Space Flight Center, Greenbelt, MD, via NASA's JavaScript Solar Eclipse Explorer, https://eclipse.gsfc.nasa.gov/JSEX/JSEX-index .html, accessed July 9, 2017. Note, however, that the uncertainty of this estimate is substantial. For the eclipse of 1338 BC, uncertainty in the quantity ΔT may be as high as half an hour, corresponding to longitude uncertainties of upwards of 7° (Espenak and Meeus, "Five Millennium Catalog," 16). Nevertheless, the largely east–west pattern of this eclipse path suggests that it's not at all unreasonable to entertain the hypothesis that a major solar eclipse was visible in ancient Egypt that day.

Egyptologists are notoriously fickle when it comes to assigning specific years to the regnal dates of the pharaohs. A death date of 1336 BC for Akhenaten is given, for example, in *The*

Oxford History of Ancient Egypt, edited by Ian Shaw (Oxford and New York: Oxford University Press, 2003), 485. Freud wanted Moses to be a follower of Akhenaten, in which case we should have expected Akhenaten's death before the eclipse of 1338 BC. On the other hand, I reckon an equally lively story could be crafted in which Akhenaten himself is cast in the role of the Exodus pharaoh.

The Pyramid of the Pharaoh Unis

For an astronomical interpretation of early archaeological sites, see Giulio Magli, *Archaeoastronomy: Introduction to the Science of Stars and Stones* (New York: Springer, 2016).

The Ancient Egyptian Pyramid Texts, translated by James P. Allen, 2nd ed. (Atlanta: SBL Press, 2015), 44, 65.

An Ancient Egyptian Coffin Lid with a Map of the Stars

Otto Neugebauer and Richard A. Parker, *Egyptian Astronomical Texts*, vol. 1, *The Early Decans* (Providence, RI: Brown University Press, 1960), 6. See also Otto Neugebauer, *The Exact Sciences in Antiquity*, 2nd ed. (New York: Dover, 1969), 82–89. And see especially Sarah Symons, Robert Cockcroft, Jesse Bettencourt, and Cody Koykka, "Ancient Egyptian Astronomy Database," http://aea.physics.mcmaster.ca, accessed July 15, 2017. The term *decan* is not Egyptian but Greek. The word, which derives from *deka* = 10, refers to the leader of a group of ten and is the origin of the modern word "dean."

The International Earth Rotation and Reference System (IERS) announces upcoming leap seconds in IERS Bulletin C, https://www.iers.org/IERS/EN/Publications/Bulletins/bulletins.html.

Fragments of the MUL.APIN Astronomy Tablets

Hermann Hunger and David Pingree, *MUL.APIN: An Astronomical Compendium in Cuneiform*, Archiv für Orientforschung, Supplement 24 (Horn, Austria: Ferdinand Berger & Söhne, 1989). See also Hermann Hunger and David Pingree, *Astral Sciences in Mesopotamia* (Leiden and Boston: Brill, 1999), 57–83.

The literature presents a few minor inconsistencies regarding the modern analogs of the MUL.APIN constellations. Our list follows Francesca Rochberg, *The Heavenly Writing: Divination, Horoscopy, and Astronomy in Mesopotamian Culture* (New York: Cambridge University Press, 2004), 127–28, note 21. Rochberg, however, lists 18 constellations instead of 17, with Pisces divided into three constellations instead of two.

A Collection of Eclipse Omens

Some 44 individual prognosticators are attested by name in royal dispatches. Hermann Hunger, *Astrological Reports to Assyrian Kings*, State Archives of Assyria vol. 8 (Helsinki: Helsinki University Press, 1992), xx.

On these and other divinatory traditions in an ancient Mesopotamia, see Rochberg, *Heavenly Writing*, 10, 45, 55, 66, and throughout.

A full translation of tablet K.3563 can be found in Francesca Rochberg-Halton, "The Assumed 29th Ahu Tablet of Enuma Anu Enlil," in *Language, Literature, and History: Philological and*

Historical Studies Presented to Erica Reiner, edited by Francesca Rochberg-Halton (New Haven: American Oriental Society, 1987), 327–50.

A Cuneiform Horoscope

Ptolemy, *Almagest*, 3.7. Translation by Gerald J. Toomer in Claudius Ptolemy, *Ptolemy's Almagest*, (Princeton: Princeton University Press, 1998), 166.

Hunger and Pingree, *Astral Sciences*, 144.

Translation from Francesca Rochberg, *Babylonian Horoscopes* (Philadelphia: American Philosophical Society, 1998), 56–57. Rochberg lists tablet AB 251 as the second oldest personal horoscope. The oldest, dated to January, 410 BC, is in a different format and lacks a prognostication. It seems forgivable, then, to transfer the title of oldest horoscope to tablet AB 251.

Rochberg cites Astronomical Diary No. -453 iv 2 for the earliest use of the zodiac as an evenly-spaced celestial coordinate system. Rochberg, *Babylonian Horoscopes*, 30.

Tablet AB 251 was dated to April 29, 410 BC, by Abraham Sachs in "Babylonian Horoscopes," *Journal of Cuneiform Studies* 6, no. 2 (1952): 54–57. (Note that the first line, which is missing, is a reconstruction and the "Pincer of the Scorpion" refers to Libra.) Sachs presents both linguistic and astronomical arguments for his assertion. Having the benefit of more modern ephemerides, I disagree that a date of March 22/23, 173 BC, can be discarded on purely astronomical grounds.

An Astronomical Diary Chronicling the Conquest of Alexander the Great

Abraham J. Sachs and Hermann Hunger, *Astronomical Diaries and Related Texts from Babylonia*, vol. 1, *Diaries from 652 B.C. to 262 B.C.* (Vienna: Österreichischen Akademie der Wissenschaften, 1988), 176–79.

A connection, however indirect, between K.3563, which is from the seventh century BC, and contemporary Babylonian interpretations of the eclipse of 331 BC is suggested by Robartus J. van der Spek, "Darius III, Alexander the Great and Babylonian Scholarship," in *A Persian Perspective: Essays in Memory of Heleen Sancisi-Weerdenburg*, edited by Wouter Henkelman and Amélie Kuhrt (Leiden: Nederlands Instituut voor het Nabije Oosten, 2003).

Fred Espenak and Jean Meeus, "Five Millennium Catalog of Lunar Eclipses: −1999 to +3000 (2000 BCE to 3000 CE)," NASA Technical Publication TP-2009–214173 (Greenbelt, MD: NASA, 2009), Catalog Number 4036, Canon Plate 202.

3: A QUICK SPIN AROUND THE CELESTIAL SPHERE

The World in Rome's Hands

"*Urbem Syracusas maximam esse Graecarum, pulcherrimam omnium saepe audistis. Est, iudices, ita ut dicitur.*" Cicero, *In Verrem*, 2.4.117.

The principal ancient sources for the siege of Syracuse are Polybius, *Histories*, 8 (ca. 100 BC); Livy, *History of Rome*, 24–25 (ca. 1 BC); and Plutarch, *Life of Marcellus* (ca. 100). Archimedes' boast of being able to lift the Earth is recounted in Plutarch, *Marcellus*, 14.7. Archimedes'

"Iron Hands" are mentioned in Polybius, *Histories*, 8.6.2–4; Plutarch, *Marcellus*, 15.2; and Livy, *History*, 24.34.10–11. The death of Archimedes is described in Livy, *History*, 25.31.9–10, and Plutarch, *Marcellus*, 19.4–6.

A date of April 1, 212 BC, for the Roman assault on Syracuse is merely a guess based on my reconstruction of Livy's vague timeline. (Archimedes' death likely occurred some months later, when the Romans stormed the central part of the city.) For a reconstruction of the ancient Syracusan calendar, and the placement of Artemisios in springtime, see Paul A. Iversen, "The Calendar on the Antikythera Mechanism and the Corinthian Family of Calendars," *Hesperia* 86 (2017): 129–203. As a point of contrast, the Nemoralia, the ancient Italian festival to Diana (the Roman counterpart to Artemis), was celebrated in mid-August. This is the festival described so unforgettably in James Frazer's *The Golden Bough*. If we were to let our imagination get carried away, we might even picture Archimedes in the role of the *Rex Nemorensis*, the "King of the Wood," whose powers are transferred to another only through his ritual murder.

Cicero's description of Archimedes' celestial models and their predecessors is found in *De re publica*, 1.21–2. Compare also Cicero, *De natura deorum*, 2.88, and *Tusculanae disputationes*, 1.63. It's not clear from Cicero's wording whether Thales' globe was celestial or terrestrial. For a modern account of the Antikythera Mechanism, see Alexander Jones, *A Portable Cosmos: Revealing the Antikythera Mechanism, Scientific Wonder of the Ancient World* (New York: Oxford University Press, 2017). The small celestial globe belonging to the Galerie J. Kugel in Paris is described in Elly Dekker, *Illustrating the Phaenomena: Celestial Cartography in Antiquity and the Middle Ages* (Oxford: Oxford University Press, 2013), appendix 2.1, G1.

Star Law and Star Lore

On the Babylonians lacking a conception of the celestial sphere, see Francesca Rochberg, *The Heavenly Writing: Divination, Horoscopy, and Astronomy in Mesopotamian Culture* (New York: Cambridge University Press, 2004), 126–27.

According to the *Thesaurus Linguae Graecae*, the oldest attestation of the word *astronomia* is in the play *The Clouds* by Aristophanes (ca. 420 BC), while *astrologia* first appears a few decades later, in the writings of Isocrates and Xenophon. Xenophon, in fact, makes use of both words. Thesaurus Linguae Graecae® Digital Library, edited by Maria C. Pantelia, University of California, Irvine, http://www.tlg.uci.edu, accessed March 13, 2019.

Archimedes mentions the heliocentric system of Aristarchus of Samos in "The Sand Reckoner." In this treatise, Archimedes is not interested in the question of whether the Sun orbits the Earth or vice versa. Instead, he wants to demonstrate that it is possible to compute the total number of grains of sand needed to fill up the universe. Archimedes notes correctly that the heliocentric cosmos proposed by Aristarchus would need to be much, much larger than the standard geocentric cosmos due to the apparent lack of observable stellar parallax. For Archimedes' use of the term *astrologos*, see Archimedes, "Arenarius," in *Archimedis Opera Omnia*, edited by J. L. Heiberg, 3 vols. (Leipzig: B. G. Teubner, 1880–81), 2:245, 249.

Mapping the Sky

For an overview of the basic astronomical coordinate systems and formulas for transforming between them, see, for example, Jean Meeus, *Astronomical Algorithms*, 2nd ed. (Richmond, VA: Willmann–Bell, 1998), chap. 13.

Sun-Based or Star-Based Astrology?

In accord with the traditional sources, a northern hemisphere perspective, in which Aries is a spring sign, is adopted throughout this book.

For an excellent and very readable explanation of the International Celestial Reference Frame (ICRF), see George H. Kaplan, *The IAU Resolutions on Astronomical Reference Systems, Time Scales, and Earth Rotation Models: Explanation and Implementation*, United States Naval Observatory Circular no. 179 (Washington, DC: U.S. Naval Observatory, 2005), chap. 3.

Ptolemy adopts the convention of defining Aries by the spring equinox in the *Almagest*, 2.7, entirely without comment. In the *Tetrabiblos*, 1.10, he acknowledges that it is customary to define Aries this way without acknowledging the significant implications of this custom for astrology. Prior to Ptolemy, there was a well-attested tradition of assigning the vernal point to Aries 8°. See Otto Neugebauer, *A History of Ancient Mathematical Astronomy*, 3 vols. (Berlin, Heidelberg, and New York: Springer, 1975), 2:593–600.

One example of a star appearing in a horoscope is Girolamo Cardano's birth chart for King Henry VIII, presented in the introduction of this book. Cardano notes that the star Aldebaran was positioned alongside Venus in the Ninth House.

A Thirteenth Zodiac Sign?

In English, at least, the zodiac signs of Scorpio and Capricorn have distinct spellings from the IAU constellations of Scorpius and Capricornus.

Zodiac systems consisting of more than twelve signs date back at least as far as 1970, when Steven Schmidt proposed 14 signs. Steven Schmidt, *Astrology 14: Your New Sun Sign* (Indianapolis: Bobbs–Merrill, 1970). The year 2016 saw another flare-up of these speculations. See, for example, Tess Koman, "Everything You Need to Know About the Controversial 13th Zodiac Sign," *Cosmopolitan*, September 20, 2016 (online only), http://www.cosmopolitan.com/lifestyle/a3614109/everything-you-need-to-know-about-13th-zodiac-sign-constellation-ophiucus.

The modern list of 88 constellations was introduced in *Transactions of the International Astronomical Union* 1 (1922): 158. Curiously, 89 constellations are listed, since Argo appears as a single constellation alongside its three component constellations, Carina, Puppis, and Vela. The constellation boundaries were first specified by Eugène Delporte, *Délimitation scientifique des constellations (tables et cartes)*, Report of Commission 3 of the International Astronomical Union (Cambridge, U.K.: Cambridge University Press, 1930). The updated J2000.0 boundaries of the IAU constellations used in figure 3.5 are taken from the IAU's website, https://www.iau.org/public/themes/constellations, accessed May 2, 2017.

4: SIGNS FROM ABOVE

F. R. Stephenson, L. V. Morrison, and C. Y. Hohenkerk, "Measurements of the Earth's Rotation: 720 BC to AD 2015," *Proceedings of the Royal Society A*, 472:20160404, http://dx.doi.org/10.1098/rspa.2016.0404.

Details of Caesar's assassination are taken from Suetonius, *Life of the Divine Julius*, 80–82, and Plutarch, *Life of Caesar*, 63–66. The utterance, "Beware the Ides of March," is from Shakespeare's *Julius Caesar*, 1.2.

For the modern site of Caesar's assassination, see Filippo Coarelli, *Rome and Environs: An Archaeological Guide*, translated by James J. Clauss and Daniel P. Harmon (Berkeley: University of California Press, 2014), 283–84.

An Empire of Astrology

Compare Suetonius's account of the omens predicting the death of Julius Caesar with his account of the explicitly astrological forecast of the death of the emperor Domitian. And, most famously, there are the magi in the Gospel of Matthew.

Caesar's comet is examined from both a literary and astronomical perspective in John T. Ramsey and A. Lewis Licht, *The Comet of 44 B.C. and Caesar's Funeral Games*, American Philological Association American Classical Studies no. 39 (Atlanta: Scholars Press, 1997).

Although most Roman legions had emblems such as lions and bulls that need not have been astrological, several chose the explicitly astrological Capricorn. A stone relief from Hadrian's wall, for example, names the Legio II Augusta and depicts its emblem, Capricorn, together with a Pegasus (British Museum no. OA.250).

Silver *cistophorus* of Augustus, Ephesus, 25 BC, from the collection of the American Numismatic Society, 1944.100.39182.

The feast of Trimalchio appears in Petronius, *Satyricon*, 27–78. For a detailed disquisition on the difficulties of deciphering Trimalchio's delicacies, see K. F. C. Rose and J. P. Sullivan, "Trimalchio's Zodiac Dish (Petronius, *Sat.* 35. 1–5)," *Classical Quarterly* 18, no. 1 (May 1968): 180–84.

Thrasyllus & Son, Astrologers

The careers of Thrasyllus and Balbillus are traced in Frederick H. Cramer, *Astrology in Roman Law and Politics*, Memoirs of the American Philosophical Society 37 (Baltimore: J. H. Furst, 1954), part 1, chap. 3. Part 2 of this monograph surveys the Roman edicts against astrology, the earliest of which dates to 139 BC.

The Poetry of Heaven

An excellent account of the rise of Greek astrology is Cramer, *Astrology in Roman Law and Politics*, part 1, chap. 1. For direct source material (most of which, however, dates to the later Roman Empire), there is the monumental *Catalogus Codicum Astrologorum Graecorum* (*CCAG*), edited by Franz Boll, Franz Cumont, Wilhelm Kroll, and Alessandro Olivieri, 12 vols. (Brussels: Henricus Lamertin, 1898–1953).

The majority (*maxima ac plurima*) of Nechepso–Petosiris fragments are preserved in the writings of Vettius Valens. See Ernst Riess, "Nechepsonis et Petosiridis fragmenta magica," *Philologus*, Supplementband 6 (1891–93): 329.

The chapter summary of Thrasyllus's *Pinax* is found in *CCAG*, 8.3.99–101. An English translation appears in Robert H. Schmidt, *Antiochus, with Porphyry, Rhetorius, Serapio, Thrasyllus, Antigonus et al., Definitions and Foundations* (Cumberland, MD: Golden Hind Press, 2009), 341–45. In this summary we learn, for example, that Thrasyllus belonged to the camp who put the equinox at Aries 8°.

The fragments of Balbillus are found in *CCAG*, 8.3.103–4, and *CCAG*, 8.4.233–38. A partial translation appears in Otto Neugebauer and Henry Bartlett van Hoesen, *Greek Horoscopes*, Memoirs of the American Philosophical Society 48 (Philadelphia: American Philosophical Society, 1959), 76–78.

Bouché-Leclercq also puts Manilius first in his chronological list of Greco-Roman astrologers. Auguste Bouché-Leclercq, *L'astrologie grecque* (Paris: Ernest Leroux, 1899), xx–xxi.

"Haec ego divino cupiam cum ad sidera flatu / ferre, nec in turba nec turbae carmina condam / sed solus, vacuo veluti vectatus in orbe / liber agam currus non occursantibus ullis / nec per iter socios commune regentibus actus, / sed caelo noscenda canam, mirantibus astris/ et gaudente sui mundo per carmina vatis, / vel quibus illa sacros non invidere meatus / notitiamque sui, minima est quae turba per orbem." Manilius, *Astronomica*, edited and translated by G. P. Goold (Cambridge, MA: Harvard University Press, 1997), 2.136–44.

"Fata regunt orbem . . ." Manilius, *Astronomica*, 4.14.

Hostility toward Epicureans was preserved in Jewish tradition, where the term "Epikoros" or "Apikoros" signified an especially noxious type of atheist. See Gotthard Deutsch, "Apikoros," *The Jewish Encyclopedia*, 12 vols. (New York and London: Funk and Wagnalls, 1901–06), 1:665–66.

Zodiac First Impressions

Manilius describes the zodiac personality types in *Astronomica*, 4.122–293. Petronius, *Satyricon*, 39, relates a humorous version of the same. Fittingly, Trimalchio's sign is Cancer.

What's Your Sign?

An excellent article exploring the enigma of Augustus's zodiac sign is Tamsyn Baron, "Augustus and Capricorn: Astrological Polyvalency and Imperial Rhetoric," *Journal of Roman Studies* 85 (1995): 33–51.

The method of computing the length of life via the starter (ἀφέτης, *aphetes*) and destroyer (ἀναιρέτης, *anairetes*) is described by Ptolemy, *Tetrabiblos*, 3.10, and also Balbillus, *CCAG*, 8.4.235–38. This method is known as the method of *aphesis*, prorogation, or primary directions. See Martin Gansten, "Balbillus and the Method of *aphesis*," *Greek, Roman, and Byzantine Studies* 52 (2012): 587–602.

On the length of the year 46 BC, "the last year of confusion," see Thomas Hewitt Key and A. S. Wilkins, "Calendarium," in *A Dictionary of Greek and Roman Antiquities*, 3rd ed., edited by William Smith, William Wayte, and G. E. Marindin (London: J. Murray, 1890–91), 343–45. Among the valiant, modern efforts to fix the dating of the pre-Julian Roman calendar, see Chris Bennett, "Two Notes on the Chronology of the Late Republic," *Zeitschrift für Papyrologie und Epigraphik* 147 (2004): 169–74.

Perhaps the strongest argument that Manilius 4.122–293 concerns Sun signs is that he explicitly treats the influence of the signs when rising in a separate section, 4.505–84.

Signs and Significance

More accurately, it turns out that the staff at the newspaper *Le Monaco*, which was the source of Pearson's roulette data, were too lazy to record the actual roulette results and simply made them up. See Adam Kucharski, *The Perfect Bet: How Science and Math are Taking the Luck out of Gambling* (New York: Basic Books, 2016), 4–7.

The critical values of the chi-squared distribution can be found, for instance, in *NIST/SEMAT-ECH e-Handbook of Statistical Methods*, 1.3.6.7.4, http://www.itl.nist.gov/div898/handbook, accessed December 18, 2018. For an experiment with 12 classes, there are 11 degrees of freedom. Note that the chi-squared test, which has the advantage of simplicity, suffers from low statistical power, meaning that, compared to other tests, larger sample sizes are needed to detect deviations from uniformity.

U.S. Supreme Court justice birth dates are from Wikipedia, accessed December 18, 2018.

NHL player birthdays are from Ralph Slate, "hockeydb.com: The Internet Hockey Database," http://www.hockeydb.com, accessed December 13, 2018.

For a discussion of the relative age effect, see Malcolm Gladwell, *Outliers: The Story of Success* (New York: Little, Brown, 2008), chap. 1.

Baseball, basketball, and football player birthday data are from Greg Spira, "The Boys of Late Summer: Why do so many pro baseball players have August birthdays?," *Slate*, April 16, 2008, https://slate.com/culture/2008/04/why-do-so-many-pro-baseball-players-have-august-birthdays.html, accessed December 18, 2018. The data are compiled by month, not by day, so it's not possible to analyze the data by sign. Curiously, Spira claims there is no relative age effect in the NFL data, but a chi-squared value of 29.2 is significant even at the 99% confidence level. The baseball data ($\chi^2 = 93.1$ = significant) and basketball data ($\chi^2 = 4.5$ = not significant) are much less equivocal.

England men's national football team player birthday data are from Chris Goodwin and Glen Isherwood, "England Football Online," http://www.englandfootballonline.com, accessed December 16, 2018.

"If you need to use statistics . . ." is a quip commonly attributed to Ernest Rutherford, although without any solid sourcing.

U.S. birth data, 1994–2014, are from the National Center for Health Statistics, Centers for Disease Control and Prevention (1994–2003), and the Social Security Administration (2000–14). These data sets were compiled and made available by *FiveThirtyEight* as supporting material for Carl Bialik, "Some People Are Too Superstitious to Have a Baby on Friday the 13th," *FiveThirtyEight*, May 13, 2016, https://fivethirtyeight.com/features/some-people-are-too-superstitious-to-have-a-baby-on-friday-the-13th, accessed December 18, 2018. The data files themselves were taken from https://github.com/fivethirtyeight/data/tree/master/births, accessed December 18, 2018.

Olympic sailing medalist birth dates are from Wikipedia, accessed August 29, 2017.

See "The Story Behind the Seal," United States Naval Observatory, http://www.usno.navy.mil/USNO/library/library-history/the-story-behind-the-seal-1, accessed November 1, 2017. The USNO seal was designed in the mid-1800s, prior to Housman's major and Goold's minor emendations of Manilius's text. The modern variant, with Goold's translation, reads: *"adde gubernandi studium, quod venit in astra / et pontum caelo vincit.*" "There is also the art of navigation, which has reached out to the stars and binds the sea to heaven." Manilius, *Astronomica*, 4.279–80.

5: CLAUDIUS PTOLEMY'S ASTROLOGICAL TRAVEL GUIDE

"cuius similitudinem et formam non alia magis arbor quam pinus expresserit. Nam longissimo velut trunco elata in altum quibusdam ramis diffundebatur." Pliny the Younger, *Letters*, 6.16. His account of the eruption is continued in 6.20.

C. Barbante et al., "Greenland Ice Core Evidence of the 79 AD Vesuvius Eruption," *Climate of the Past*, June 13, 2013.

The *Hou Hanshu* ("History of the Later Han") records the arrival of a Roman delegation to China in the year 166. See John E. Hill, *Through the Jade Gate – China to Rome: A Study of the Silk Routes 1st to 2nd Centuries CE*, 2 vols. (CreateSpace, 2015), 1:23–27.

The Pompeiian Lakshmi is described, for instance, in Mary Beard, *The Fires of Vesuvius: Pompeii Lost and Found* (Cambridge, MA: Belknap Press, 2008), 24.

"ultima Thule." Virgil, *Georgics*, 1.30.

The earliest account of Thule describes it as a place having the consistency of a sponge or jellyfish: Strabo, *Geographica*, 2.4.1. I'm partial to the opinion that Thule originally referred to the Scandinavian mainland and that an echo of its name is preserved in the modern region of Telemark, Norway. See Olaus Magnus, *Ain kurze Auslegung und Verklerung der neuuen Mappen von den alten Gœttenreich und andern Nordlenden* (Venice: Giovanni Tommaso, 1539), §E, A.

The Greatest

Otto Neugebauer, *The Exact Sciences in Antiquity*, 2nd ed. (New York: Dover, 1969), 145. Neugebauer attributes the adage to the mathematician David Hilbert.

For Ptolemy's biography, see Gerald J. Toomer, "Ptolemy," in *Dictionary of Scientific Biography*, edited by Charles Coulston Gillispie, 18 vols. (New York: Charles Scribner's Sons, 1970–81), 11:186–206.

As Above, So Below

Ptolemy announces his intention to write a geographical treatise in *Almagest*, 2.13.

See, in general, J. Lennart Berggren and Alexander Jones, *Ptolemy's Geography* (Princeton: Princeton University Press, 2000). The eclipse at Gaugamela is discussed in 1.4; the Greco-Roman expeditions to Africa and Asia are discussed in appendices A, B, and E; the "metropolis of the Sinai [Chinese]" (μητρόπολις Σινῶν), in 1.14; the latitude of Thule, in 1.7.

Squashing the Sphere

The figure of "roughly 8,000 localities" is from Berggren and Jones, *Ptolemy's Geography*, 19. Ptolemy was not the first to make a map of the world since he was preceded by Eratosthenes and others. Nor was he the first to develop projections of the sphere, which were of interest to astronomers and makers of sundials. But Ptolemy appears to be the first to meaningfully apply these methods to the problem of terrestrial cartography.

John P. Snyder, *Flattening the Earth: Two Thousand Years of Map Projections* (Chicago: University of Chicago Press, 1993).

Within the *Geography*, Ptolemy introduces three separate map projections. See Berggren and Jones, *Ptolemy's Geography*, 35–40.

An Image of the World

Nathan Sidoli and J. L. Berggren, "The Arabic Version of Ptolemy's *Planisphere* or *Flattening the Surface of the Sphere*: Text, Translation, Commentary," *SCIAMVS* 8 (2007): 37–139.

Neugebauer argues that Hipparchus is the probable inventor of the stereographic projection, although the evidence for this is circumstantial. Otto Neugebauer, *A History of Ancient Mathematical Astronomy*, 3 vols. (New York, Heidelberg, and Berlin: Springer, 1975), 2:868–69.

The stereographic projection is sometimes referred to by its Ptolemaic name, the planisphere projection. Note, however, that the planispheres commonly found in planetarium gift shops use a different projection, the azimuthal equidistant projection.

A rare and curious astrolabe showing a stereographic map of the Earth, including the coastlines of North and South America and some impish-looking sea monsters, is the geographical astrolabe by Gillis Coignet, made in Antwerp in 1560, in the collection of the Museum of the History of Science, University of Oxford, Inv. 53211.

A Means to an End?

Otto Neugebauer, *Exact Sciences in Antiquity*, 191.

Jon D. Giorgini and JPL Solar System Dynamics Group, "NASA/JPL Horizons On-Line Ephemeris System," http://ssd.jpl.nasa.gov/?horizons.

Ptolemy's Astrology

The oldest known degree requirements of any university are documented for the University of Bologna, in 1405. These include a detailed reading list "*ad astrologiam*" consisting of both astronomical and astrological authors. See Domenico Maria da Novara, *I Pronostici di Domenico Maria da Novara*, edited by Fabrizio Bònoli, Giuseppe Bezza, Salvo de Meis, and Cinzia Colavitta (Florence: Leo S. Olschki, 2012), 8–10.

"Τῶν τὸ δι' ἀστρονομίας προγνωστικὸν τέλος παρασκευαζόντων, ὦ Σύρε, δύο τῶν μεγίστων καὶ κυριωτάτων ὑπαρχόντων." Ptolemy, *Tetrabiblos*, 1.1.

Aristotle (*Metaphysics*, 6.1026a) famously divided all of "theoretical philosophy" into three branches: physics, mathematics, and what he named theology but his followers called metaphysics—that is, the thing you studied "after physics." These three branches were differentiated according to where their subject matter fell along the axes of changeable vs. eternal, and material vs. immaterial. However (*Physics*, 2.2.194a), Aristotle included within mathematics disciplines that he acknowledged were somewhat more physical, specifically, optics, harmonics, and astronomy (*astrologia*). Ptolemy opens the *Almagest* by echoing

Aristotle's threefold division of physics, mathematics, and theology, and categorizes his book as a work of mathematics.

Ptolemy does not use the word *astrologia*, but within the *Tetrabiblos* he does employ the terms "astrologer" (ἀστρολόγους, 4.4) and "astrological" (ἀστρολογικάς, 3.13). For specific instances of Ptolemy's use of the terms "mathematics" and "mathematician" in the *Almagest*, see Claudius Ptolemy, *Syntaxis Mathematica*, in *Claudii Ptolemai Opera quae exstant omnia*, edited by J. L. Heiberg, 3 vols. (Leipzig: B. G. Teubner, 1898–1919), 1.1, 4.2, 9.1, 9.2.

Ptolemy makes the distinction between general and genethlialogical astrology in *Tetrabiblos*, 2.1. The description of the zodiac and planetary genders, influences, and rulerships is in *Tetrabiblos*, 1.5, 1.6, 1.17.

Astral Geography

Aspects are treated in *Tetrabiblos*, 1.13. Ptolemy does not acknowledge an association between the triplicities and the classical elements, but this linkage can be found, for example, in Ptolemy's contemporary Vettius Valens, *Anthologies*, 2.1.

On the Babylonian sense of astral geography, see Francesca Rochberg, *The Heavenly Writing: Divination, Horoscopy, and Astronomy in Mesopotamian Culture* (New York: Cambridge University Press, 2004), 68–69. Manilius treats this topic in *Astronomica*, 4.711–817. Ptolemy's system is in *Tetrabiblos*, 2.3.

The fact that the *ecumene* described in *Tetrabiblos*, 2.3, is less extensive than that of the *Geography* is one of the arguments for considering the *Tetrabiblos* an earlier work than the *Geography*. Berggren and Jones, *Ptolemy's Geography*, 21.

Troglodytes and Pamphylians: Ptolemy, *Tetrabiblos*, 2.3. Translation by F. E. Robbins in Ptolemy, *Tetrabiblos*, Loeb Classical Library 435 (Cambridge, MA: Harvard University Press, 1940), 155, 149.

"Do not unlike places produce unlike men?" This objection to astrology is raised explicitly by Cicero. Cicero, *De divinatione*, 2.96; translation by W. A. Falconer, in Cicero, *On Old Age, On Friendship, On Divination*, Loeb Classical Library 154 (Cambridge, MA: Harvard University Press, 1923), 479.

Around the Aegean Sea, Ptolemy regards Thrace, Macedonia, Hellas, Achaia, Crete, the Cyclades, and the coastal region of Asia Minor as distinct regions with distinct ethnicities. Ptolemy, *Tetrabiblos*, 2.3.

Jared Diamond, *Guns, Germs, and Steel: The Fates of Human Societies*, 20th anniversary edition (New York: W. W. Norton, 2017).

Ptolemy, *Tetrabiblos*, 2.3. Translation by Robbins, 135, 141.

In the Eye of the Beholder

"Spartacus Gay Travel Index," *Spartacus International Gay Guide* (Berlin: Bruno Gmünder, 2017), https://spartacus.travel/gaytravelindex.pdf, accessed February 28, 2017.

Tyler Vigen, *Spurious Correlations: Correlation Does Not Equal Causation* (New York and Boston: Hachette, 2015), 57.

Burton introduces the "Sotadic Zone" in Richard F. Burton, translator, *The Book of The Thousand Nights and a Night: A Plain and Literal Translation of the Arabian Nights Entertainments*, 10 vols. (Privately Printed by the Burton Club, 1885), 10:179.

Ptolemy, *Tetrabiblos*, 2.8. Translation by Robbins, 189.

6: HOW UNIQUE IS A HOROSCOPE?

The only indication that the renewal of the 1,460-year "canicular year" was acknowledged by anyone is from Censorinus (third century), *De die natali*, 18.10, 21.10–11. In older texts, the date given is *"ante diem XII kal. Aug."* (July 21) of the year 139. However, from the large number of exact dates known in the Egyptian calendar, in particular from Ptolemy, there's no question that 1 Thoth in the year 139 fell on July 20. The suggestion, however speculative, that Ptolemy may have been involved is made in Alexander Jones, ed., *Time and Cosmos in Greco-Roman Antiquity* (Princeton: Princeton University Press, 2017), 42.

The technical term for "dawn-rising" is "heliacal rising."

The idea that the chronology of ancient Egypt could be organized around the Sothic cycle was first proposed by Eduard Meyer, "Aegyptische Chronologie," *Abhandlungen der Königlich Preussischen Akademie der Wissenschaften*, Philosophische und Historische Abhandlungen, Abh. 1 (1904): 1–212. Some decades later, Otto Neugebauer provided a more measured assessment of the antiquity and importance of this cycle. See Jim Ritter, "Otto Neugebauer and Ancient Egypt," in *A Mathematician's Journeys: Otto Neugebauer and Modern Transformations of Ancient Science*, edited by Alexander Jones, Christine Proust, and John M. Steele (New York: Springer, 2015), 153–55.

Each coin image in figure 6.2 shows the reverse of a bronze drachm of Antoninus Pius, minted in Alexandria, and dated to 144–45, in the collection of the American Numismatic Society. Their collection identifiers are: (i) Aries and Mars: 1944.100.60335; (ii) Taurus and Venus: 1944.100.60338; (iii) Gemini and Mercury: 1944.100.60339; (iv) Cancer and the Moon: 1944.100.60342; (v) Leo and the Sun: 1944.100.60348; (vi) Virgo and Mercury: 1944.100.60349; (vii) Libra and Venus: 1944.100.60350; (viii) Scorpio and Mars: 1944.100.60352; (ix) Sagittarius and Jupiter: 1944.100.60355; (x) Capricorn and Saturn: 1944.100.60358; (xi) Aquarius and Saturn: 1944.100.60364; (xii) Pisces and Jupiter: 1944.100.60367.

Virgil, *Aeneid*, 6.847–53.

The Lighthouse of the World

Ancient assertions about the age of astrology can be found in Frederick H. Cramer, *Astrology in Roman Law and Politics*, Memoirs of the American Philosophical Society 37 (Baltimore: J. H. Furst, 1954), 18.

See, for instance, John Dillery, "Hellenistic Historiography," in *The Oxford History of Historical Writing*, vol. 1, *Beginnings to AD 600*, edited by Andrew Feldherr and Grant Hardy (Oxford: Oxford University Press, 2011), 172–74.

On Hipparchus's use of Babylonian data and the assertion that, contrary to what is often asserted, it is unlikely that he ever lived in Alexandria, see Gerald J. Toomer, "Hipparchus," in *Dictionary of Scientific Biography*, edited by Charles Coulston Gillispie, 18 vols. (New York: Charles Scribner's Sons, 1970–81), vol. 15, supplement 1, 207–24.

Isaiah 47:13.

The origins of Thrasyllus are not unambiguous, but Cramer (*Astrology in Roman Law and Politics*, 92–93) insists that he hailed from Alexandria.

A Bouquet of Astral Flowers

The authoritative Greek text of the *Anthologies* is David Pingree, ed., *Vettii Valentis Atiocheni Anthologiarum Libri Novem* (Leipzig: B. G. Teubner, 1986). No complete English edition has been published. However, Mark T. Riley has placed his invaluable unpublished translation online at http://www.csus.edu/indiv/r/rileymt/vettius%20valens%20entire.pdf. The horoscopes, treated on their own, are translated and analyzed in Otto Neugebauer and Henry Bartlett van Hoesen, *Greek Horoscopes*, Memoirs of the American Philosophical Society 48 (Philadelphia: American Philosophical Society, 1959).

Pingree, *Anthologiae*, xviii–xx, includes an index (*Thematum Index*) of the 123 unique horoscopes (*themata*) that occur within the *Anthologies*.

Quotations are from Neugebauer and van Hoesen, *Greek Horoscopes*, 81, 93, 122, 121, 101, 102. These correspond to Pingree, *Anthologiae*, 4, 24, 95, 94, 47, 49. For the dancer's horoscope (*thema* 94), Pingree's corrected text places these events in the dancer's 20th, not 25th, year.

The details of Valens's own biography are from *Anthologiae*, 4.11.4–5. The word Valens uses to describe his ascetic life is ἐγκρατέστερον, which, in general, means "self-sufficient" or "disciplined." However, within Valens's milieu, the word may imply a connection with the Encratites (Ἐγκρατίτες), a gnostic Christian sect whose members abstained from, among other things, relations with women and eating meat.

The conjecture that *thema* 83 is Valens's own nativity is made by Pingree, *Anthologiae*, v. The additional information cited comes from *Anthologiae*, 1.21.17–26, 2.31.8–14; 5.6.70–2, and 7.6.135–40. Valens is one of a group of six individuals examined who all survived the same maritime mishap: *Anthologiae*, 7.6.159–60.

Vettius Valens, *Anthologies*, 5.6.72, 9.12.19. Translation by Riley, 105, 162.

On the doctrine of cosmic sympathy, see, for instance, René Brouwer, "Stoic Sympathy," in *Sympathy: A History*, edited by Eric Schliesser (Oxford: Oxford University Press, 2015), 15–35.

Astrology as an Experimental Science

Olivia Koski and Jana Grcevich, with art by Steve Thomas, *Vacation Guide to the Solar System: Science for the Savvy Space Traveler!* (New York: Penguin, 2017).

At Mars's closest approach, which is about 54.5 million kilometers from Earth, the gravitational force exerted by the red planet on a 70 kg Earthling is only about 1×10^{-6} N, that is, 1 micronewton.

See especially Karl Popper, "Science: Conjectures and Refutations," Thomas Kuhn, "Logic of Discovery or Psychology of Research," and Imre Lakatos, "The Popperian versus the Kuhnian

Research Programme," reprinted in *Philosophy of Science and the Occult*, edited by Patrick Grim, 2nd ed. (Albany: State University of New York Press, 1990).

Vettius Valens, *Anthologies*, 6.9.7–8. Translation by Riley, 122.

The horoscope in question is Vettius Valens, *Anthologiae*, 2.41.85–89 (*thema* 35). The Greek verb used by Valens, θηριομαχέω, "fight with wild beasts," is the same used by Paul in 1 Cor. 15:32. Note that Neugebauer and van Hoesen, *Greek Horoscopes*, 96, have corrected the position of Mercury from Aries to Pisces in order to yield a plausible first-century date.

The Meanings of a Horoscope

"If *hora* is the time when everything happens concurrently, *chronos* is close to its opposite . . . it is restricted to specialized contexts where it signifies duration of time. It is time in which nothing happens, or at least nothing that can register passage of time." Norman Austin, *Archery at the Dark of the Moon: Poetic Problems in Homer's Odyssey* (Berkeley: University of California Press, 1975), 89.

This same eight-sign sequence can also be found in the horoscopes of the first-century astrologer Dorotheus of Sidon. See David Pingree, ed., *Dorothei Sidonii carmen astrologicum* (Leipzig: BSB Teubner, 1976). Similarly, this is the format for the majority of the horoscopes among the astronomical papyri of Oxyrhynchus (first century BC through sixth century CE). Alexander Jones, ed., *Astronomical Papyri from Oxyrhynchus*, Memoirs of the American Philosophical Society 233, 2 vols. (Philadelphia: American Philosophical Society, 1999), 1:247–95.

The Astrology Machine

The history of the astrolabe's origin and early development is chronicled in Otto Neugebauer, *A History of Ancient Mathematical Astronomy*, 3 vols. (Berlin and New York: Springer, 1975), 2:868–78. In this early context, it's important to note that *astrolabos* (ἀστρολάβος), which translates literally to "star-taker," was a generic term which referred to any instrument equipped with a sighting device for taking elevations. Ptolemy devotes section 6.1 of the *Almagest* to describing an "astrolabe" that, in fact, more closely resembles an armillary sphere.

A translation of John Philoponus's astrolabe treatise can be found in Robert T. Gunther, *The Astrolabes of the World*, 2 vols. (Oxford: Oxford University Press, 1932), 1:61–81.

How Unique Is a Horoscope, Really?

The angular separation between a planet and the Sun is called its elongation. The maximum elongations of Mercury and Venus are 28° and 48°, respectively.

The United Nations estimates the 2017 population at 7.55 billion, and the 2015–20 crude birth rate at 18.6 per 1,000 population. The product of these numbers yields an estimate for births per year, which can then be converted to births per day. United Nations, Department of Economic and Social Affairs, Population Division, *World Population Prospects: The 2017 Revision*, vol. 1, *Comprehensive Tables* (ST/ESA/SER.A/399), Tables 1 and A.19.

The story of the potter's wheel of Nigidius Figulus is recounted in Augustine, *City of God*, 5.3.

More precisely, my list of Z-codes begins on March 17, 9999 BC. Why this date? Because this is the highest negative value which can be submitted to the NASA/JPL Horizons online ephemeris system.

In general, it's necessary to know the precise UTC time of someone's birth in order to specify their Z-code. However, certain calendar dates are such that regardless of the hour, there is no ambiguity in the Z-code. This is the case for the birthdays of Drew Brees, Norah Jones, Heath Ledger, Lance Bass, Jason Momoa, Pink (Alecia Beth Moore), John Krasinski, and Michael Owen, whose date and city of birth were obtained from Wikipedia, accessed March 26, 2019. The Z-code of Markus Persson's birthday is not free of ambiguity, but the ambiguous period amounts to only 19 minutes out of 24 hours. For the remaining five individuals, I have relied upon the birth times reported at the Astro-Databank (http://www.astro.com/astro-databank, last accessed March 26, 2019), which maintains a database of celebrity birth times verified, where possible, from official birth certificates.

7: PATTERNS, PATTERNS, EVERYWHERE!

For descriptions of al-Mansur's Baghdad, complete with reconstructed maps, see Guy Le Strange, *Baghdad during the Abbasid Caliphate* (Oxford: Clarendon Press, 1900), chaps. 1, 2. Taking as a guide map 2, "The Round City in the Time of Mansur," the site of the Palace of the Golden Gate can be plausibly located near modern-day Baghdad's 14th of July Street, at a point opposite to where the Utafiyah neighborhood juts into the Tigris.

"Les fondations furent jetées à un moment choisi par l'astronome Nawbakht et par Māshallah ibn Sāriya." Ya'kūbī, *Les Pays*, translated by Gaston Wiet (Cairo: Imprimerie de l'Institut Français d'Archéologie Orientale, 1937), 11–12.

The horoscope of Baghdad's foundation can be found in *The Chronology of Ancient Nations: An English Version of the Arabic Text of the Athâr-ul-Bâkiya of Albîrûnî*, translated and edited by Edward Sachau (London: published for the Oriental Translation Fund of Great Britain & Ireland by W. H. Allen, 1879), 262–63. Biruni, who mentions only Nawbakht but not Masha'allah, presents this horoscope within an account of the Julian calendar and gives the foundation date explicitly as July 23. It has, however, long been noted that the horoscope diagram itself refers unambiguously to July 30. Whether this discrepancy represents Biruni's own error, a copyist's error or, indeed, indicates that there may have been multiple foundation moments is a question for which there may not be an answer.

A Golden Age?

Baghdad is listed as the world's most populous city beginning in the year 900, when its population reached an estimated 900,000 inhabitants. George Modelski, *World Cities: –3000 to 2000* (Washington, DC: Faros, 2000), 219.

On Baghdad's Bayt al-Hikma, see especially Dimitri Gutas, *Greek Thought, Arabic Culture: The Graeco-Arabic Translation Movement in Baghdad and Early 'Abbāssid Society (2nd–4th/8th–10th centuries)* (New York: Routledge, 1998), 53–60.

Al-Kindi's epithet "Philosopher of the Arabs" is found in Muhammad ibn Ishaq ibn al-Nadim, *The Fihrist: A 10th Century AD Survey of Islamic Culture*, translated and edited by Bayard Dodge ([S.L.]: Great Books of the Islamic World, Inc.; Chicago: Distributed by KAZI Publications, 1998), 615.

On the observatories established by al-Mamun and Arabic science generally, see Jim al-Khalili, *The House of Wisdom: How Arabic Science Saved Ancient Knowledge and Gave Us the Renaissance* (New York: Penguin, 2011), chap. 6 and throughout.

Regarding the characterization of science as a sequence of metaphysical paradigm shifts, I have in mind, of course, Thomas S. Kuhn, *The Structure of Scientific Revolutions* (Chicago: University of Chicago Press, 1962).

The early history of coffee is shrouded in mystery. It's quite likely that it was known for its medicinal uses by Razi (ninth century) and Ibn Sina (tenth century), but it does not appear to have become a common beverage in the Islamic world until the fifteenth century. See Bennett Alan Weinberg and Bonnie K. Bealer, *The World of Caffeine: The Science and Culture of the World's Most Popular Drug* (New York: Routledge, 2001), chap. 1.

Naming the Stars

The list of Arabic astronomers cited by Copernicus is taken from Nidhal Guessoum, "Copernicus and Ibn al-Shatir: Does the Copernican Revolution have Islamic Roots?" *Observatory* 128 (June 2008): 235.

Surprisingly, the International Astronomical Union (IAU) did not get around to regularizing the proper names of the stars, as distinct from their well-established designations, until 2016. Equally surprising is that not all of the 100 brightest stars have been assigned names, such that a list of the 110 brightest stars needed to be consulted in order to obtain 100 star names. These names, and their officially sanctioned spellings, are listed at "Naming Stars," International Astronomical Union, https://www.iau.org/public/themes/naming_stars, accessed April 11, 2018.

The origins and etymologies for the names of stars have been adapted from Paul Kunitzsch and Tim Smart, *A Dictionary of Modern Star Names: A Short Guide to 254 Star Names and Their Derivations*, 2nd ed. (Cambridge, MA: Sky & Telescope, 2006). Visual magnitude values are those of the Hipparcos catalog, which, in general, differ slightly from those listed on the website of the IAU.

The Museum of the History of Science at Oxford University possesses an especially old astrolabe from Syria (Inv. no. 47632) made by Khafif, apprentice to Ali ibn Isa al-Asturlabi (that is, Ali, son of Isa the astrolabist), dated to the latter half of the ninth century. The oldest unambiguously dated astrolabe, signed by a certain Nastulus in the year 927–28 (AH 315), is part of the al-Sabah collection of the Kuwait National Museum (LNS 36 M).

English, Latin, and Arabic names for the parts of an astrolabe can be found in *The Planispheric Astrolabe* (Greenwich, U.K.: National Maritime Museum, 1976), appendix 1.

Planets that Pass in the Night

On the significance of astrology to the imperial ideology of the Sasanians and, subsequently, the Abbasids, see Gutas, *Greek Thought, Arabic Culture*, 34–52.

Three sentences in the *Fihrist* constitute most of what is known of Masha'allah's biography: "*Mā Shā' Allāh ibn Athrā*, whose name Mā Shā' Allāh, was Mīshā, which means *yithro*. He was a Jew, and lived from the time of al-*Manṣūr* to the time of al-*Ma'mūn*. He was a man of distinction and during his period the leading person for the science of the judgment of the stars." Al-Nadim, *Fihrist*, 650.

Paul Kunitzsch, "On the Authenticity of the Treatise on the Composition and Use of the Astrolabe Ascribed to Messahalla," *The Arabs and the Stars: Texts and Traditions on the Fixed Stars, and Their Influence in Medieval Europe* (Northampton: Variorum Reprints, 1989).

Masha'allah's astrological world history was called "On Conjunctions, Religions, and Peoples." This has survived only as an extended fragment within the work of a ninth-century Christian astrologer named Ibn Hibintā. A translation of this fragment, along with extensive commentary, including reconstructed dates for the conjunction years, is given by E. S. Kennedy and David Pingree, *The Astrological History of Māshā'allāh* (Cambridge, MA: Harvard University Press, 1971).

The names "small," "middle," and "great" for the different types of Jupiter–Saturn conjunctions do not appear in the fragment of Masha'allah's "On Conjunctions, Religions, and Peoples." These terms are used throughout Abraham ibn Ezra, *The Book of the Word*, translated and edited by Shlomo Sela (Leiden and Boston: Brill, 2010). Pierre d'Ailly distinguishes four types of Jupiter–Saturn conjunctions: small (*minor*) conjunctions, occurring every 20 years; great (*magna*) conjunctions, occurring every 60 years, when the conjunction returns to the same zodiac sign; major (*maior*) conjunctions, when the sequence shifts triplicities, a period he overestimates at 240 years; and maximal (*maxima*) conjunctions, when the sequence cycles through all four triplicities from Aries to Aries, a period he overestimates at 960 years. Pierre d'Ailly, *Concordantia astronomie cum hystorica narratione* (Venice: Erhardus Ratdolt, 1490), chap. 1.

Matthew 3:11.

The Abbasid revolt occurred during the conjunction year 749, the last of that watery triplicity. Masha'allah apparently believed that the Abbasids would be overthrown by a fully Persian dynasty from Isfahan in the year 815. Kennedy and Pingree, *The Astrological History of Māshā'allāh*, 111–13.

Cracking the Code

Abū Ma'šar, *On Historical Astrology: The Book of Religions and Dynasties* (*On the Great Conjunctions*), edited and translated by Keiji Yamamoto and Charles Burnett (Leiden and Boston: Brill, 2000).

Abraham ibn Ezra, *The Book of the Word*, 271–79.

Kepler's account of the fiery trigon appears in Johannes Kepler, *De stella nova* (Prague: Paul Sessius, 1606), 10–57.

"*nec restituetur Iudaeis libertas ante tertiam revolutionem Michaelis spiritus, haecque fiet post Christi nativitatem anno 1880, mense 8.*" Johannes Trithemius, *De septem secundeis* (Frankfurt: Cyriacus Jacobus, 1545).

The astrological assessment of the University of Paris physicians regarding the Black Plague is reprinted in *Étude Historique et Critique sur la Peste*, edited and translated by H. Émile Rébouis (Paris: A. Picard, Crovill-Morant et Foucard, 1888).

D'Ailly, *Concordantia astronomie*, chaps. 60, 61.

Al-Kindī, *Scientific Weather Forecasting in the Middle Ages: The Writings of Al-Kindī*, edited and translated by Gerrit Bos and Charles Burnett (London and New York: Kegan Paul, 2000).

Marie-Thérèse d'Alverny and Françoise Hudry, "Al-Kindi: De Radiis," *Archives d'histoire doctrinale et littéraire du moyen âge* 41 (1974): 139–260.

Among the list of al-Kindi's works, which occupies twelve whole pages in the modern translation of the *Fihrist*, there appears the title of a lost work: "The Use of Indian Arithmetic, four sections" (Al-Nadim, *Fihrist*, 617). Al-Khwarizmi's book on the use of Hindu numerals has not survived in Arabic, but it was preserved in an influential Latin translation from the twelfth century, *Algoritmi de numero Indorum*.

Leonardo Pisano, better known by his nickname Fibonacci, introduced the word *zephirum* in his *Liber abbaci* in the year 1202. *Scritti di Leonardo Pisano*, edited by Baldassarre Boncompagni, vol. 1, *Il Liber Abbaci di Leonardo Pisano* (Rome: Tipografia delle Scienze Matematiche e Fisiche, 1857), 2.

Al-Kindi's pioneering cryptological work is described in Ibrahim A. Al-Kadit, "Origins of Cryptology: The Arab Contributions," *Cryptologia* 16, no. 2 (April 1992): 97–126.

Knowledge Is Power

Book 3 of Trithemius's *Steganographia*, which had long been taken as evidence for his necromancy, was deciphered independently by Thomas Ernst and James A. Reeds in 1996–97. Thomas Ernst, "Schwarzweisse Magie: Der Schlussel zum dritten Buch der Steganographia des Trithemius," *Daphnis* 25 (1996): heft 1; James A. Reeds, "Solved: The Ciphers in Book III of Trithemius's Steganographia," *Cryptologia* 22, no. 4 (October, 1998): 291–313.

Ronald Clark, *The Man Who Broke Purple: The Life of Colonel William Friedman, Who Deciphered the Japanese Code in World War II* (Boston: Little, Brown, 1977).

William F. Friedman and Elizebeth S. Friedman, *The Shakespearean Ciphers Examined* (Cambridge, U.K.: Cambridge University Press, 1957), 145, 163, 22.

The correlation of Jupiter–Saturn conjunctions and the deaths of U.S. presidents has long been noted, even before the attempted assassination of Ronald Reagan in 1981. See, for example, John Gribbin, "Lunatic Fringe: Presidential Cycles," *New Scientist*, October 18, 1979, 212.

This extraordinary photograph of William and Elizebeth Friedman is discussed in a fascinating article by William H. Sherman, "How to Make Anything Signify Anything," *Cabinet* 40 (Winter 2010–11), http://www.cabinetmagazine.org/issues/40/sherman.php, accessed April 11, 2018.

8: WHEN YOU WISH UPON A STAR, WHICH ALGORITHM SHOULD YOU USE?

"Climbing Mount Everest is Work for Supermen," *New York Times*, March 18, 1923.

"sola videndi insignem loci altitudinem cupiditate ductus, ascendi." Francesco Petrarca, *Selected Letters*, translated by Elaine Fantham, 2 vols. (Cambridge, MA: Harvard University Press, 2017), 1:44–45. Today, Mount Ventoux is famous as one of the mountain stages of the Tour de France.

"Man is the measure of all things" is attributed to Protagoras of Abdera by Diogenes Laertius, *Lives of the Eminent Philosophers*, 9.8.2 [51]. Petrarch, in his letter, cites a similar sentiment of Seneca: *"nichil praeter animum esse mirabile, cui magno nichil est magnum."* For the association of this expression with the Renaissance humanists, see especially *Civilisation: A Personal View by Kenneth Clark*, episode 4, "Man: The Measure of all Things" (BBC-TV, 1969).

"Et eunt homines mirari alta montium et ingentes fluctus maris et latissimos lapsus fluminum et oceani ambitum et gyros siderum, et relinquunt se ipsos." Augustine, *Confessions*, 10.8.15.

On Jung, Petrarch, and synchronicity, see Richard Tarnas, *Cosmos and Psyche: Intimations of a New World View* (New York: Plume, 2007), 50–60.

Carl Jung, "In Memory of Richard Wilhelm," appendix to *The Secret of the Golden Flower: A Chinese Book of Life*, translated and explained by Richard Wilhelm with a commentary by C. G. Jung, translated from the German by Cary F. Baynes (New York: Harcourt Brace, 1962), 142.

Wanderers

"Chaucer's text of A.D. 1391 has the supreme importance of being the first good description of the construction and use of a Scientific Instrument to be written for Englishmen in their own language. It is therefore the *doyen* of English Scientific Text-books." Robert T. Gunther, *The Astrolabes of the World*, 2 vols. (Oxford: Oxford University Press, 1932), 1:vii.

"In the eighth year of his reign, which was in the Era of 1298 and the year 1260 after the birth of Jesus Christ, this King Alfonso ordered everything translated from Latin to Castilian Spanish so that he might have knowledge of all writings." *Chronicle of Alfonso X*, translated by Shelby Thacker and José Escobar (Lexington, KY: University Press of Kentucky, 2002), 46.

See especially Bernard R. Goldstein, "Astronomy among Jews in the Middle Ages," in *Science in Medieval Jewish Cultures*, edited by Gad Freudenthal (New York: Cambridge University Press, 2011), 136–46.

The University of Paris medical faculty's diagnosis that the Black Death was caused by a triple conjunction of Saturn, Jupiter, and Mars in 1345 is reprinted in *Étude Historique et Critique sur la Peste*, edited and translated by H. Émile Rébouis (Paris: A. Picard, Crovill-Morant et Foucard, 1888).

"How many people perished in the Black Death is unknown; for Europe, the most widely cited figure is 33 percent." John Kelly, *The Great Mortality: An Intimate History of the Black Death, the Most Devastating Plague of All Time* (New York: HarperCollins, 2005), 11.

Petrarca, *Selected Letters*, 1:367.

The Heavens—and Hell

"l'amor che move il sole e l'altre stelle." Dante, *Paradiso*, 33.145. The word *stelle*, "stars," is the final word in each of the three *cantiche* of the *Divina Commedia*: *Inferno, Purgatorio*, and *Paradiso*.

For the life of Guido Bonatti, see Lynn Thorndike, *A History of Magic and Experimental Science*, 8 vols. (London: Macmillan, 1923-58), 2:825-40. Bonatti's astrology book has no fixed name and is variously referred to as the *Decem tractatus astronomiae* (Augsburg, 1491), *De astronomia tractatus x* (Basel, 1550), or sometimes just the *Liber astronomicus* (Thorndike). A modern and very helpful translation is Guido Bonatti, *Book of Astronomy*, translated by Benjamin N. Dykes (Minneapolis: Cazimi Press, 2010). My citations refer to the Basel edition of 1550.

Ezzelino da Ramano appears in Dante, *Inferno*, 12.109-10.

"sicut fuit ille tyrannus Ycilinus de Romano, et erat quidam eius Astrologus nomine Salionus quem credo assensisse sibi, potius ex timore quam quod crederet ita esse. Et hoc credo propterea, quia Ycilinus habebat quendam eius fratrem in compedibus, de quo ipse timebat ne occideret eum." Bonatti, *De astronomia*, col. 144.

"Verum est tamen quod ego elegi quadam vice comiti Guidoni Novello de Tuscia contra Florentinos . . . et tamen debellavimus eos et vicimus ex toto: et fuit hoc in valle Arbiae apud montem apertum." Bonatti, *De astronomia*, col. 393.

The traitorous Bocca degli Abati, who gets a kick in the head from Dante, appears in *Inferno*, 32.73-114. Bonatti appears in *Inferno*, 20.118.

Dante, *Inferno*, 20.37-39. Translation by Robert Hollander and Jean Hollander in Dante, *The Inferno: A Verse Translation* (New York: Random House, 2000), 363.

An Algorithm for Every Occasion

The standard description of judicial astrology appears in the *Speculum astronomiae* of Albertus Magnus (thirteenth century). Albertus divides *astronomia iudiciaria* into four parts: (i) revolutions; (ii) nativities; (iii) interrogations; and (iv) elections, to which he appends the science of "images." Bonatti, however, uses the word "judgment," *iudicium*, when referring to interrogations but not elections.

On Cecco d'Ascoli, see Thorndike, *Magic and Experimental Science*, 2:948-68. Bonatti, in return, labels as heretics those who deny that "fortune rules over everything" (*"fortuna dominatur in omni re"*), since the only alternative, he asserts, would be to hold God responsible for all of the world's injustices. Bonatti, *De astronomia*, col. 388.

These questions about food are treated under judgments pertaining to the Twelfth House. Bonatti, *De astronomia*, cols. 380-83.

The Houses of Heaven

Designations for the Greek Houses are those listed in Ptolemy, *Tetrabiblos*, translation by F. E. Robbins in Ptolemy, *Tetrabiblos*, Loeb Classical Library 435 (Cambridge, MA: Harvard University Press, 1940), 272-73, note 2.

Will It Be a Boy or a Girl?

A very early forerunner of judicial astrology is the first-century *Carmen astrologicum* of Dorotheus. See David Pingree, ed., *Dorothei Sidonii carmen astrologicum* (Leipzig: BSB Teubner, 1976).

Giovanni Petrarca was born sometime in 1337; so it's not clear whether his unnamed mother was actually pregnant or merely soon-to-be-pregnant when the child's father ascended Mount Ventoux in April 1336.

The algorithm regarding the gender of an unborn child is Bonatti, *De astronomia*, col. 250: "*Si mulier portat masculum vel fœminam.*"

Cheating Fate

An English edition is Muhammad ibn Musa al-Khwarizmi, *The Algebra of Mohammed ben Musa*, edited and translated by Frederic Rosen (London: Oriental Translation Fund, 1831).

Bonatti stipulates that an astrologer ought not to cast horoscopes for his own questions in Bonatti, *De astronomia*, col. 225: "*Quod Astrologus non debet aspicere sibijpsi.*"

Bonatti explicitly acknowledges the role of free will in astrological elections. "Electing is the desire of the intellect resulting from an act of free will" ("*Eligere autem, est appetitus intellectus resultans ex actu liberi arbitrij*"). Bonatti, *De astronomia*, col. 385.

On employing both an interrogation and an election prior to the Battle of Montaperti, Bonatti writes, "*veruntamen ego habebam primo per quæstionem quod debebamus obtinere, et post habuimus electionem fortissimam in eundo ad prælium.*" Bonatti, *De astronomia*, cols. 393–94.

When to Buy and Sell

"*si non poteris eos aptare omnes, apta illos quos aptare potes, quia non aptabis ita paucos ex eis, quin prosint electioni tuae, licet non tantum quantum velles.*" Bonatti, *De astronomia*, col. 395.

"*sed nos ut plurimum non habemus tempus expectandi: unde oportet quod eligamus in spaciis quae habemus et commiscere illud boni quod possumus in electione nostra.*" Bonatti, *De astronomia*, col. 396.

Bonatti's buy-and-sell algorithms are "*De emptione causa lucrandi*" and "*Quando aliquis voluerit vendere rem aliquam ut lucretur cum precio eius.*" *De astronomia*, cols. 429–30. Bonatti's instructions for how to "accommodate" a planet are described under "*Qualiter aptetur planeta,*" cols. 399–402.

The specific parameters of the Bonatti Fund, such as starting year, initial allocation percentage, and buy/sell fractions, have no effect on the overall result. In general, the longer you have your money in the Bonatti Fund, the worse off you are.

On the rate of success (or lack thereof) of managed funds to beat the market, see Daniel Kahneman, *Thinking, Fast and Slow* (New York: Farrar, Straus and Giroux, 2011), 215.

When to Take a Drive

FARS (Fatality Analysis Reporting System), https://www-fars.nhtsa.dot.gov/Main/index .aspx, accessed May 10, 2018.

"*sitque Luna in 11. vadens ad 10. et nunquam ponas eam sub terra.*" Bonatti, *De astronomia*, col. 475.

The total number of fatal crashes reported in 2012–16 was 158,242. Incidents which lack time or location data are dropped from our analysis, which accounts for the slightly reduced sample of 155,544. Note that the time when a crash occurs is not, of course, the same as when the journey began. However, my assumption has been that the edge cases where a journey began with the Moon below the horizon yet the crash occurs when the Moon was above the horizon are, by and large, balanced out by the scenarios where the opposite is the case.

Dividing the Houses

As a guide to how this topic is dealt with by modern astrologers, I have followed Ralph William Holden, *The Elements of House Division* (Romford, U.K.: L. N. Fowler, 1977).

Ernst Zinner, *Regiomontanus: His Life and Work*, translated by Ezra Brown (Amsterdam and New York: North–Holland, 1990), 9–12, 51–5.

Regiomontanus's treatise on House division is the *Tabulae directionum*, undertaken at the behest of János Vitéz, archbishop of Esztergom and chancellor of Hungary. "It was first printed posthumously in 1490 by Erhard Ratdolt in Augsburg, and went through eleven editions up to 1626; The number of copies is not insignificant . . . Among those who used these tables were . . . Nicholas Copernicus . . . and Kepler." Zinner, *Regiomontanus*, 93.

Regarding the popularity of Placidus Houses among modern astrologers, see Holden, *Elements of House Division*, 91–92.

Regiomontanus dismisses the Campanus method in one brief remark: "But this method is so foreign to the minds of the ancients and so useless since it relies on an imaginary vertical circle which has no power that we deem it best to pass it over in silence" (*"Modus tamen ille quam alienus sit a mentibus antiquorum et quam futilis quod circulo verticali imaginario ac nihil virtutis habenti innititur: silencio praetereundum censemus"*). Regiomontanus, *Tabulae directionum* (Augsburg: Erhard Ratdolt, 1490), 14th problem.

Ptolemy's description of how the Houses should be divided, which is limited to a brief remark at the beginning of *Tetrabiblos*, 3.10, most closely resembles the Equal-House system. This may be why Cardano, who had no small opinion of his own mathematical abilities, rejected the more mathematically sophisticated Regiomontanus Houses. Ptolemy's very reasonable suggestion, that the cusp of the First House be placed 5° above the horizon, instead of exactly on the horizon, does not seem to have been incorporated into any of the standard House systems.

Ex Iis Unam Cave: "Beware of One of Them"

This and many other charming sundial inscriptions can be found in René R. J. Rohr, *Sundials: History, Theory, and Practice*, translated by Gabriel Godin (New York: Dover, 1996), 126–29.

Medieval clock terminology was sufficiently generic that the transition from water clocks to weight-driven mechanical clocks was not captured very well in contemporary documents. See Gerhard Dohrn-van Rossum, *History of the Hour: Clocks and Modern Temporal Orders*, translated by Thomas Dunlap (Chicago: University of Chicago Press, 1996).

The assertion, however tenuous, is that Dante, *Paradiso*, 10.139–43, *"che l'una parte e l'altra tira e urge,"* may refer to the back-and-forth motion of a mechanical verge-and-foliot ("twig-

and-leaf'') escapement. A separate clock metaphor, albeit one that could apply equally well to a water clock, is *Paradiso*, 24.13–15. See Dohrn-van Rossum, *History of the Hour*, 92–94.

Isaac Newton, *The Principia: Mathematical Principles of Natural Philosophy*, translated by I. Bernard Cohen and Anne Whitman (Berkeley: University of California Press, 1999), Scholium to the Definitions 1, 408.

An excellent reference for understanding the technical details of astrolabe design is James E. Morrison, *The Astrolabe* (Tallmadge, OH: Good Place, 2007). Placidus cusps are equivalent to an astrolabe's unequal hour lines, even though the location of these arcs will differ. On the Prague clock, the astrolabe face appears upside down, since the clock uses a North Pole projection instead of a South Pole projection. Morrison, *Astrolabe*, 79–82, 306–9.

The Wheel of Fortune (*rota Fortunae*) metaphor dates back at least as far as Cicero (*In Pisonem*, 10). A century and a half later, Tacitus notes that it had already become a rhetorical cliché (*Dialogus de oratoribus*, 23). A few Roman-era astrologers' boards (*pinakes*) have survived. See Stephan Heilen and Dorian Gieseler Greenbaum, "Astrology in the Greco-Roman World," in *Time and Cosmos in Greco-Roman Antiquity*, edited by Alexander Jones (Princeton: Princeton University Press, 2017), 126–31. On the survival of these wheels into the Middle Ages, see Thorndike, *Magic and Experimental Science*, 1:682–84.

9: WHAT'S IN A NAME?

The authoritative modern biography is Victor E. Thoren, *The Lord of Uraniborg: A Biography of Tycho Brahe* (Cambridge, U.K.: Cambridge University Press, 1990). Tycho's nose is discussed on 22–26.

Tycho describes the night he discovered his new star in two works: *De nova stella* (Copenhagen, 1573) and, posthumously, *Astronomiae instauratae progymnasmata*, part 2, chap. 3 (Prague, 1602). See Tycho Brahe of Denmark, *Tychonis Brahe Dani Opera Omnia*, edited by J. L. E. Dreyer, 15 vols. (Copenhagen: Libraria Gyldendaliana, 1913–29), 1:16, 2:307–8. The accounts are inconsistent as to whether the new star equaled or exceeded the brightness of Venus.

"*cumque mihi, qui inde fere a pueritia, omnia coeli sidera perfecte (non enim magna huic scientiae inest difficultas) cognita haberem, satis evidenter constaret, nullam in eo coeli loco unquam ante extitisse, vel minimam, nedum tam conspicuae claritatis stellam . . .*" Tycho Brahe, *De nova stella*, in *Tychonis Brahe Opera Omnia*, 1:16.

"*Omnibus enim Philosophis constat, et res ipsa non obscure declarat, in aethera coelestis mundi regione, nullam fieri alterationem generationis vel corruptionis: sed coelum et quae in eo continentur aetherea corpora, non augeri, non imminui, non variari aut numero, aut magnitudine, aut lumine, aut quavis alia ratione: sed semper idem, sibique in omnibus simile, nullis terentibus annis permanere.*" Tycho Brahe, *De nova stella*, in *Tychonis Brahe Opera Omnia*, 1:16.

The account of Hipparchus's new star ("*novam stellam*") is preserved in Pliny, *Natural History*, 2.24 [95]. Pliny writes that it was this discovery which prompted Hipparchus to compile his star catalog. Because Pliny refers to the star's motion, the ancient and modern consensus is that the object was a comet. However, Tycho makes the cogent point that this interpretation presumes that Hipparchus, the greatest observational astronomer of antiquity, didn't know what a comet looked like. *Tychonis Brahe Opera Omnia*, 1:17.

David H. Clark and F. Richard Stephenson, *The Historical Supernovae* (Oxford: Pergamon Press, 1977), is a superb reference. Although Tycho made the most detailed observations of the supernova of 1572, he was not the first to sight it. Wolfgang Schüler of Wittenberg noted it five nights earlier, on November 6.

Tycho observed the new star with an inverted sextant. Thoren, *Lord of Uraniborg*, 58.

Tycho records that the nova ceased to be visible in March 1574. *Tychonis Brahe Opera Omnia*, 2:308.

On the miraculousness of his own discovery, *Tychonis Brahe Opera Omnia*, 1:16.

Adam S. Burrows, "Baade and Zwicky: 'Super-novae,' neutron stars, and cosmic rays," *Proceedings of the National Academy of Sciences of the United States of America* (*PNAS*) 112, no. 5 (February 3, 2015): 1241–42, https://doi.org/10.1073/pnas.1422666112.

Oliver Krause et al., "Tycho Brahe's 1572 supernova as a standard type Ia as revealed by its light-echo spectrum," *Nature* 456 (December 4, 2008): 617–19, http://dx.doi.org/10.1038/nature07608.

A Stage for All the World

For a comprehensive tally of Shakespeare's characters, I have consulted Eric M. Johnson, "Open Source Shakespeare: An Experiment in Literary Technology," https://www.opensourceshakespeare.org, accessed September 1, 2018. Open Source Shakespeare generates a list of 1,224 characters with speaking parts. Ignoring the trickier questions as to which plays are genuine, this number is still a slight overcount, since it includes instances of "All" or "Both" as entries. Pruning this list yields a number closer to 1,175 unique characters.

Shakespeare citations are *Hamlet*, 3.2.23–26; *Romeo and Juliet*, Prologue, 6; *Julius Caesar*, 1.2.231–32; *Hamlet*, 2.2.273–75 and 2.2.124–27.

For *Hamlet* as a cosmological allegory, see Peter D. Usher, *Shakespeare and the Dawn of Modern Science* (Amherst, NY: Cambria Press, 2010). Usher attributes the hypothesis of a link between *Hamlet* and Tycho Brahe's portrait to Johan Huizinga in 1910 (p. 124). Thoren, *Lord of Uraniborg*, suggests a 1592 legation to England which included both a Rosenkrantz and a Gyldenstierne as the likely origin of the characters' names (pp. 428–29).

"*Universum hoc et amplissimum totius Machinae mundanae Theatrum, Viri inclyti, Coelos, Terram, Maria, et quae in his comprehenduntur, Solem, Lunam, Stellas, Animantia, Vegetabilia, et Mineralia, per Divini numinis sapientiam, non in suimetipsius, sed hominis, quem suae imagini conformem reddidit, commodum necessitatemque creata et instituta esse, nemo sapiens ire potest inficias. Deus enim, cum sit incorporeus, immensus, aeternus, incomprehensibilis, ubique et nullibi, non indiget, corporea, finita, temporanea, comprehensibili, et locali, Mundi forma. Sed hominem, Mundo, quo ad haec consimilem, in terra, centro totius Universitatis, propterea statuit, ut inde, quasi ex specula, universi orbis Naturam et constitutionem contemplaretur: eaque ratione Dei invisibilis et incorporei, per visibilia et creata corpora, Maiestatem, Sapientiamque in hac mortali vita quodammodo agnosceret.*" Tycho Brahe, *De nova stella*, in *Tychonis Brahe Opera Omnia*, 1:35.

Hamlet, 2.2.321–33.

Words, Words, Words

On the seven heavens, see Kaufmann Kohler, "Angelology," in *The Jewish Encyclopedia*, 12 vols. (New York and London: Funk and Wagnalls, 1901-06), 1:583-97. For Talmudic views on astrology in general, see Kaufmann Kohler, "Astrology," in *The Jewish Encyclopedia*, 2:241-45.

Dante's description of "seventh heaven" is in *Paradiso*, cantos 21-22.

The *Oxford English Dictionary* has the word "influenza" entering English through Italian descriptions of an outbreak that began in 1743.

Hamlet, 3.1.4.

The Pith and Marrow of Its Attribute

Geoffrey Chaucer, *The Riverside Chaucer*, edited by Larry D. Benson, 3rd ed. (Oxford and New York: Oxford University Press, 2008), "General Prologue," A.414; "The Miller's Tale," A.3192, 3451, 3457, 3514; "The Wife of Bath's Prologue," D.324; "The Franklin's Tale," F.1266.

George Polya's maxim does not appear to be a direct quote, although it is widely treated as such. It does, however, capture the basic spirit of George Polya, *How to Solve It: A New Aspect of Mathematical Method* (Princeton: Princeton University Press, 1945).

"The Incunabula Short Title Catalogue is the international database of 15th-century European printing created by the British Library with contributions from institutions worldwide . . . The database records nearly every item printed from movable type before 1501, but not material printed entirely from woodblocks or engraved plates. 30,518 editions are listed as of August 2016, including some 16th-century items previously assigned incorrectly to the 15th century." https://data.cerl.org/istc, accessed September 1, 2018.

Ernst Zinner, *Regiomontanus: His Life and Work*, translated by Ezra Brown (Amsterdam and New York: North-Holland, 1990), 110-30.

There are several ways to analyze the data of a 2×2 contingency table, such as Fisher's exact test, a chi-squared test, or a binomial test of two proportions. Alternatively, the "astronomy" books can be compared against the null hypothesis of a 50-50 split. Regardless of the test employed, it's not possible to reject the null hypothesis that all of the book titles come from the same population.

The Time Is Out of Joint

"*Erunt etiam mulieres multe ultra solitum impudice et multa comittent adulteria et in omnibus actibus libidinis vexabuntur.*" Domenico Maria da Novara, *I Pronostici di Domenico Maria da Novara*, edited by Fabrizio Bònoli, Giuseppe Bezza, Salvo de Meis, and Cinzia Colavitta (Florence: Leo S. Olschki, 2012), 147.

Aloysius Lilius, *Compendium novae rationis restituendi kalendarium* (Rome: The Heirs of Antonio Blado, 1577), 1-2.

The figure of 365.242374 as the average length in days between successive March equinoxes around the year 2000 comes from J. Meeus and D. Savoie, "The History of the Tropical Year," *Journal of the British Astronomical Association* 102, no.1 (February 1992): 40–42.

Nicolaus Copernicus, *De revolutionibus orbium coelestium* (Nuremberg: Johannes Petreius, 1543). Calendar reform is discussed in the preface addressed to Pope Paul III.

For a general overview of the Julian calendar, Gregorian calendar, and Julian day, see Leofranc Holford-Strevens, *The History of Time: A Very Short Introduction* (Oxford: Oxford University Press, 2005). For a more detailed discussion of Universal Time (UT), Barycentric Dynamical Time (TDB), and ΔT = TDB–UT, see Jean Meeus, *Astronomical Algorithms*, 2nd ed. (Richmond, VA: Willmann–Bell, 1998), chap. 10.

The translation "Astronomy is written for astronomers" appears in *On the Revolutions / Nicholas Copernicus*, edited by Jerzy Dobrzycki, translation and commentary by Edward Rosen (Baltimore: Johns Hopkins University Press, 1978), 5. This edition incorporates parts of Copernicus's manuscript draft, which differs significantly from the 1543 printed edition, notably in the inclusion of an unprinted introduction to chapter 1. There Copernicus writes, "If then the value of the arts is judged by the subject matter which they treat, that art will be by far the foremost which is labeled astronomy by some, astrology by others, but by many of the ancients, the consummation of mathematics" (p. 7). This may be the only instance in which Copernicus writes the word *astrologia*.

In his *De nova stella*, Tycho outlines a planetary and meteorological "Diary for the year 1573." *Tychonis Brahe Opera omnia*, 1:74–130.

Kepler emphasizes the importance of planetary aspects throughout *Harmonice Mundi*, 4. Johannes Kepler, *Gesammelte Werke*, edited by Walther von Dyck and Max Caspar, 21 vols. (Munich: C. H. Beck, 1938–), 6:208–86. A direct statement that only planetary aspects should be retained in astrology can be found in his account of the supernova of 1604. Johannes Kepler, *De stella nova in pede serpentarii*, in *Gesammelte Werke*, 1:166–67.

Cardano's astrology is discussed in Anthony Grafton, *Cardano's Cosmos: The Worlds and Works of a Renaissance Astrologer* (Cambridge, MA: Harvard University Press, 2001).

In 1629, Kepler added a brief section to the *Rudolphine Tables* with the colorful title "*Sportula genethliacis missa*" ("A Gift Basket Sent to the Genethliac Astrologers"), in which he explains how the *Tables* can be used for casting horoscopes. It begins with the surprising admission, "*Quia plerique opus hoc Tabularum expetunt propter Astrologiam, quaeruntque, Num etiam Genethliaca Themata integra per nostra Praecepta possint erigi*" ("Since most seek out these Tables on account of astrology, and enquire whether genethliac horoscopes can also be cast complete according to our precepts"). Kepler, *Gesammelte Werke*, 10:244.

"*Mathematici officium vulgò putatur, annua scribere Prognostica*." Johannes Kepler, *De fundamentis astrologiae certioribus*, in *Gesammelte Werke*, 4:12.

Kepler's *prognostica* are collected in *Gesammelte Werke*, 11.2; his horoscopes (well over 1,000) are collected in 21.2.2.

For a description of the horoscopes cast by Kepler upon the birth of his son, see Dorian Gieseler Greenbaum, "Kepler's Personal Astrology: Two Letters to Michael Maestlin," in *From Māshā'allāh to Kepler: Theory and Practice in Medieval and Renaissance Astrology*, edited by

Charles Burnett and Dorian Gieseler Greenbaum (Ceredigion, U.K.: Sophia Centre Press, 2015), 177–200.

"tum deinde per somnia et nugas praedictionum genethliacarum educate." Johannes Kepler, *Tabulae Rudolphinae*, in *Gesammelte Werke*, 10:36. In contrast to his unequivocal rejection of genethliac astrology, it's much less clear whether Kepler's mature view of the universe left any room for "general" astrology, for instance, planetary influences over the weather.

Kepler's metaphor of astronomy as the daughter of astrology is introduced in the preface to the *Tabulae Rudolphinae* (*Gesammelte Werke*, 10:36), Kepler reprises the metaphor to conclude the astrological *"Sportula"* of his Tables: *"Haec hactenus, in gratiam gentis astrologicae, ne mater vetula (qua similitudine sum usus in praefatione ad lectorem) se destitutam et despectam a filia ingrata et superba queratur"* (10:254).

For a detailed account of the witchcraft proceedings against Kepler's mother, see Max Caspar, *Kepler*, translated and edited by C. Doris Hellman (New York: Dover, 1993), 240–58.

On the possibility of Vermeer's use of optics, see David Hockney, *Secret Knowledge: Rediscovering the Lost Techniques of the Old Masters* (New York: Viking Studio, 2001). And see especially *Tim's Vermeer*, directed by Teller, written by Penn Jillette and Teller (High Delft Pictures, 2013).

Noel M. Swerdlow, "Galileo's Horoscopes," *Journal for the History of Astronomy* 35, part 2, no. 119 (May 2004): 135–41.

Hamlet, 1.5.87–88.

10: BIG ASTROLOGY

"Apollo 11 Mission Report," NASA SP-238 (Washington, DC: Scientific and Technical Information Office, NASA, 1971).

Occultation

Bernard Capp, *Astrology and the Popular Press: English Almanacs 1500–1800* (London: Faber and Faber, 2008 [1979]), 36, 89.

Regarding the date and location of the inaugural meeting of the Theosophical Society, see Henry Steel Olcott, "Inaugural Address by Colonel H. Steel Olcott, President of the Theosophical Society, Delivered at Mott Memorial Hall in the City of New York, at the First Regular Meeting of the Society, November 17th, 1875," reprinted in *The Theosophist* 53 (August 1932): 502–16.

"We have not long to wait, and many of us will witness the Dawn of the New Cycle, at the end of which not a few accounts will be settled and squared between the races." Helena P. Blavatsky, *The Secret Doctrine: The Synthesis of Science, Religion, and Philosophy*, unabridged verbatim edition, 2 vols. (Pasadena, CA: Theosophical University Press, 2014 [1888]), 1:xliv.

Blavatsky, *The Secret Doctrine*, 1:viii.

Nicholas Campion, *A History of Western Astrology*, vol. 2, *The Medieval and Modern Worlds* (London and New York: Continuum, 2009), 233.

R. H. Naylor, "What the Stars Foretell for the New Princess and a Few Hints on the Happenings of this Week," *Sunday Express*, August 24, 1930, 11.

Campion discusses the origins of the 12-paragaph horoscope in *A History of Western Astrology*, 2:261.

On Blavatsky's evolutionary sequence of "root-races," see, for example, Blavatsky, *The Secret Doctrine*, 2:6–12. For an account of how this and many other occult ideas found their way into Nazi ideology, see especially Eric Kurlander, *Hitler's Monsters* (New Haven: Yale University Press, 2017), chap. 1.

Wassily Kandinsky, *Concerning the Spiritual in Art*, translated with an introduction by M. T. H. Sadler (New York: Dover, 1977 [1914]), chap. 3, "Spiritual Revolution," 13–14.

Richard Greene, *Holst: The Planets* (Cambridge, U.K.: Cambridge University Press, 1995), 41.

Martin Bernheimer, "Pop! John Williams on Philharmonic Podium," *Los Angeles Times*, November 12, 1983, as quoted in Emilio Audissino, *John Williams's Film Music: Jaws, Star Wars, Raiders of the Lost Ark, and the Return of the Classical Hollywood Music Style* (Madison, WI: The University of Wisconsin Press, 2014), 141.

Audissino, *John Williams's Film Music*, 76. And see especially Rick Beato, "John Williams vs. Gustav Holst or Star Wars vs. The Planets," *YouTube*, November 13, 2016, https://youtu.be/8IX1jSVmaAs.

Oh the Weather Outside Is . . . Radioactive?

Blavatsky, *The Secret Doctrine*, 1:viii.

Benedict Carey, "A Princeton Lab on ESP Plans to Close Its Doors," *New York Times*, February 10, 2007.

The Freud/Jung Letters: The Correspondence between Sigmund Freud and C. G. Jung, edited by William McGuire, translated by Ralph Manheim and R. F. C. Hull (Princeton: Princeton University Press, 1974), letter 259J, 427.

Carl Jung, "In Memory of Richard Wilhelm," appendix to *The Secret of the Golden Flower: A Chinese Book of Life*, translated and explained by Richard Wilhelm with a commentary by C. G. Jung, translated from the German by Cary F. Baynes (New York: Harcourt Brace, 1962), 142.

An excellent overview of cosmic rays written for a general audience is Michael W. Friedlander, *A Thin Cosmic Rain: Particles from Outer Space* (Cambridge, MA: Harvard University Press, 2000).

Clyde W. Tombaugh, "The Search for the Ninth Planet, Pluto," *Astronomical Society of the Pacific Leaflets* 5, no. 209 (April 1946): 73–80.

The 26th International Astronomical Union General Assembly held in Prague, Czech Republic, ratified Resolution B5, "Definition of a Planet in the Solar System," and Resolution B6, "Pluto," whereby Pluto was officially designated a dwarf planet, on August 24, 2006. There are currently five objects denominated as dwarf planets: Eris, Pluto, Haumea, Sedna, and Ceres.

The 2006 IAU categories of "dwarf planet" and "small solar system body" supersede the previous but still recognized category of "minor planet." A database of minor planets (785,045 as of October 20, 2018) is available at the International Astronomical Union Minor Planet Center, https://www.minorplanetcenter.net.

A comprehensive review of the sunspot record can be found in Frédéric Clette, Leif Svalgaard, José M. Vaquero, and Edward W. Cliver, "Revisiting the Sunspot Number: A 400-Year Perspective on the Solar Cycle," *Space Science Reviews* 186, no. 1-4 (December 2014): 35-103.

The sunspot data of figure 10.3 are from the World Data Center Sunspot Index and Long-Term Solar Observations (WDC-SILSO), Royal Observatory of Belgium, Brussels, http://www.sidc.be/silso/home. The plotted data series are: (i) Monthly mean total sunspot number (January 1749-September 2018) (SN_m_tot_V2.0.csv, accessed October 1, 2018); (ii) 13-month smoothed monthly total sunspot number (January 1749-September 2018) (SN_ms_tot_V2.0.csv, accessed October 8, 2018); and (iii) Archive of raw daily sunspot group counts (January 1, 1610-December 31, 2020) (GNobservations_JV_V1-12.csv, accessed September 24, 2018). Monthly mean sunspot group counts were computed from the raw daily group counts and scaled by a factor of 12.08 (from the original definition of the Group Number in Douglas V. Holt and Kenneth H. Schatten, "Group Susnpot Numbers: A New Solar Activity Reconstruction," *Solar Physics* 179, no. 1 (April 1998): 189-219) and by a factor of 1/0.6 (in accordance with the sunspot series revision of July 1, 2015). The sunspot number and scaled group number series are in close agreement only from about 1878 (Solar Cycle 12) to the present; prior group counts are systematically smaller.

Measurements of the variation of total solar irradiance (TSI) over three solar cycles (1978-2004) can be found in Claus Fröhlich, "Solar Irradiance Variability Since 1978," *Space Science Reviews* 125, no. 1-4 (August 2006): 53-65.

A modern debunking of Herschel's sunspot and wheat price correlation is Jeffrey J. Love, "On the Insignificance of Herschel's Sunspot Correlation," *Geophysical Research Letters* 40, no. 16 (August 16, 2013): 4171-76.

Two of Chizhevsky's articles translated into English appear in *Russian Cosmism*, edited by Boris Groys (Cambridge, MA: EFlux-MIT Press, 2018).

John A. Eddy, "The Maunder Minimum," *Science* 192, no. 4245 (June 18, 1976): 1189-1202.

A history of the solar wind concept can be found, for example, in Nicole Meyer-Vernet, *Basics of the Solar Wind* (Cambridge, U.K., and New York: Cambridge University Press, 2007), chap. 1.

In the United States, space weather information is coordinated through the Space Weather Prediction Center in Boulder, CO (https://www.swpc.noaa.gov), which is part of the National Weather Service and the National Oceanographic and Atmospheric Administration.

The inverse correlation of cosmic rays and sunspot numbers was first noted by Scott E. Forbush, "World-Wide Cosmic Ray Variations, 1937-1952," *Journal of Geophysical Research* 59, no. 4 (December 1954): 525-42. More recent and extended measurements can be found in H. S. Ahluwalia, "Timelines of Cosmic Ray Intensity, *Ap*, IMF, and Sunspot Numbers since 1937," *Journal of Geophysical Research* 116 (December 2011): A12106.

Compelling evidence that at least some cosmic rays originate in supernova remnants was recently published in Ackermann et al., "Detection of the Characteristic Pion-Decay Signature in Supernova Remnants," *Science* 339, no. 6121 (February 15, 2013): 807–11.

Cosmos: A Personal Voyage, written by Carl Sagan, Ann Druyan, and Steven Soter (PBS, 1980), episode 9, "The Lives of the Stars."

"Estimated contributions to public exposure from different sources for different countries, and UNSCEAR estimates of worldwide average exposure," annex B, figure 36, in *Sources and Effects of Ionizing Radiation: United Nations Scientific Committee on the Effects of Atomic Radiation: UNSCEAR 2008 Report to the General Assembly with Scientific Annexes*, 2 vols. (New York: United Nations, 2010), 1:404.

Cosmos, episode 9, "The Lives of the Stars."

More accurately, Jupiter and Saturn have the largest magnetospheres, with Uranus and Neptune in close competition. See Margaret Galland Kivelson and Fran Bagenal, "Planetary Magnetospheres," in *Encyclopedia of the Solar System*, 3rd ed., edited by Tilman Spohn, Doris Breuer, and Torrence V. Johnson (Amsterdam and Boston: Elsevier, 2014), 141.

We Are Living in an Empirical World

Isabel Briggs Myers with Peter B. Myers, *Gifts Differing: Understanding Personality Type*, 2nd ed. (Mountain View, CA: Davies–Black, 1995), preface.

C. G. Jung, "A Psychological Theory of Types (1931)," in C. G. Jung, *Psychological Types*, a revision by R. F. C. Hull of the translation by H. G. Baynes (Princeton: Princeton University Press, 1971), 531.

"Ezra Solomon," in *Oxford Essential Quotations*, 6th ed., edited by Susan Ratcliffe (Oxford University Press online, 2018), http://www.oxfordreference.com/view/10.1093/acref/9780191866692.001.0001/q-oro-ed6-00017202?rskey=CJPBUk&result=2, accessed April 29, 2019.

"It's tough to make predictions. . . ." Variations of this adage have been attributed to such colorful characters as Niels Bohr, Yogi Berra, and Mark Twain.

For an overview of the Mars Effect, see Michel Gauquelin, "Spheres of Influence," in *Philosophy of Science and the Occult*, edited by Patrick Grim, 2nd ed. (Albany: State University of New York Press, 1990), 37–50, originally published in *Psychology Today* 7 (October 1975): 22–27.

Arthur Mather as quoted in I. W. Kelly, G. A. Dean, and D. H. Saklofske, "Astrology: A Critical Review," in *Philosophy of Science and the Occult*, 66.

For a debunking of Gauquelin's findings, see Paul Kurtz, Jan Willem Nienhuys, and Ranjit Sandhu, "Is the 'Mars Effect' Genuine?," *Journal of Scientific Exploration* 11, no. 1 (March 1997): 19–39. For a fascinating postscript suggesting that birth records in Europe pre-1950 were widely fudged to give a more auspicious day and hour, see Geoffrey A. Dean, Arthur Mather, David K. B. Nias, and Rudolf H. Smit, *Tests of Astrology: A Critical Review of Hundreds of Studies* (Amsterdam: AinO, 2016), §6.9.

Skepticism and Wonder

In fact, during the eighteenth century, James Bradley discovered stellar aberration, a phenomenon that, like stellar parallax, is caused by the Earth's annual motion around the Sun. Unlike parallax, however, aberration (which is an effect of the finite speed of light) was not a test of the Earth's motion expected by classical astronomers.

Geoffrey A. Dean, Arthur Mather, David K. B. Nias, and Rudolf H. Smit, *Tests of Astrology: A Critical Review of Hundreds of Studies* (Amsterdam: AinO, 2016).

A notable website that maintains a database of to-the-minute celebrity birth times verified, where possible, from official birth records is the Astro-Databank, http://www.astro.com/astro-databank, last accessed March 26, 2019.

"Objections to Astrology: A Statement by 186 Leading Scientists," *Humanist* 35, no. 5 (September/October 1975): 4–6.

Carl Sagan, *The Demon-Haunted World: Science as a Candle in the Dark* (New York: Ballantine, 1996), chap. 17, "The Marriage of Skepticism and Wonder," 302–3.

Paul Feyerabend, "The Strange Case of Astrology," in *Philosophy of Science and the Occult*, 23–27, originally published in Paul Feyerabend, *Science in a Free Society* (London: New Left Books, 1978).

Cosmos, episode 5, "Blues for a Red Planet."

The Final Frontier?

John Lear, *Kepler's Dream*, with the full text and notes of *Somnium, sive astronomia lunaris Joannis Kepleri*, translated by Patricia Frueh Kirkwood (Berkeley: University of California Press, 1965), notes 130, 135, 147, 213–14, and throughout.

CONCLUSION: UPON THE WORDS OF NO ONE

Horace, *Epistles*, 1.1.14. And see especially Michael Hunter, *Establishing the New Science: The Experience of the Early Royal Society* (Woodbridge, U.K., and Wolfeboro, NH: Boydell Press, 1989), xiv, 17, 41–42.

Otto Neugebauer, "The Study of Wretched Subjects," *Isis* 42, no. 2 (June 1951): 111.

INDEX